LAN Protocol
Handbook

M&T BOOKS

LAN Protocol Handbook

Mark A. Miller

M&T Books
A Division of M&T Publishing, Inc.
501 Galveston Drive
Redwood City, CA 94063

Library of Congress Cataloging in Publication Data

Miller, Mark, 1955-
    LAN protocol handbook / Mark A. Miller.
       p.   cm.
    Includes bibliographical references and index.
    ISBN 1-55851-099-0 (book) : $34.95
    1. Local area networks (Computer networks) 2. Computer network protocols. I. Title.
TK5105.7.M54 1990
005.7'13--dc20
                                 90-6135
                                    CIP

93 92 91 90   4   3   2

Project Editor: David Rosenthal

Trademarks

3+, 3+Open, 3+Mail, 3+Open/Mail, and 3Com are trademarks of 3Com Corp.

Apple, Appleshare, and AppleTalk are registered trademarks of Apple Computer, Inc.

ARCNET is a trademark of Datapoint Corp.

CompuServe is a trademark of CompuServe Information Services

DEC is a trademark of Digital Equipment Corp.

ETHERAND is a trademark of International Business Machines Corp.

Ethernet is a trademark of Xerox Corp.

EtherTalk is a trademark of Apple Computer, Inc.

Hewlett-Packard is a trademark of Hewlett-Packard Company

IBM is a registered trademark of International Business Machines Corp.

Intel is a trademark of Intel Corporation

Internetwork Packet Exchange (IPX) is a trademark of Novell, Inc.

LANalyzer is a trademark of Novell, Inc.

LAN Manager is a trademark of International Business Machines Corp.

LANVista is a trademark of Digilog, Inc.

LANWatch is a trademark of FTP Software, Inc.

LocalTalk is a trademark of Apple Computer, Inc.

MicroChannel is a trademark of International Business Machines Corp.

MS-DOS is a trademark of Microsoft

NetBIOS is a trademark of International Business Machines Corp.

NetWare and Novell are registered trademarks of Novell, Inc.

PC LAN Program is a trademark of International Business Machines Corp.

PC Network is a trademark of International Business Machines Corp.

Proteon is a trademark of Proteon, Inc.

PS/2 is a trademark of International Business Machines Corp.

Sequenced Packet Exchange is a trademark of Novell, Inc.

SFT is a trademark of Novell, Inc.

SNA is a registered trademark of International Business Machines Corp.

Sniffer is a trademark of Network General Corp.

SpiderAnalyzer and SpiderMonitor are trademarks of Spider Systems, Inc.

StarLAN is a trademark of AT&T

Systems Application Architecture and SAA are trademarks of International Business Machines Corp.

Token-Ring is a trademark of International Business Machines Corp.

UNIX is a registered trademark of AT&T

VAX is a registered trademark of Digital Equipment Corp.

VINES is a registered trademark of Banyan Systems Inc.

Contents

Chapter 7. Analyzing Apple Computer's AppleTalk 261

Illustrations

Chapter 1. LAN Protocols: An Overview

Chapter 2. LAN Protocol and Performance Analysis

Chapter 3. Analyzing Novell's NetWare

Chapter 4. Analyzing 3Com's 3+ and 3+Open

Chapter 5. Analyzing IBM Token-Ring Related Protocols

Tables

Chapter 6. Analyzing Banyan VINES

Chapter 7. Analyzing Apple Computer's AppleTalk

Why this Book Is for You

This book has been written to address software difficulties among Local Area Networks and to provide a comprehensive reference on the most popular LAN Operating System software. In reading the *LAN Protocol Handbook*, you will gain insight into the operation of six vendors' protocol analyzers, so that your selection of this most important analysis tool will be appropriate for your network applications. In individual chapters, we will examine in detail the software structure of Novell's NetWare, 3Com's 3+ and 3+Open, IBM's Token-Ring related protocols, Banyan VINES, and Apple Computer's AppleTalk.

This book is of particular interest to the following:

- Network administrators who are responsible for the software troubleshooting and maintenance of their LAN

- Application developers that are writing application programs that will operate on a particular Network Operating System, such as NetWare or AppleTalk

- Network managers who are considering the purchase of a LAN protocol analyzer, and need further information on some of the different vendors' products

- End users who need in-depth knowledge of the internal protocols that are operating on their LAN

- Readers of the companion *LAN Troubleshooting Handbook* who have realized that the hardware failures are only one part of the total LAN analysis story

Preface

I have always wondered what motivates otherwise rational people to write a book. Perhaps some insight into the origin of this text might be of interest to you.

This book is a companion volume to the *LAN Troubleshooting Handbook* (M&T Books, 1989). At the time that the first book was finished, I concluded that only part of the LAN analysis story had been told. The *Troubleshooting Handbook* focuses on the Ethernet, ARCNET, Token-Ring, and StarLAN network topologies; their proper operation, cabling, and other installation-related issues; troubleshooting tools; and typical network problems and solutions. Between 70–90 percent of all network failures are attributable to the hardware issues discussed in the *Troubleshooting Handbook*. The nagging question for many, however, is how to understand and correct the remaining 10–30 percent of network failures that can be blamed on the network operating system and its related protocols? Therefore, the complete LAN analysis and optimization story requires consideration of both the hardware and software issues. Hence the need for a second volume.

Let me provide you with a road map in the Preface to assist in your study of network protocols. Chapter 1 provides a review of the OSI Reference Model, the various LAN standards, and the Data Link Layer frame formats. Those who need further LAN architectural information should consult the *Troubleshooting Handbook*. Chapter 2 discusses the role of LAN protocols and the effective use of a protocol analyzer. It also includes profiles of six different analyzers that are currently available on the market and lists some guidelines for those network users who are considering an analyzer purchase.

Chapters 3–7 are devoted to individual networking software architectures. In the order presented, they are: Novell's NetWare, 3Com's 3+

and 3+Open, IBM's Token-Ring related protocols, Banyan Systems' VINES, and Apple Computer's AppleTalk. Each chapter is relatively independent of the others -- pick and choose those that are of interest to you.

Chapter 8 concludes with some guidelines for networking software evaluation. It also considers some issues (other that those related to protocols) that should be considered in diagnosing your local area network.

Tackling the subject of LAN software is a very rigorous task, and I owe a debt to several groups of individuals who assisted in preparing different portions of the text. The first group is the LAN software vendors. Apple Computer, Inc., Banyan Systems Inc., IBM, Novell, Inc., and 3Com Corporation were each very helpful in providing the technical documentation necessary to dissect their networking protocols.

The second group, the selected protocol analyzer manufacturers, provided a great deal of input into Chapter 2, which discusses each of their products in detail. The contributions of John Bennett, Bruce Campbell, Mike Cookish, Sue Fairchild, Soccoro Land, Jay Seaton, Frances Selkirk, and Kent Sterling were greatly appreciated.

The third group helped me prepare the examples offered in Chapters 3–7. These Denver-area network administrators graciously allowed me to analyze their live networks using a Sniffer protocol analyzer from Network General Corporation, and to simulate many typical network conditions. In the process, we also identified some real problems. These administrators include Jack Kilian, Margery Komninos, Marc Lansky, Gary Peterson, John Urban, and Michael Wilcox. Many thanks for this much-needed assistance.

The last group are the technical experts who provided comments and technical details for individual sections of the manuscript. These contributors include Christian Fahlbusch, Sue Fairchild, Paul Ferguson, J.

Scott Haugdahl, Kerry Lynn, Carl Shinn, Jr., David Trousdale, Michael Wilcox, and a number of individuals from Banyan Systems Inc. Thanks to you all for your expert opinions.

Three editors at M&T Books kept the project moving and on schedule. Thanks to Brenda McLaughlin, Tom Woolf, and David Rosenthal for your encouragement.

Krystal Valdez again demonstrated her expert secretarial skills (and adept hieroglyphic interpretation!) in making the many pages of handwritten manuscript into a readable text. Thanks again, Krys, for another job well done.

Finally, I owe a special thanks to my family. For a number of reasons, this project was more demanding than the first book. Holly, Nathan, and Nicholas provided their love and support during the long hours. Thanks for your love.

CHAPTER ONE

LAN Protocols: An Overview

Many local area network (LAN) managers claim that between 70 and 90 percent of their network failures are attributable to hardware failures. That means from 10 to 30 percent of these problems are to be blamed on software. Unfortunately, even though software difficulties occur less frequently, they are usually more difficult to diagnose. In many cases, the use of rather expensive test equipment is required. However, the test equipment alone cannot solve either hardware or software failures. The network administrator must do that, and he or she must be well-educated in both network hardware operation and the intricacies of the software in order to be effective.

Since software bugs won't disappear on their own, the network administrator must be able to identify and correct these problems when they arise. In order to do so, two things are required: an understanding of the tools and techniques needed for LAN software analysis (which will be explored in Chapter 2), plus a knowledge of the specific LAN software in use (covered in Chapters 3 through 7).

In this chapter, we will lay a foundation of understanding how network-specific applications operate. First we will review the Open System Interconnection (OSI) Reference Model that forms the basis for computer network communication. Next, we'll look at the IEEE Project 802 standards. Then, most importantly, we will explore how the various LAN protocol suites, such as Novell's NetWare, Banyan Systems' VINES, Apple Computer's AppleTalk, and others, fit into the model. First, let's define some terms.

The *IBM Dictionary of Computing* defines the term "protocol" as: "A set of semantic and syntactic rules that determines the behavior of functional units in achieving communication." Translated, this means that the form (syntax) and meaning (semantics) of a communication system (between computers in the case of a LAN) are defined by a set of rules, and we can implement these rules in either hardware or software. Thus, it is equally correct to consider EIA-232-D (hardware) and TCP/IP (Transmission Control Protocol/Internet Protocol) (software) to be protocols. The focus of this handbook, however, is on understanding software communications to facilitate LAN troubleshooting — in other words, the analysis of the software protocols.

To methodically solve a software problem, first you must define the problem — that is, get a clear understanding of *what doesn't work*. Next, you must narrow the field of possible problems by determining *what does work*. To do this quickly, some order must be imposed on a potentially chaotic situation. This order can be assisted by using the benchmark reference for all computer communication, the OSI reference model.

1.1 | How the OSI Reference Model Applies to LANs

The familiar, seven-layer OSI reference model can be divided into three sections (see reference [1-1]). The lower three layers are collectively called the communication subnet, the upper three layers are collectively called the host process, and the middle layer, called the Transport Layer, acts as a buffer between the communication subnet and the host process. We'll briefly summarize the functions of each layer from the lowest to the highest (see Figure 1-1).

The **Physical Layer** is responsible for bit transmission between one node (host, workstation, etc.) and the next node. As such, it is concerned with the interface to the transmission media (or the LAN backbone cable), the encoding of the data signal, voltage or current magnitudes, connector sizes, shapes and pinouts, and generally anything associated with the physical transmission of the bit stream.

Figure 1-1
The Open System Interconnection (OSI) reference model

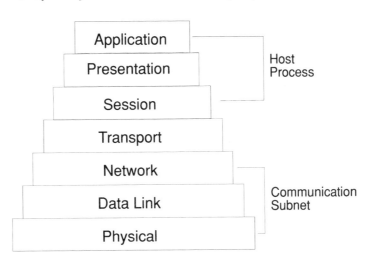

The **Data Link Layer** is responsible for providing reliable communication between adjacent nodes. As such, it assumes that the physical layer is noisy or prone to errors. Data Link provides a mechanism to transmit the frame (or package) of data bits and assures reliable delivery of that frame to the next node. Therefore, a means of addressing that frame (both its source and its destination) becomes necessary, as well as providing error control for the data within that frame, which is implemented with a Cyclic Redundancy Check (CRC).

The **Network Layer** establishes the path (or route) from the source node to the destination node via the communication subnet. The packet is the package of information at this layer, and problems such as switching, routing, and controlling the congestion of these packets within the subnet are addressed at the Network Layer.

The **Transport Layer** provides for reliable delivery of host messages originating at Layer 7, the Application Layer, in a fashion similar to the way in which the Data Link Layer assures reliable delivery of bits between adjacent nodes. The major difference between the Data

Link and Transport layers is that the Data Link domain is defined between adjacent nodes, whereas the Transport Layer's domain is from the source to the destination or end-to-end via the communication sub-net. Message-related issues become important in the Transport Layer. For example, the Transport Layer segments a long message into smaller units (packets) prior to transmission, and assures the reassembly of those packets into the original message at the receiver.

The **Session Layer** establishes and terminates process-to-process communication sessions between hosts. To manage that session, translation between name and address databases, plus synchronization between the two hosts, may be required.

The **Presentation Layer** is responsible for the syntax (or form) in which data exchanged between the two hosts is exchanged. As such, the Presentation Layer provides a data manipulation function, not a communication function. Data compression and data encryption are two examples of Presentation Layer services.

The **Application Layer** provides end-user services, such as file transfer, electronic mail, virtual terminal emulation, and remote database access. It is the Application Layer with which the end user interacts.

While theory can be interesting, a practical example of how the OSI model applies to a LAN is more useful (Figure 1-2). The Physical Layer is implemented with the cable, connectors, and transmitter/receiver circuitry of the Network Interface Card (NIC). The Data Link Layer functions are performed with protocol handler integrated circuits on the NIC, such as Intel Corporation's 82586 (for IEEE 802.3 networks) or Texas Instruments' TMS380 (for IEEE 802.5 networks). The Network and Transport layers are necessary for internetworking, but may have minimal responsibilities for a single LAN since there is only one "route," the cable, and so no routing, switching, or communication subnet reliability issues exist.

Examples of protocols that are implemented at these layers are the Department of Defense's Transmission Control Protocol/Internet Protocol (TCP/IP), Novell's Sequenced Packet Exchange/Internetwork Packet Exchange (SPX/IPX), or Xerox Corporation's Networking Services (XNS) protocols. The Session Layer is typically implemented with NetBIOS, which is the Network Basic Input/Output System developed by IBM and Sytek, Inc. Presentation and Application layer functions are performed by a combination of DOS, the Network Operating System (NOS), and various application protocols such as X.400, which is used for electronic mail.

Figure 1-2
The OSI model applied to LANs

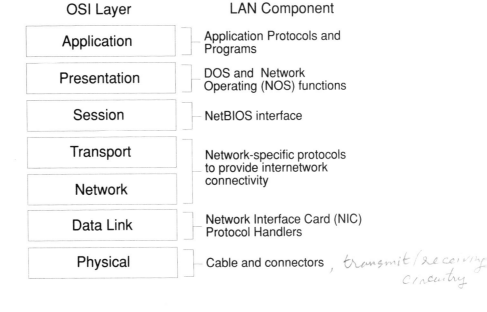

OSI Layer	LAN Component
Application	Application Protocols and Programs
Presentation	DOS and Network Operating (NOS) functions
Session	NetBIOS interface
Transport	Network-specific protocols to provide internetwork connectivity
Network	
Data Link	Network Interface Card (NIC) Protocol Handlers
Physical	Cable and connectors , *transmit/receiving circuitry*

1.2 | IEEE Project 802

Recognizing a need for standards in the LAN market, the Institute of Electrical and Electronics Engineers (IEEE) undertook Project 802. Named for the month (February) and year (1980) of its inception, Project 802 addresses LAN standards at the Physical and Data Link layers of the OSI model, (Figure 1-3). Service Access Points (SAPs) provide addressing between communicating adjacent layers.

The Physical Layer of the IEEE LAN model is similar to its OSI counterpart. Its responsibilities include signal encoding and decoding, serial bit transmission and reception, and providing the physical connection to the transmission medium via twisted-pair, coaxial, or fiber-optic cable.

Figure 1-3
Comparing IEEE Project 802 with OSI

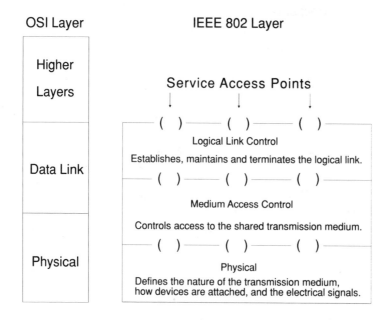

Overlapping the OSI Data Link/Physical boundary is the IEEE Medium Access Control (or MAC) layer. This layer, as its name implies, controls access to the transmission medium, and is also further subdivided into other standards:

- 802.3: Carrier Sense Multiple Access Bus with Collision Detection (CSMA/CD)

- 802.4: Token Passing Bus

- 802.5: Token Passing Ring

Each of these MAC standards defines a unique frame format, discussed in section 1.4 and detailed in references [1-2], [1-3], and [1-4].

IEEE 802.1 defines architectural and internetworking issues that are universal to the LAN Model. The highest layer of the IEEE LAN Model is Logical Link Control (LLC), defined by the IEEE 802.2 standard. While it bears a great deal of resemblance to the OSI Data Link Layer, there are also some important differences. Both Data Link and LLC must reliably transmit frames of information between adjacent stations. In the LAN model, however, there is no real need for the network layer functions of routing and switching. Since there is only one "route" (the cable), the addressing defined in the MAC-layer frame is sufficient for delivery of the frame. Other functions such as flow control (which assures that a fast sender does not overwhelm a slow receiver), and error control also are handled by the Data Link Layer without any requirements from the Network Layer.

The one major difference between OSI Data Link and IEEE 802.2 LLC is that multiple endpoints to the data link can exist in the IEEE model. With a LAN, communicating between one source and multiple SAPs is often required. SAPs function in a manner somewhat analogous to ports. Thus, a workstation that has one MAC-layer address (provided by the hardware or NIC) can communicate with several higher layer processes. Each of these processes would have a unique

SAP address. Both source (SSAP) and destination (DSAP) addresses are specified in the 802.2 LLC frame. These will be discussed in Section 1.4.

Two types of LLC operations are defined:

- Type 1 (unacknowledged, connectionless services): the sending and receiving of frames in a datagram fashion. Point-to-point, multi-point, and broadcast transmissions are supported by Type 1.

- Type 2 (connection-oriented services): a logical connection between SAPs providing sequence control, flow control, error control, and acknowledgments.

- Type 3 (acknowledged connectionless services): a datagram, point-to-point service with acknowledgements.

For further information, see reference [1-5].

1.3 | Building a Frame for Transmission

Before any protocols can be analyzed, the LAN manager must have a clear understanding of the transmission process that takes place between two workstations. Figure 1-4 illustrates this operation. For example, let Application X be an electronic mail message destined for its peer process, Application Y. The message contents, "Can you join me for lunch at 11:30?," is transferred to the Application Layer as data (Application data). The Application Layer then appends an Application Header (AH) and transfers the AH and the Application data to the Presentation Layer. The Presentation Layer treats the AH and Application data as its data unit, appends the Presentation Header (PH), and passes the data unit down to the Session, Transport, and Network layers in turn.

Figure 1-4
Building a frame for transmission

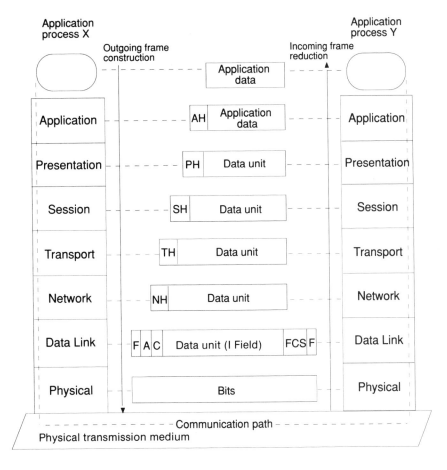

When the encapsulated electronic mail message reaches the Data Link Layer, Framing (F), Address (A), and Control (C) information is added as the Data Link Layer header. The Frame Check Sequence (FCS) and possibly additional Framing (F) characters are appended as the Data Link Layer trailer. The assembled frame is then handed to the Physical Layer. The Physical Layer encodes the data for transmission, accesses the transmission medium, and monitors the serial bit transmission.

At the destination node, a similar process occurs, except this time in reverse. The Physical Layer hands its bits to the Data Link Layer, which decodes and then strips off the Data Link Layer header and trailer. The Data Link Layer data unit is then passed to the Network, Transport, Session, and other layers in turn. The process is completed when the electronic message (shown again as Application data) is delivered to Application Y.

Figure 1-5
The encapsulated message

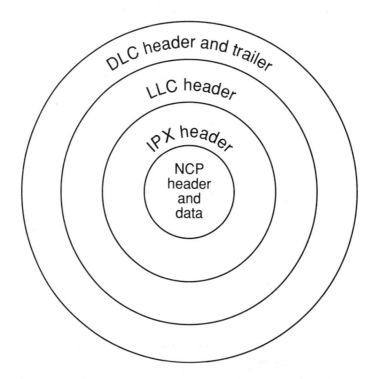

Another way to view the process is given in Figure 1-5, showing a sample transmission from a Novell NetWare server to a workstation. The actual message (data) is encapsulated with the NetWare Core Protocol (NCP) header. Next is the IPX header and message, the LLC header and message, and finally the Data Link Control (DLC) header and message. Not shown is the DLC trailer. For LANs, the DLC trailer consists of a 32-bit FCS which is recalculated at the receiver and must achieve the proper result, otherwise the entire frame will be rejected.

Using the encapsulation model above, the message (or data) from the server is at the core of a hypothetical onion. The next layer of the onion is the NCP header, followed by the next layer (IPX header), and so on. Using this analogy, the essence of protocol analysis is to "peel the onion," examining each layer in turn, until the core information is exposed. We'll look at this onion model closer in Chapter 2.

1.4 | LAN Frame Formats

As we saw in Figure 1-4, the heart of data transmission on the LAN is the unique frame format which originates at the Data Link Layer and is implemented on the NIC. Considerable detail was given to the formats of the IEEE 802.2, 802.3, 802.5, Ethernet, and ARCNET Data Link Layer frames in the companion volume, *LAN Troubleshooting Handbook* (reference [1-7]). A summary of these frame formats is also presented here.

1.4.1 | IEEE 802.2

The IEEE 802.2 LLC Protocol Data Unit (PDU) is shown in Figure 1-6a. The first two fields are the DSAP and SSAP addresses, each or which are one octet in length. (Throughout this text, we will use the term "octet," which is *defined* as 8 bits, and avoid the term "byte," which *usually* means 8 bits.) The least significant bit (LSB) of the DSAP indicates whether it is a group or individual address, while the LSB of the SSAP indicates whether the data in that LLC frame is a command or a response. The Control field is next, containing either one or two octets. Last is the Information field, an integral num-

ber of octets of information that has been passed down from the
higher layers.

The LLC PDU Control field format is shown in Figure 1-6b. There are
three different types of LLC PDUs: I, S, and U. The Information (I)
format (shown in Figure 1-6c) is used for sequential data transfer and
includes a sequence number, N(S), of the transmitted frame, plus an
acknowledgement, N(R), indicating the next expected I frame from
the remote station. The I format is used for Type 2 operation only.
The Supervisory (S) format (see Figure 1-6d) is used to supervise the
exchange of I-frames, and includes N(R), the receive sequence counter.
The S format is used for Type 2 operation only. The Unnumbered (U)
format (see Figure 1-6e) is used to establish and disconnect the logical
link. The U format can be used with either Type 1 or Type 2 operation depending on the application.

Figure 1-6a
The Logical Link Control Protocol Data Unit

DSAP address	SSAP address	Control	Information
8 bits	8 bits	8 or 16 bits	M*8 bits

DSAP Address = destination service access point address field
SSAP Address = source service access point address field
Control = control field (16 bits for formats that include sequence
    numbering, and 8 bits for formats that do not)
Information = information field
* = multiplication
M = an integer value equal to or greater than 0. (Upper bound of
    M is a function of the medium access control methodology used.)

Figure 1-6b
The LLC PDU Control Field Formats

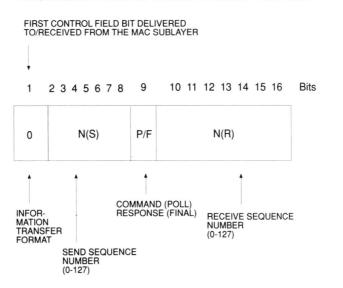

	1	2 3 4 5 6 7 8	9	10 - 16	Bits

INFORMATION TRANSFER COMMAND/RESPONSE (I-FORMAT PDU): `0 | N(S) | P/F | N(R)`

SUPERVISORY COMMANDS/RESPONSES (S-FORMAT PDUs): `1 | 0 | S S | X X X X | P/F | N(R)`

UNNUMBERED COMMANDS/RESPONSE (U-FORMAT PDUs): `1 | 1 | M M | P/F | M M M`

where:

N(S) = Transmitter send sequence number (Bit 2 = low-order bit)
N(R) = Transmitter receive sequence number (Bit 10 = low-order bit)
S = Supervisory function bit
M = Modifier function bit
X = Reserved and set to zero
P/F = Poll bit - command LLC PDU transmissions
Final bit - response LLC PDU transmissions
(1 = Poll/Final)

Figure 1-6c
Information transfer format Control Field bits

FIRST CONTROL FIELD BIT DELIVERED
TO/RECEIVED FROM THE MAC SUBLAYER

1	2 3 4 5 6 7 8	9	10 11 12 13 14 15 16	Bits
0	N(S)	P/F	N(R)	

INFOR-MATION TRANSFER FORMAT

SEND SEQUENCE NUMBER (0-127)

COMMAND (POLL) RESPONSE (FINAL)

RECEIVE SEQUENCE NUMBER (0-127)

19

Figure 1-6d
Supervisory format Control Field bits

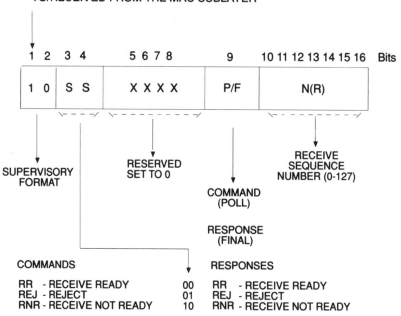

FIRST CONTROL FIELD BIT DELIVERED
TO/RECEIVED FROM THE MAC SUBLAYER

| 1 2 | 3 4 | 5 6 7 8 | 9 | 10 11 12 13 14 15 16 | Bits |

1 0   S S   X X X X   P/F   N(R)

SUPERVISORY
FORMAT

RESERVED
SET TO 0

COMMAND
(POLL)

RESPONSE
(FINAL)

RECEIVE
SEQUENCE
NUMBER (0-127)

COMMANDS

RR - RECEIVE READY   00
REJ - REJECT   01
RNR - RECEIVE NOT READY   10

RESPONSES

RR - RECEIVE READY
REJ - REJECT
RNR - RECEIVE NOT READY

Figure 1-6e
Unnumbered format Control Field bits

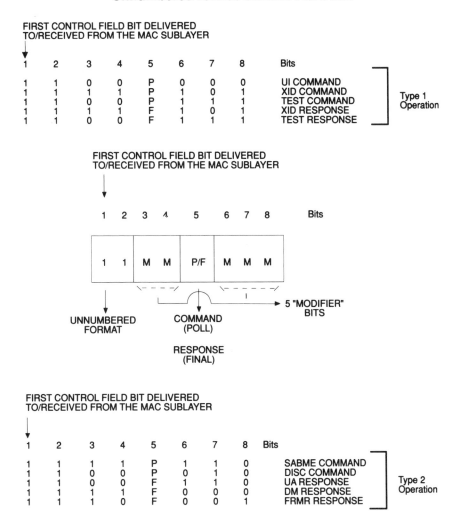

FIRST CONTROL FIELD BIT DELIVERED
TO/RECEIVED FROM THE MAC SUBLAYER

1	2	3	4	5	6	7	8	Bits	
1	1	0	0	P	0	0	0	UI COMMAND	
1	1	1	1	P	1	0	1	XID COMMAND	Type 1
1	1	0	0	P	1	1	1	TEST COMMAND	Operation
1	1	1	1	F	1	0	1	XID RESPONSE	
1	1	0	0	F	1	1	1	TEST RESPONSE	

FIRST CONTROL FIELD BIT DELIVERED
TO/RECEIVED FROM THE MAC SUBLAYER

1	2	3	4	5	6	7	8	Bits
1	1	M	M	P/F	M	M	M	

UNNUMBERED
FORMAT

COMMAND
(POLL)

RESPONSE
(FINAL)

→ 5 "MODIFIER"
BITS

FIRST CONTROL FIELD BIT DELIVERED
TO/RECEIVED FROM THE MAC SUBLAYER

1	2	3	4	5	6	7	8	Bits	
1	1	1	1	P	1	1	0	SABME COMMAND	
1	1	0	0	P	0	1	0	DISC COMMAND	
1	1	0	0	F	1	1	0	UA RESPONSE	Type 2
1	1	1	1	F	0	0	0	DM RESPONSE	Operation
1	1	1	0	F	0	0	1	FRMR RESPONSE	

Ethernet

The Ethernet frame format was developed by DEC, Intel Corporation, and Xerox Corporation and is slightly different from the IEEE 802.3 format (see reference [1-8]). The specific fields are shown in Figure 1-7a. The Ethernet frame begins with a Preamble (eight octets) that is an alternating 1010 ... pattern that ends in ... 10101011. The Preamble provides synchronization. The Destination address is a six-octet field that can either define a Physical address or a multicast address, which is determined by the LSB (P/M) of the first byte of that field. A physical address (usually burned into a ROM chip) sets that LSB=0, and is unique across all Ethernet networks. A multicast address can be to a group or broadcast to all stations, and has the LSB=1. In the case of a broadcast address, the destination field is set to all 1's — that is, FFFFFFFFFFFFH. (Throughout this text we will use a capital "H" to designate hexidecimal notation.)

The Physical addresses are further subdivided: the first three octets (A, B, and C in Figure 1-7b) are administered by the IEEE, and the last three octets (D, E, and F) are assigned by the manufacturer. Should the NIC become defective but the node address needs to remain consistent (such as a well-known address for a gateway), the ROM chip containing the original address can be removed from the old board and inserted on the new board; or the address can be set in a register using the diagnostic disk. Regardless of the technique used, care should be taken when human intervention is needed to replace the automated address administration safeguards.

Figure 1-7a
The Ethernet frame format

Preamble	Destination	Source	Type	Data	FCS	
8	6	6	2	46-1500	4	Octets

|◄─────────────────────── 64-1518 ───────────────────►|

Figure 1-7b
The Ethernet address fields

P/M	OCTET A	OCTET B	OCTET C	OCTET D	OCTET E	OCTET F

LSB   MSB

The Source address, that is the address of the station originating the frame, is specified next.

The Type field, sometimes referred to as the Ethertype, is a two-octet field that specifies the higher layer protocol used in the Data field. Some familiar Ethertypes would be 0800H (TCP/IP) and 0600H (XNS). A listing of Ethertypes is given in Appendix 1.

The Data field is the only variable-length field, and can range from a minimum of 46 to a maximum of 1500 octets. The contents of this field is completely arbitrary, as determined by the higher layer protocol currently in use.

The last field is an FCS that is a 32-bit CRC based upon the contents of the Address, Type, and Data fields.

The allowable frame length, not including the Preamble, ranges from 64 to 1518 octets. Frames outside that range are considered invalid. Short frames (sometimes called fragments or runts) generally arise from collisions. Long frames (sometimes called jabbers) usually indicate a defective transmitter at the NIC.

1.4.3 | IEEE 802.3

Figure 1-8a depicts the IEEE 802.3 MAC frame format. Note that the 802.2 LLC PDU would be completely encapsulated within the Data Unit of the MAC frame. The 802.3 frame begins with a Preamble (seven octets) that is an alternating pattern 1010 ... . The Start Frame

Delimiter (SFD) is next, defined as 10101011. Note that if the 802.3 Preamble and Start Frame Delimiter fields are combined, a pattern identical to the Ethernet Preamble will result.

Next is the Destination Address fields shown in Figure 1-8b, which can be either two or six octets in length, although six octets is the most common. The Individual/Group (I/G) field corresponds to the Physical/Multicast designation of Ethernet; the Universal/Local (U/L) field indicates whether the address is administered universally (by the IEEE) or locally (by the network administrator). The Source Address comes next, and must match the Destination Address field in length (either two for Destination and two for Source, or six for Destination and six for Source, but not two and six).

Figure 1-8a
The IEEE 802.3 MAC frame format

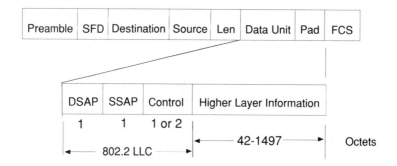

Figure 1-8b
The IEEE 802.3 address fields

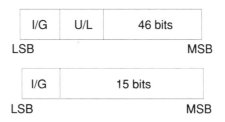

LSB = Least Significant Bit
MSB = Most Significant Bit
I/G = Individual/Group Field
U/L = Universal/Local Field

The Length field is two octets long and indicates the number of LLC octets in the Data field. A minimum of 46 octets of data is required; when the LLC data is less than 46, the Pad field is used. Maximum length of the Data and Pad fields combined is 1500 octets.

Finally, the FCS, which is based upon a 32-bit CRC, is computed based upon the contents of the Destination Address, Source Address, Length, Data, and Pad fields. (See Reference [1-2] for further details.)

Again referring to Figures 1-7a and 1-8a, note the differences between the Ethernet and IEEE 802.3 frames. First, the Type field of Ethernet has been replaced with a Length field for 802.3. This implies several things. First, the frames are the same length at the Data Link Layer, but are incompatible at the Network Layer and above. Second, if the length of the data must be specified within an Ethernet frame, some parameter defined by the Network Layer and contained within the Data Link Layer Information field must convey that quantity.

In addition, Ethernet has no provision to pad the data to its required 46-octet minimum, but 802.3 does. This implies that for Ethernet the Network Layer will give this parameter some attention and take responsibility for any necessary padding.

1.4.4 IEEE 802.5

Because of the nature of token ring network operation, three different frame formats are required. The three-octet Token, shown in Figure 1-9a, circulates around the ring, passing network access control to the various workstations. The multi-octet Frame, shown in Figure 1-9b, contains either user data or ring management data. The two-octet Abort Sequence in Figure 1-9c, is used for error conditions, such as hard errors internal to the workstation. We'll look at each transmission type individually.

The 24 bits of the Token (Figure 1-9a) are divided into three octets: the Starting Delimiter, which contains violations to the Differential Manchester code plus binary 0's; the Access Control field, which grants network access; and the Ending Delimiter, which contains Differential Manchester Code violations, binary 1's, plus two additional bits, Intermediate and Error detect, described below.

The Access control field begins with three Priority (P) bits that set the priority of that Token. Each workstation is assigned a priority for its transmissions, 000 being the lowest and 111 being the highest. The Reservation (R) bits can be used by a workstation to request the reservation of the next Token as a transmission passes by. In order for a workstation to transmit, its priority must be greater than or equal to the priority of that Token. The Token (T) bit delineates either a Token (T=0) or a Frame (T=1).

The Monitor Count (M) bit is used to prevent high-priority Tokens or any Frames from continuously circulating around the ring. It is set to M=0 by the transmitting station, and set to M=1 by the Active Monitor. If the monitor sees an incoming priority Token or Frame with M=1, it assumes that the transmitting station did not remove the token or frame after one round trip, and removes that Token or Frame, purges the ring, and issues a new Token.

The Ending Delimiter includes Differential Manchester code violations and binary 1's; an Intermediate frame (I) bit which, when it is set, indicates that this Frame is part of a multi-frame transmission; and an Error detect (E) bit that is set when a Frame contains an FCS error, a non-integral number of bytes, or a Differential Manchester code violation between Starting and Ending delimiters.

The variable-length Frame shown in Figure 1-9b is transmitted by the workstation following the successful capture of the Token. The first two octets of the Frame, the Starting Delimiter and Access Control, are taken from the Token format described above. The Frame Control field defines two types of frames, either LLC frames that carry user data, or MAC frames that carry ring management data. The Destination and Source address fields, either two or six octets in length, follow the same formats as the 802.3 address fields shown in Figure 1-8b.

Figure 1-9a
The IEEE 802.5 Token format

Starting Delimiter	Access Control	Ending Delimiter	
1	1	1	octets
VV0VV000	PPPTMRRR	VV1VV1IE	

V	= Differential Manchester Violations	P = Priority Mode T = Token Bit M = Monitor Count R = Priority Reservation	V	= Differential Manchester Violations
0	= Binary ZERO		1	= Binary ONE
			I	= Intermediate
			E	= Error Detect

Figure 1-9b
The IEEE 802.5 MAC Frame format

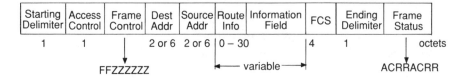

Starting Delimiter	Access Control	Frame Control	Dest Addr	Source Addr	Route Info	Information Field	FCS	Ending Delimiter	Frame Status
1	1		2 or 6	2 or 6	0 – 30		4	1	octets

FFZZZZZZ ◄── variable ──► ACRRACRR

F = Frame Format
    00 = MAC (Ring data)
    01 = LLC (User data)
    1X = future use
Z = Control bits
A = Address recognized; initially 0, changed to 1 when station recognizes its address
C = Frame copied; initially 0, changed to 1 when station copies frame to its RX buffer
R = Reserved bits
RI = Route Information; used for additional routing when a frame traverses multiple rings via bridges. When RI is present, the I/G bit of the Source address = 1, and the RI is placed in all messages:

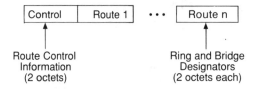

| Control | Route 1 | • • • | Route n |

Route Control Information (2 octets) Ring and Bridge Designators (2 octets each)

FCS = Frame Check Sequence

Figure 1-9c
The IEEE 802.5 Abort Sequence format

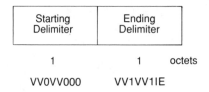

Starting Delimiter	Ending Delimiter
1	1 octets

VV0VV000 VV1VV1IE

An optional Routing Information (RI) field (added by IBM) precedes the variable-length Information field. The RI field is used when the transmitting frame must go between multiple rings via bridges. A source-routing protocol, which defines route control information plus ring and bridge designators, is used for these multiple ring topologies.

For LLC frames, the Information field contains the LLC PDU that was shown in Figure 1-6b. The PDU includes the DSAP and SSAP address, control information, plus the data from the higher layers (Network and above). For MAC Frames, the Information field contains Commands and Parameters for ring management. We will elaborate further on these fields in Chapter 5, which discusses the IBM Token-Ring related protocols.

An FCS follows the Information field. The Ending Delimiter field is taken from the Token frame. The Frame Status field ends the 802.5 frame. It includes the Address Recognized (A) and Frame Copied (C) bits that verify that the receiving station has properly processed the Frame.

The Abort Sequence format shown in Figure 1-9c is used when certain error conditions occur, such as hard errors at the workstation. The Starting and Ending Delimiter fields are identical to the corresponding fields in the Token.

1.4.5 Sub-Network Access Protocol

An extension to the IEEE 802.2 LLC header has been defined by the Internet community, known as the Sub-Network Access Protocol, or SNAP (see reference [1-9]). This extension was made in order to encapsulate Internet Protocol (IP) datagrams and Address Resolution Protocol (ARP) requests and replies within an 802.X (802.3, 802.4, or 802.5) frame.

The SNAP header immediately follows the 802.2 header, and is encapsulated within the 802.X frame (see Figure 1-10). For the 802.2 header, both DSAP and SSAP fields are set to AAH, and the Control field is set to 03H (for Unnumbered Information). The Protocol ID or Organization Code is three octets, and is specified in RFC-1042 (see reference [1-9]) as all ZEROs. The Ethertype (two octets) completes the SNAP header.

By using 802.2 LLC and SNAP within the same 802.X MAC frame, both SAP addresses and Ethertypes can be specified. Both 3Com (in 3+ and 3+Open) and AppleTalk use SNAP within their respective frames. Banyan's literature (see reference [6-2]) indicates that future VINES releases may incorporate SNAP.

Figure 1-10
Sub-Network Access Protocol (SNAP) header
encapsulated within an IEEE 802.X frame

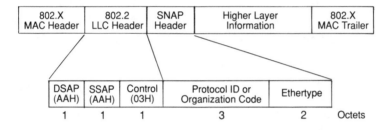

1.4.6   ARCNET

ARCNET, originally developed by Datapoint Corporation, is not part of the IEEE Project 802 standards. It bears some resemblance to the IEEE 802.4 Token Passing Bus architecture, but specifics such as node addressing reveal incompatibilities. For example, the original 2.5 megabit-per-second (Mbit/sec) ARCNET uses eight-bit addresses, where the IEEE standard uses 48-bit addresses. Nevertheless, the ARCNET architecture has received wide acceptance in the industry and continues to experience growth.

ARCNET has five frame formats, as depicted in Figure 1-11. The Invitation to Transmit (ITT) is the token that passes control of the network from one workstation to another. The FBE is a query from a station desiring to transmit to determine if the intended receiver has sufficient buffer space available to hold the incoming frame. The

Packet (PAC) is the frame itself, and can contain up to 508 octets of data. An Acknowledgement (ACK) confirms the receipt of a packet or offers a positive response to an FBE. The Negative Acknowledgement (NAK) indicates a refusal to accept a packet or a negative response to a Free Buffer Enquiry. (For further information on the ARCNET protocols, see reference [1-10].)

Figure 1-11
The ARCNET frame formats

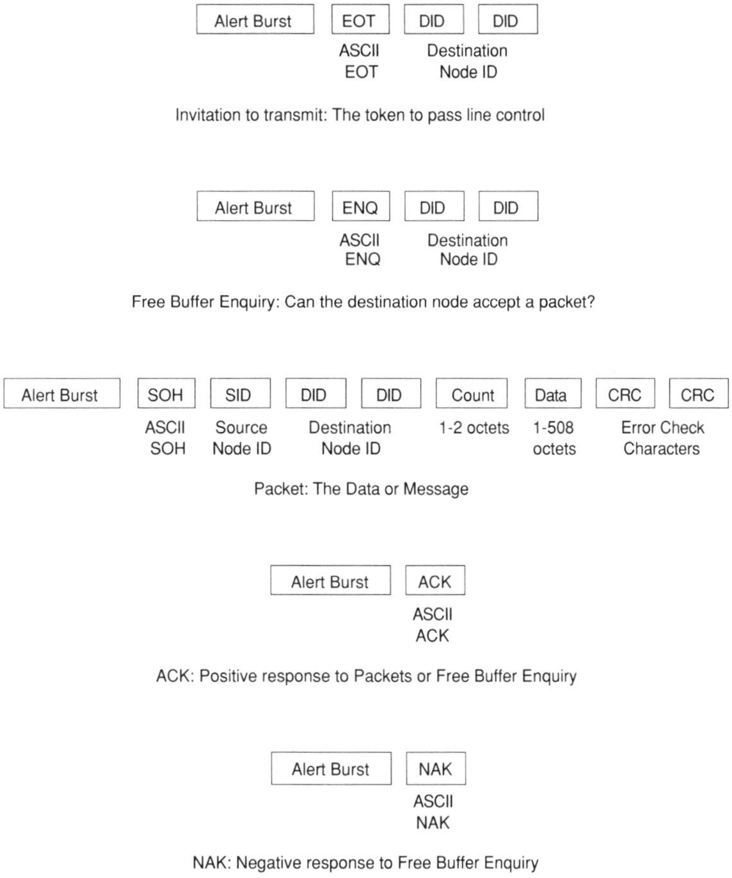

Alert Burst	EOT	DID	DID
	ASCII EOT	Destination Node ID	

Invitation to transmit: The token to pass line control

Alert Burst	ENQ	DID	DID
	ASCII ENQ	Destination Node ID	

Free Buffer Enquiry: Can the destination node accept a packet?

Alert Burst	SOH	SID	DID	DID	Count	Data	CRC	CRC
	ASCII SOH	Source Node ID	Destination Node ID		1-2 octets	1-508 octets	Error Check Characters	

Packet: The Data or Message

Alert Burst	ACK
	ASCII ACK

ACK: Positive response to Packets or Free Buffer Enquiry

Alert Burst	NAK
	ASCII NAK

NAK: Negative response to Free Buffer Enquiry

31

1.5 | LAN Protocol Implementations

The next logical question becomes, "How do all of the LAN protocols fit into the overall scheme of the OSI Reference Model?" Figure 1-12 provides an explanation. The lower two layers, Physical and Data Link, are hardware-dependent. As such, they define the type of transmission medium (twisted-pair, coax, or fiber-optic cable), the network topology (bus, star, or ring), medium-access technique (CSMA/CD or token passing), and the transmission frame format.

Figure 1-12
LAN protocol implementation

Application	Application Programs and Protocols for file transfer, electronic mail, etc.				
Presentation	Novell NetWare Core Protocols (NCP)	3Com 3+ Redirector and Server Message Block (SMB)	IBM PC LAN Program Redirector and Server Message Block (SMB)	Banyan VINES	Apple Computer AppleTalk Filing Protocol (AFP)
Session	NetBIOS	NetBIOS	NetBIOS	Remote Procedural Calls (Net RPC)	AppleTalk Session Protocol (ASP)
Transport	NetWare SPX	Sequenced Packet Protocol (SPP)	PC LAN	VINES Interprocess Communications Protocol (VIPC)	AppleTalk Transaction Protocol (ATP)
Network	NetWare IPX	Internetwork Datagram Protocol (IDP)	Support Program	VINES Internet Protocol (VIP)	Datagram Delivery Protocol (DDP)
Data Link	Network Interface Cards: Ethernet, Token-Ring, ARCNET, StarLAN				
Physical	Transmission Media: Twisted Pair, Coax, or Fiber Optics				

Starting at the Network Layer and extending to the Application Layer are the various protocols associated with each NOS, such as Novell's NetWare, Banyan Systems' VINES, or Apple Computer's AppleTalk. As can be seen from Figure 1-12, not all NOSs implement each layer. Indeed, the strengths and weaknesses of each protocol suite are revealed when compared to the benchmark of OSI. Rather than trying to argue that Brand X is superior or inferior to Brand Y, we will dissect each NOS individually, starting with Novell's NetWare in Chapter 3. Subsequent chapters will discuss 3Com Corporation's 3+ and 3+ Open, IBM's Token-Ring related protocols such as NetBIOS and Server Message Block, Banyan Systems' VINES, and Apple Computer's AppleTalk. Once armed with the technical details of each network operating system, the reader can determine the strengths and weaknesses of each product for himself or herself and apply that information to his or her own network environment.

1.6 References

[1-1] International Organization for Standardization, Information Processing Systems — Open Systems Interconnection-Basic Reference Model, ISO 7498 — 1984.

[1-2] Institute of Electrical and Electronics Engineers, Carrier Sense Multiple Access with Collision Detection (CSMA/CD) Access Method and Physical Layer Specifications, ISO 8802-3, ANSI/IEEE Std 802.3 — 1988.

[1-3] Institute of Electrical and Electronics Engineers, Token Passing Bus Access Method, ISO/DIS 8802/4, ANSI/IEEE Std 802.4 — 1985.

[1-4] Institute of Electrical and Electronics Engineers, Token Ring Access Method, IEEE Standard 802.5 — 1989.

[1-5] Institute of Electrical and Electronics Engineers, Logical Link Control, ISO 8802.2, IEEE Std 802.2 — 1989.

[1-6] John Voelcker, "Helping Computers Communicate", *IEEE Spectrum*, Volume 23, Number 3, March 1986 pp. 61–70, (also reprinted in *Computer Communications: Architectures, Protocols and Standards*, Second Edition, IEEE Computer Society Press, 1987, pp. 9–18).

[1-7] Miller, Mark A., *LAN Troubleshooting Handbook*, M&T Books, 1989.

[1-8] Digital Equipment Corporation, Ethernet Data Link Layer and Physical Layer Specifications, 1982.

[1-9] A Standard for the Transmission of IP Datagram Over IEEE 802 Networks, RFC-1042, DDN Network Information Center, February 1988.

[1-10] Datapoint Corporation, ARCNET Designer's Handbook, document 61610, 1988.

Ethernet Protocol Types

The Ethernet type field contains a hexadecimal number that can be interpreted to yield a symbolic Ethernet protocol type name. A table of some of the major Ethernet protocol types and their descriptions follows. (Table Courtesy of FTP Software, Inc., and believed accurate as of February 15, 1990.)

Hexidecimal	Description	Notes
0000-05DC	IEEE802.3 Length Field	
0101-01FF	Experimental (for development)	Conflicts with 802.3 length fields
0200	Xerox PUP	Conflicts with 802.3 length fields
0201	PUP Address Translation	Conflicts with 802.3 length fields
0600	Xerox XNS IDP	
0800	DoD IP	
0801	X.75 Internet	
0802	NBS Internet	
0803	ECMA Internet	
0804	CHAOSnet	
0805	X.25 Level 3	
0806	ARP (for IP and for CHAOS)	
0807	XNS Compatibility	
081C	Symbolics Private	
0888-088A	Xyplex	
0900	Ungermann-Bass Network Debugger	
0A00	Xerox 802.3 PUP	
0A01	PUP 802.3 Address Translation	
0BAD	Banyan Systems	
1000	Berkeley trailer negotiation	
1001-100F	Berkeley Trailer encapsulation	
1600	VALID	
4242	PCS Basic Block Protocol	
5208	BBN Simnet Private	
6000	DEC Unassigned	
6001	DEC MOP Dump/Load Assistance	
6002	DEC MOP Remote Console	

Hexidecimal	Description
6003	DEC DECnet Phase IV
6004	DEC LAT
6005	DEC DECNet Diagnostics
6006	DEC DECNet Customer Use
6007	DEC DECNet SCA
6009	DEC Unassigned
6010-6014	3Com Corp.
7000	Ungermann-Bass Download
7001	UB NIU
7002	UB NIU
7020-7029	LRT (England)
7030	Proteon
8003	Cronus VLN
8004	Cronus Direct
8005	HP Probe protocol
8006	Nestar
8008	AT&T
8010	Excelan
8013	SGI diagnostic type (obsolete)
8014	SGI network games (obsolete)
8015	SGI reserved type (obsolete)
8016	SGI "bounce server" (obsolete)
8019	Apollo
802E	Tymshare
802F	Tigan, Inc.
8035	Reverse ARP
8036	Aeonic Systems
8038	DEC LANBridge
8039	DEC Unassigned
803A	DEC Unassigned
803B	DEC Unassigned
803C	DEC Unassigned
803D	DEC Ethernet CSMA/CD Encryption Protocol
803E	DEC Unassigned
803F	DEC LAN Traffic Monitor
8040	DEC Unassigned
8041	DEC Unassigned
8042	DEC Unassigned
8044	Planning Research Corp.
8046	AT&T
8047	AT&T
8049	ExperData (France)
805B	Versatile Message Translation Protocol RFC-1045 (Stanford)
805C	Stanford V Kernel production
805D	Evans & Sutherland

Hexidecimal	Description
8060	Little Machines
8062	Counterpoint Computers
8065	University of Massachusetts, Amherst
8066	University of Massachusetts, Amherst
8067	Veeco Integrated Automation
8068	General Dynamics
8069	AT&T
806A	Autophon (Switzerland)
806C	ComDesign
806D	Compugraphic Corp
806E-8077	Landmark Graphics Corp.
807A	Matra (France)
807B	Dansk Data Elektronic A/S (Denmark)
807C	Merit Internodal
807D	VitaLink Communications
807E	VitaLink Communications
807F	VitaLink Communications
8080	VitaLink Communications bridge
8081	Counterpoint Computers
8082	Counterpoint Computers
8083	Counterpoint Computers
8088	Xyplex
8089	Xyplex
808A	Xyplex
809B	Kinetics Ethertalk - Appletalk over Ethernet
809C	Datability
809D	Datability
809E	Datability
809F	Spider Systems, Ltd. (England)
80A3	Nixdorf Computer (West Germany)
80A4-80B3	Siemens Gammasonics Inc.
80C0	Digital Communications Assoc.
80C1	Digital Communications Assoc.
80C2	Digital Communications Assoc.
80C3	Digital Communications Assoc.
80C6	Pacer Software
80C7	Applitek Corp.
80C8-80CC	Integraph Corp.
80CD	Harris Corp.
80CE	Harris Corp.
80CF-80D2	Taylor Inst.
80D3	Rosemount Corp.
80D4	Rosemount Corp.
80D5	IBM SNA Services Over Ethernet
80DD	Varian Assoc.

Hexidecimal	Description
80DE	Integrated Solutions TRFS (Transparent Remote File System)
80DF	Integrated Solutions
80E0	Allen-Bradley
80E3	Allen-Bradley
80E4-80F0	Datability
80F2	Retix
80F3	Kinetics, AppleTalk ARP (AARP)
80F4	Kinetics
80F5	Kinetics
80F7	Apollo Computer
80FF-8103	Wellfleet Communications
8107	Symbolics Private
8108	Symbolics Private
8109	Symbolics Private
8130	Waterloo Microsystems
8131	VG Laboratory Systems
8137	Novell (old) NetWare IPX (ECONFIG E Option)
8138	Novell
8139-813D	KTI
9000	Loopback (Configuration Test Protocol)
9001	Bridge Communications XNS Systems Management
9002	Bridge Communications TCP/IP Systems Management
9003	Bridge Communications
FF00	BBN VITAL LANBridge cache wakeup

CHAPTER TWO

LAN Protocol and Performance Analysis

Network analysis and troubleshooting have become really hot topics. For several years now, a number of vendors have advertised their network products as "plug and play." With modular cabling systems, LAN components can certainly be plugged together. Unfortunately, they don't always play as they should. This has led to an increased demand for diagnostic tools that can isolate network compatibility problems.

The companion volume to this book, *LAN Troubleshooting Handbook*, focused primarily on finding and fixing hardware failures: cables, connectors, network interface cards (NICs), etc. This book will address software difficulties, examining different network operating systems within the context of the OSI Reference Model. As we study the different protocols, we will approach analysis and diagnosis from the point of view of a layered architecture as well. Therefore, we must begin by looking at the role that these layered protocols perform within a LAN.

2.1 The Role of Protocols

As we discussed in Chapter 1, a protocol is merely a set of rules. In society, protocols govern the way we shake hands. In the military, protocols govern when (and to whom) you salute. In local area networks, protocols govern the interaction between each individual workstation (or client) and the file server.

We will assume that each network node (workstation, server, host, etc.) has a layered architecture which may or may not exactly fit the OSI Reference Model. Each layer of the architecture has a defined set of functions and communicates with its peer (or equal) process at the distant node (see Figure 2-1).

Figure 2-1
Peer-to-peer communication within layered systems

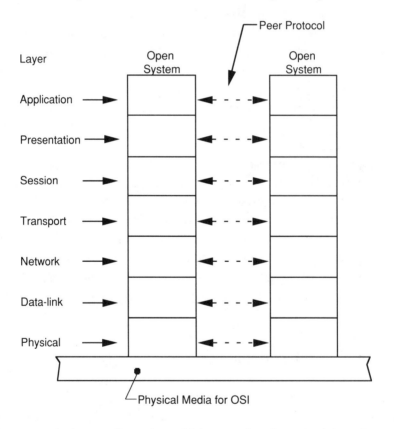

The transmission medium (or cable) provides the actual (or physical) path between nodes. When this path is damaged or disconnected, communication problems naturally arise. Architectural layers above the physical layer also have communication paths, however these paths are virtual. By virtual, we mean that they give every appearance of existing, but can only be seen by somehow tapping into the physical path. The Data Link Layer (layer 2) exists in each node; however, communication between Data Link processes at each node (a virtual connection) can only be established with the existence (and co-operation) of the underlying physical layer to which each Data Link Layer process has an interface. The hardware (Layers 1 and 2) plus the software (Layers 3 through 7) must thus function together in order for the Application data on one system (such as your workstation) to communicate with its intended destination system (such as the network server).

Several fundamental principles emerge here. First, each layer of the network architecture has a defined function, and implements that function using a protocol. Second, the various layers within a single node (and their protocols) maintain relationships to each other. These relationships are called interfaces. These interfaces are allowed certain assumptions about the nature and responsibilities of their adjacent layers (both higher and lower). Thus the Data Link Layer provides services to the Network Layer, but it uses the services made available by the Physical Layer. Finally, each layer (and therefore each protocol) has a peer (or equal) with which it is communicating at the distant node. For example, my workstation's Data Link Layer communicates with the server's Data Link Layer, just as my workstation's Network Layer communicates with the server's Network Layer, and so on.

Unfortunately, these communication paths are not always foolproof. For example, my NIC may build a transmission frame that is too short or too long for the server to recognize. Or, perhaps the hardware that computes the Cyclic Redundancy Check (CRC or checksum) is faulty at either the transmitter or the receiver, thus causing the frame to be rejected. An operating system parameter, such as a cache buffer size, may have an inappropriate size for the application, thus producing excessive delays. The process of protocol analysis helps us isolate these failures and determine exactly what has gone wrong.

Reference [2-1] (the OSI Reference Model) provides good background information about layered architectures. References [2-2] and [2-3] provide further insight into protocols and their use in a LAN environment.

2.2 | Protocol Analysis

The layered network architecture consists of various protocols that communicate with their peer processes at the distant node. Since all of these protocols must reach the destination node at the far end in order for the data at the highest layer (the Application layer) to be meaningful, the protocols must be transmitted along with that data. The protocol information is carried within the transmission (Data Link Layer) frame.

The model we used in Chapter 1 to describe this process was the onion (see Figure 2-2). Workstation data that is to be transmitted, such as a database record, is passed to the Application Layer. This process adds the Protocol Control Information (PCI) that is then used to communicate with its peer (Application Layer) process on the server. The data plus Application Layer PCI is then passed to the next lower layer, the Presentation Layer. Additional PCI is added by each layer in turn until the bits at layer 1, the Physical Layer, are actually transmitted over the cable. At the receiving end, a similar process occurs, but in reverse. The model of the onion is helpful because each layer of PCI can be peeled off and examined before passing the information on to the next higher layer.

Figure 2-2
Encapsulating data with Protocol Control Information

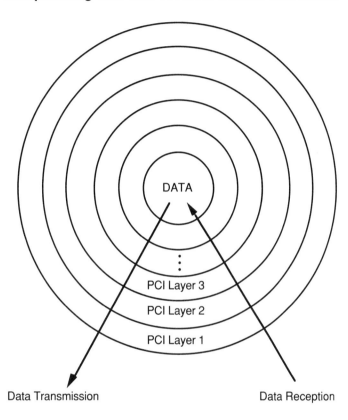

PCI: Protocol Control Information

The technique of protocol analysis is analogous to peeling the onion. We look at one layer, and then remove it to reveal the next layer that needs examination. The protocol analyzer is the tool that automatically peels the onion for us. It contains a NIC for the particular type of network to be analyzed, whether it is ARCNET, Ethernet, or token ring, and attaches to the LAN like any other node where it passively listens or eavesdrops on all network transmissions (see Figure 2-3). The protocol analyzer automatically peels off the various of layers of Protocol Control Information, decodes them, and presents them for study in some meaningful fashion, such as EBCDIC, ASCII, hexadecimal, or English.

Figure 2-3
Protocol Analyzer Attachment on a LAN

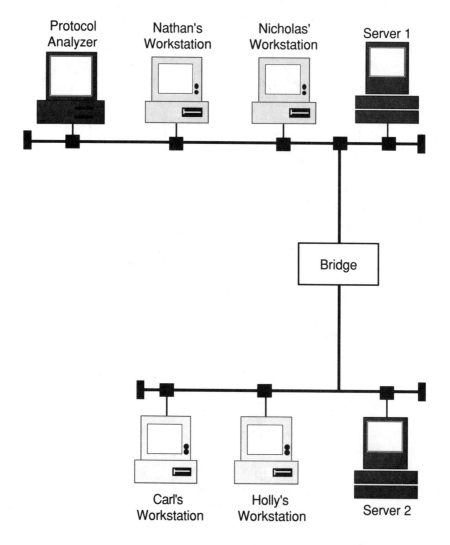

Note that the location of the protocol analyzer on the network is important; the data must pass by the analyzer's NIC in order to be captured. In Figure 2-3, data transmitted on the cable segment from Carl's workstation or Holly's workstations to Server 2 could not be captured by the protocol analyzer on the other cable segment because the analyzer and data of interest are on opposite sides of the bridge. These transactions could be analyzed, however, if some capabilities were added to the test configuration, such as a remote unit, which could report the results of the transmission to the protocol analyzer. We'll discuss several protocol analyzers that offer these capabilities in section 2.5.

The process of eavesdropping on network transmissions is called capturing. However, before using the protocol analyzer to capture data, you need to decide which frames of information are important and should be captured. This is called filtering. With different analyzers, the user can set filters to include or exclude the capture of frames based upon many different parameters, such as source or destination addresses, higher layer protocol data contained within the frame's information field, whether the CRC on the frame passed or failed, etc. The capture is also affected by the speed of the analyzer's CPU, its memory, storage capacity, etc.

The next process is the decoding and display of the filtered information. Decoding is usually invisible to the end user, and utilizes protocol interpreters that are built into the analyzer. These interpreters are specific to the particular protocols being decoded, e.g. NetWare or TCP/IP.

Acquiring a protocol analyzer is a major investment, and care must be taken to insure that your network's protocols can be analyzed with the unit or software you select. In other words, check carefully and make sure you know about all the protocol interpreters before purchasing. We'll look more at some of the different vendors tools in Section 2.5.

The analyzer's ability to set traps (capture a specific bit pattern) and triggers (recognizing an event such as the change in a control lead) that start or end a capture also is most useful. Customized tests, or applications libraries that contain test scripts, can be a real time saver.

The analyzer's storage abilities, including both RAM and hard disk, plus its ability to produce hard copy output are important considerations when it comes to analyzing a problem. For example, being able to print out a captured trace file for further analysis the next day, or being able to replay the captured data, can be vital to solving the problem.

Finally, the protocol analyzer is valuable because it allows us to benchmark the LAN, thus observing trends in network performance over an extended period of time. This makes it easier to predict what effect that adding an additional 30 workstations or a new bridge will have on network performance. We will discuss some of these network metrics in section 2.4.

2.3 | Protocol Analysis Techniques

Protocol analyzers can be used for a variety of purposes, including finding hardware and software faults, optimizing a network, and isolating bad cables. Cable faults, for example, can be varied:

- cable is shorted, open, or frayed
- connector is bad or improperly seated
- cross-connect field is miswired
- cable tap is faulty
- cable is improperly grounded

Hardware faults (other than those that are cabling related) are usually associated with a defective NIC or repeater. Examples of such faults would be:

- a workstation that can transmit but not receive
- excessive data packet collisions
- improperly framed transmissions, known as fragments (frames that are too short) or jabbers (frames that are too long)
- high error rates resulting from a failure of the CRC calculation at either transmitter or receiver

Software faults can be especially elusive, and can have several causes:

- failure of the software itself (affectionately known as a bug)
- parameters (such as workstation cache buffers) that are improperly configured
- incompatibilities between two nodes, such as transmit and receive buffers or window sizes

Routing and addressing problems can also occur for extended LANs or internetworks. These kinds of errors can include:

- duplicate node addresses
- network congestion at a bridge, router, or gateway
- broadcast storms where nodes broadcast queries for routing information and do not allow sufficient time for a response

We'll look at software difficulties associated with individual LAN software suites in the detailed chapters that follow.

Of course, a protocol analyzer is not a panacea for all your network ills. In order to identify the specific LAN fault, the network analyst must do several things:

1. Remain calm. No failure can be solved in a panic.

2. Make a best guess as to the nature of the failure -- hardware or software. This step is crucial because it will guide the steps in analysis and dictate what other tools might be useful, such as a Time Domain Reflectometer (TDR), tone generator and detector, breakout box, etc.

3. Mentally outline a strategy to isolate the failure.

4. Be methodical and only change one parameter or variable at a time during the troubleshooting or network optimization process. Record the effect of the previous change, and carefully consider if the change of a second parameter will interact with the first. When in doubt, restore the first parameter to its initial value, and then change another variable.

5. Take good notes during the troubleshooting process.

In order to analyze the performance of a LAN, we must know two things: 1) what characteristics should the network exhibit when it is operating properly, and 2) what conditions could be causing the abnormal behavior. We'll begin by defining the metrics used to define LAN performance.

2.4 | LAN Performance Metrics

Network metrics give the administrator a benchmark against which to gauge the overall health of LAN. While there are obvious differences in architecture that affect which metrics will apply to your LAN (e.g., token ring networks don't experience collisions), we can still divide these measurements into four general categories.

| 2.4.1 | **Network Utilization** |

Network Utilization measures the gross level of activity on the network. Mathematically, this is defined as the ratio of the number of bits transmitted during a specific period of time to the total number of bits that could have been transmitted during that period. Appendix A of reference [2-4] calculates the number of bits that represent 100% utilization for Ethernet/802.3 networks.

Let us assume that a maximum length frame (8 octet preamble + 14 octet header + 1500 octets of data + 4 octet FCS) is to be transmitted. Also remember that an interframe gap (9.6 microseconds or μsec of dead time) precedes each frame. Therefore, the time to transmit each maximum length frame will be:

$$(1526 \text{ octets} * 8 \text{ bits/octets} * 0.1 \text{ μsec/bit}) + 9.6 \text{ μsec}$$
$$= 1.23 \text{ milliseconds or ms}$$

Thus, in one second 812 frames (plus 812 interframe gaps) occur.

When these interframe gaps are considered, the actual number of bits transmitted during a one-second interval is 9,922,048, not 10,000,000 as one might intuitively expect. The lower number (9,922,048) is the correct value for 100% utilization.

Using this result, if 50 Ethernet/802.3 frames, each containing 100 octets of data, are transmitted in one second, the total number of octets transmitted would be:

$$\text{Total data} = (8 \text{ octet preamble} + 14 \text{ octet header}$$
$$+ 100 \text{ octets data} + 4 \text{ octet FCS})$$
$$* 8 \text{ bits/octet} * 50 \text{ frames}$$
$$= 50,400 \text{ bits transmitted}$$

$$\text{Network Utilization} = \frac{50,400 \text{ bits transmitted}}{9,922,048 \text{ maximum bits}}$$

$$= 0.5\%$$

While this number may seem low, it is actually fairly representative, since most LANs experience a network utilization less than 15 percent.

2.4.2 | Network Traffic

To measure network traffic you must first define the sources and destinations of the information transmitted over the LAN. The first metric to consider, sometimes referred to as Pair Counts, is the measurement of the number of frames exchanged between pairs of workstations, or between a workstation and a peripheral. This measurement determines which nodes are the busiest, who is communicating with whom, and can be useful in dividing the network into communities of interest. This determination is often required before adding a network bridge to create subnetworks.

A second, related benchmark is Throughput, which measures the number of frames or bits that have passed through the network. This measurement usually has at least two peaks per day, normally between 10:00 and 11:00 am and 2:00 and 3:00 pm. By measuring traffic and determining the peak times, it is often possible to schedule traffic so that throughput-intensive activities, such as large file transfers, can take place at off-peak times in order to smooth out the network load.

A third benchmark, Frame Statistics, establishes the minimum, maximum, and average sizes of transmitted frames. These can prove useful for determining what type of activity (e.g. database queries with short frames or file transfers with long frames) are predominantly used on the LAN.

All network analyzers have the ability to analyze the network traffic based upon the higher layer protocol used within each frame, such as TCP/IP, NetBIOS, or AppleTalk. This network traffic data can provide insights into the way in which the network resources, such as mainframe applications, are being utilized.

2.4.3 | Network Delays

Network users always seem to be in a hurry. Two measurements can be made to determine if the network is running slower or faster today than yesterday.

The Channel Acquisition Time is the time between when the frame is ready for transmission and when it is actually placed on the network. As such, it is a measure of the Media Access Control (MAC) delay, including delays, collisions, etc.

Network Response Time measures the propagation delay from the transmitter to receiver and back. It can be a useful measurement when a wide area network connection, such as leased lines, is exhibiting excessive delays.

2.4.4 | Network Errors

Frame errors cause retransmissions, and generally degrade network performance. Five different frame error situations can occur:

- A bad Frame Check Sequence (FCS) indicates that bit errors occurred that affected the Cyclic Redundancy Check (CRC).

- Misaligned Frames occur when the number of bits in the received frame is not an integral number of octets, and the frame also has a bad FCS.

- Jabbers are frames that exceed the maximum allowable frame length.

- Runts are frames that are less than the minimum frame length.

- Finally, Collisions result from the simultaneous transmission of two stations and occur in IEEE 802.3 networks.

Tracking down the sources of these network errors generally leads to a defective Network Interface Card (NIC) at one of the workstations.

2.5 | Protocol Analysis Tools

Given the assumption that Murphy's law is in effect and that disaster will eventually strike your network software, it would be prudent to have some type of analysis tool available. Fortunately, electronic test equipment for network software is available from many different manufacturers in a variety of models. Unfortunately, these tools can be quite costly. The challenge is selecting the protocol analyzer that fits your network and your budget.

In this section, we will look at six different protocol analyzers, from software-only products, to hardware/software kits to upgrade a PC to a stand-alone test units. These six analyzers are representative of what is available to the LAN administrator, but is by no means an exhaustive list. Neither is this section an attempt to provide comprehensive product reviews or endorsements of any particular unit. All of the analyzers mentioned here, as well as those not mentioned, have their strengths and weaknesses. Specifics, such as pricing and protocols supported, should be obtained directly from the vendors listed in Appendix 2.

One purpose of this section is to provide a survey of several available units, thus giving the reader enough background information to conduct additional research and find an analyzer that will meet his or her unique needs. Demonstration disks for many of these analyzers are available for those readers who wish to pursue the techniques of protocol analysis or consider the purchase of an analysis tool. (See the coupon in the back of the book for further details.)

2.5.1 | FTP Software, Inc.'s LANWatch

LANWatch is a software-only product that turns any PC or compatible having 384 kilobytes of RAM and one floppy drive into a LAN Analyzer, and is available for Ethernet, StarLAN, IEEE 802.3, and IEEE 802.5 networks. In addition to a PC, the user must supply a NIC for the particular network in use. Western-Digital, 3Com, Interlan, Proteon, and other vendors' NICs are currently supported). Because of the reliance upon the user-supplied host PC and the NIC, LANWatch capture rates and storage specifications vary. Higher layer protocol converters are available for TCP/IP, IPX, XNS, VINES, AppleTalk, DECnet and other protocol suites.

LANWatch has two principal methods of operation. Display mode provides real time capture and display of network transmissions. Examine mode allows a detailed analysis of captured data.

The Display mode gives information on each packet as it is received by LANWatch. Each line starts with a timestamp, packet length in bytes, and protocol type. Additional information is taken from the packet header and is protocol-dependent. (For most protocols, this will include source and destination addresses.) Toggle switches allow the user to select a display of seven layers of information corresponding to the ISO layers (Figure 2-1). Display mode also includes several filters:

- Background, which determines which packets are accepted from the network;

- Viewing, which determines which packets are displayed on the screen;

- Save, which determines which packets are stored to a dump file;

- Alarm, which will sound the bell on the PC when a specified event occurs; and

- End Trigger, which will wait for a specified event to reach the center of the buffer, then enter Examine mode.

Filters can be combined or modified by the operations AND, OR, and NOT. FTP supplies sufficient source code written in C so users can write their own filters and protocol interpreters.

Examine mode stops the capture of network traffic and analyzes the contents of the buffer. Previously stored information may be specified using the Load filter. It has a short display, which is like that of Display mode (Figure 2-4), and a long display (Figure 2-5), which contains additional information on each packet, and hexadecimal and ASCII dumps of the packet contents. A Search filter is available in both forward and reverse to find particular events.

Figure 2-4
FTP Software, Inc., LANWatch Examine Screen

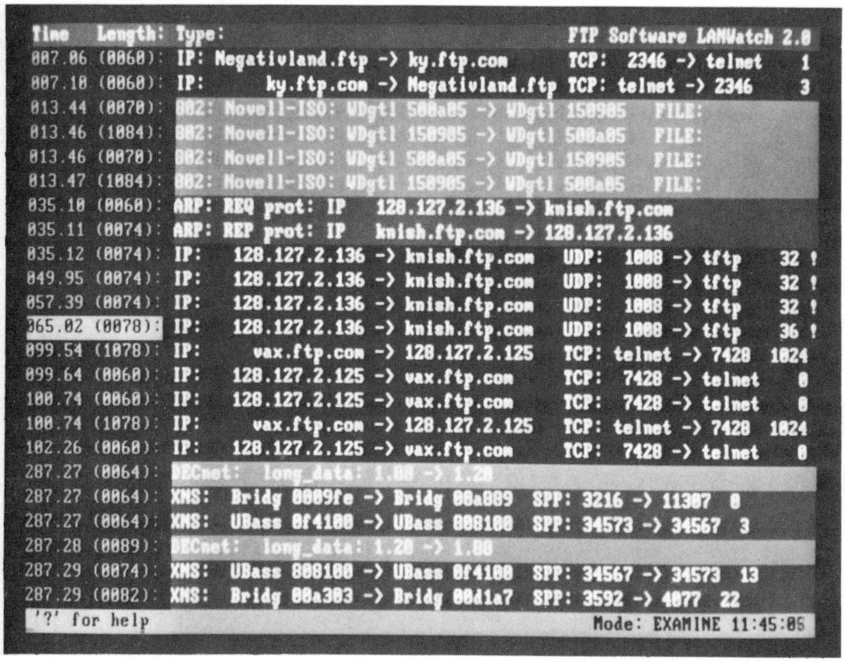

```
Time   Length: Type:                                    FTP Software LANWatch 2.0
007.06 (0060): IP: Negativland.ftp -> ky.ftp.com      TCP:  2346 -> telnet    1
007.10 (0060): IP:       ky.ftp.com -> Negativland.ftp TCP: telnet -> 2346     3
013.44 (0070): 802: Novell-ISO: WDgtl 500a05 -> WDgtl 150905    FILE:
013.46 (1004): 802: Novell-ISO: WDgtl 150905 -> WDgtl 500a05    FILE:
013.46 (0070): 802: Novell-ISO: WDgtl 500a05 -> WDgtl 150905    FILE:
013.47 (1004): 802: Novell-ISO: WDgtl 150905 -> WDgtl 500a05    FILE:
035.10 (0060): ARP: REQ prot: IP  128.127.2.136 -> knish.ftp.com
035.11 (0074): ARP: REP prot: IP     knish.ftp.com -> 128.127.2.136
035.12 (0074): IP:     128.127.2.136 -> knish.ftp.com   UDP:  1008 -> tftp    32 !
049.95 (0074): IP:     128.127.2.136 -> knish.ftp.com   UDP:  1008 -> tftp    32 !
057.39 (0074): IP:     128.127.2.136 -> knish.ftp.com   UDP:  1008 -> tftp    32 !
065.02 (0078): IP:     128.127.2.136 -> knish.ftp.com   UDP:  1008 -> tftp    36 !
099.54 (1078): IP:       vax.ftp.com -> 128.127.2.125   TCP: telnet -> 7428  1024
099.64 (0060): IP:     128.127.2.125 -> vax.ftp.com     TCP:  7428 -> telnet    0
100.74 (0060): IP:     128.127.2.125 -> vax.ftp.com     TCP:  7428 -> telnet    0
100.74 (1078): IP:       vax.ftp.com -> 128.127.2.125   TCP: telnet -> 7428  1024
102.26 (0060): IP:     128.127.2.125 -> vax.ftp.com     TCP:  7428 -> telnet    0
287.27 (0064): DECnet:  long_data: 1.88 -> 1.20
287.27 (0064): XNS:   Bridg 0009fe -> Bridg 00a809   SPP: 3216 -> 11307  0
287.27 (0064): XNS:   UBass 0f4100 -> UBass 808100   SPP: 34573 -> 34567  3
287.28 (0089): DECnet:  long_data: 1.20 -> 1.88
287.29 (0074): XNS:   UBass 808100 -> UBass 0f4100   SPP: 34567 -> 34573  13
287.29 (0082): XNS:   Bridg 00a303 -> Bridg 0041a7   SPP: 3592 -> 4077  22
'?' for help                                          Mode: EXAMINE 11:45:05
```

Figure 2-5
FTP Software, Inc. LANWatch Long Format Display Screen

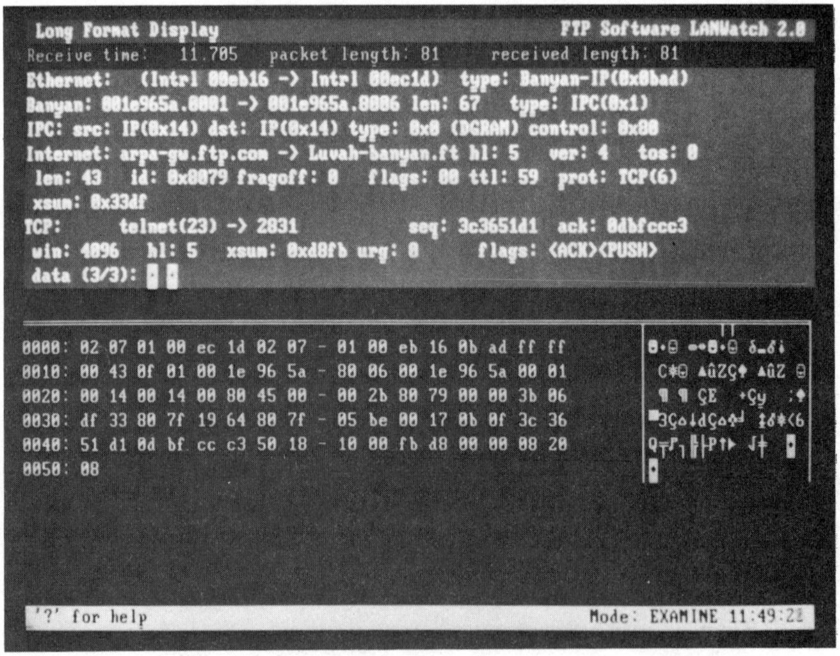

```
Long Format Display                          FTP Software LANWatch 2.8
Receive time:  11.785   packet length: 81    received length: 81
Ethernet:  (Intrl 00eb16 -> Intrl 00ec1d)  type: Banyan-IP(0x0bad)
Banyan: 001e965a.0001 -> 001e965a.0006 len: 67   type: IPC(0x1)
IPC: src: IP(0x14) dst: IP(0x14) type: 0x0 (DGRAM) control: 0x00
Internet: arpa-gw.ftp.com -> Luvah-banyan.ft hl: 5   ver: 4   tos: 0
len: 43   id: 0x0079 fragoff: 0   flags: 00 ttl: 59   prot: TCP(6)
xsum: 0x33df
TCP:        telnet(23) -> 2831        seq: 3c3651d1  ack: 0dbfccc3
win: 4096   hl: 5   xsum: 0xd8fb urg: 0      flags: <ACK><PUSH>
data (3/3):

0000: 02 07 01 00 ec 1d 02 07 - 01 00 eb 16 0b ad ff ff
0010: 00 43 0f 01 00 1e 96 5a - 00 06 00 1e 96 5a 00 01
0020: 00 14 00 14 00 00 45 00 - 00 2b 00 79 00 00 3b 06
0030: df 33 00 7f 19 64 00 7f - 05 be 00 17 0b 0f 3c 36
0040: 51 d1 0d bf cc c3 50 18 - 10 00 fb d8 00 00 00 20
0050: 08

'?' for help                                Mode: EXAMINE 11:49:2
```

LANWatch also contains a statistics package that can analyze the number of frames of each protocol received, the frame size, and histograms of network traffic. In summary, this is a powerful software package for those administrators wishing to supply their own hardware (Reference [2-5] provides further details.)

2.5.2 | Digilog, Inc.'s LANVista

LANVista is available in three different configurations. A Stand-alone System includes an add-in card plus software. The Complete System includes a Dolch 80386 portable computer (Figure 2-6). The Distributed System contains slave units (Figure 2-7) that can be attached to remote LAN segments and monitored from a central point. The master/slave software is compatible with Microsoft Windows and provides simultaneous communication between the master and various slaves.

Figure 2-6
Digilog, Inc. LANVista system

Figure 2-7
Digilog, Inc. LANVista slave units

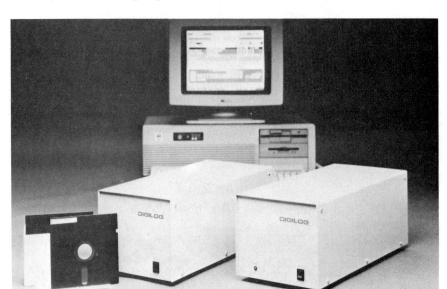

The physical communication path is via the LAN itself or an external serial (RS-232) connection. The master/slave architecture is one of LANVista's unique features and allows monitoring and analysis of remote segments connected via bridges or gateways.

LANVista is currently available for Ethernet, IEEE 802.3, and IEEE 802.5 networks. Network statistics and individual segment statistics provide details on network operation (Figure 2-8). Many statistics are available, including frame length, frame gap, network utilization, and errors.

Figure 2-8
Digilog, Inc. LANVista Network Display screen

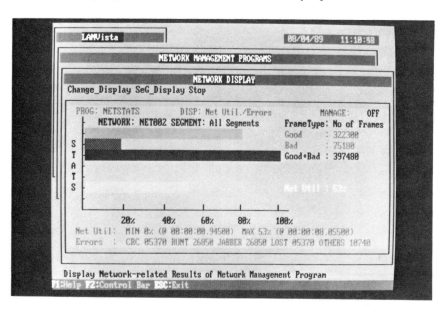

Protocol interpreters are available for TCP/IP, IPX, DECnet, XNS, and AppleTalk Phases 1 and 2. The Summary mode (Figure 2-9) delineates frame number, a time stamp, size addresses, filters, and errors. The Protocol mode (see Figure 2-10) provides a seven-layer decoded readout of the particular frame with all of its fields. TDR functions are also included, allowing the detection and analysis of cable problems. In summary, LANVista's strength is its flexible architecture and its ability to monitor remote LAN segments. (Reference [2-6] provides additional details.)

Figure 2-9
Digilog, Inc. LANVista Summary Mode screen

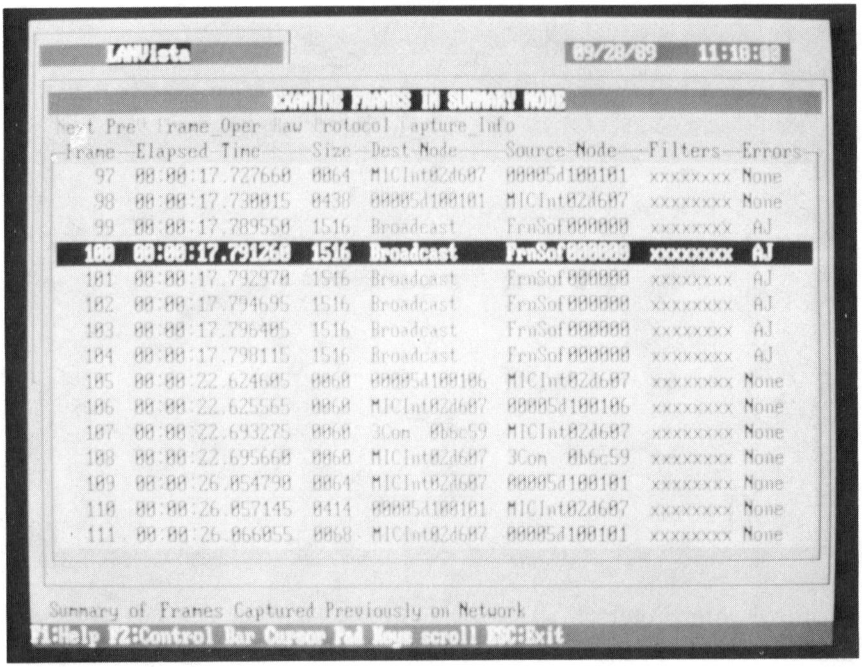

Figure 2-10
Digilog, Inc. LANVista Protocol Mode screen

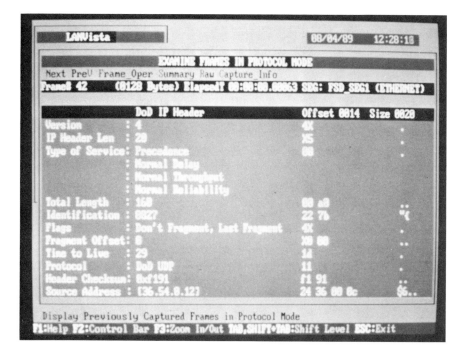

2.5.3 | Novell Inc.'s LANalyzer

The LANalyzer, from Novell was one of the first protocol analyzers. Originally developed and marketed by Excelan in an Ethernet version, the latest version of the LANalyzer supports IEEE 802.3 and IEEE 802.5 as well. This analysis tool is available in two formats: as a kit including an optimized NIC (80286 with 2 Mbytes of buffer memory and specialized networking hardware) and software for installation in a user-supplied AT-compatible PC; or as a stand-alone unit packaged in an NEC 80386SX portable computer (Figure 2-11). The specialized hardware has the capability to detect and measure important physical layer attributes, such as actual utilization, network collisions, and token rotation time, that are unobtainable on analyzers that use standard network adapters. An adapter board is available for StarLAN (IEEE 802.3 1BASE5) networks.

All operation is initiated from the Command Screen (Figure 2-12), with various annotated function keys assigned. A mouse interface is also included to simplify user operations. Up to eight channels can be activated, each having unique programmable filters. This filtering is performed as packets are received so the LANalyzer can display utilization and statistics for each channel in real time. The LANalyzer traffic generator can be activated while receiving so the unit can generate a load while simultaneously viewing the results. This function can also be used to stimulate other stations and then capturing the returned packets When used in conjunction with the high-resolution time-stamping, this technique can be useful for testing the response time of stations or transit time through gateways.

Figure 2-11
Novell, Inc. LANalyzer

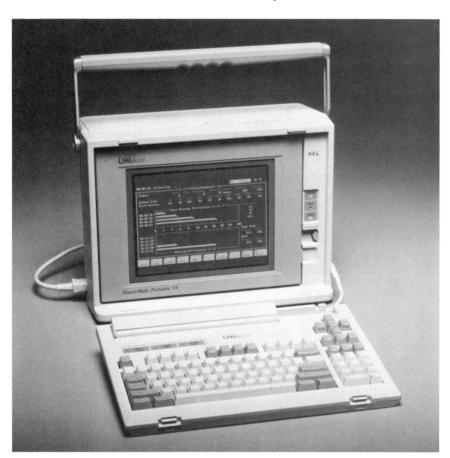

The Monitor Network screen for token ring (Figure 2-13) shows a variety of network statistics, such as token rotation time, error counts, and data throughput. Bar charts display average network utilization in 1-, 5-, 10-, and 20-second periods (user definable), as well as instantaneous utilization in the last 1 to 5 seconds. A similar screen exists for each of the defined channels. The Station Monitor screen (Figure 2-14) displays the real-time activity for up to 600 stations. The Packet Slice screen (Figure 2-15) examines the details of captured frames, including protocol details for layers 1 - 4 and a hexadecimal display of the entire frame.

Figure 2-12
Novell, Inc. LANalyzer Command screen

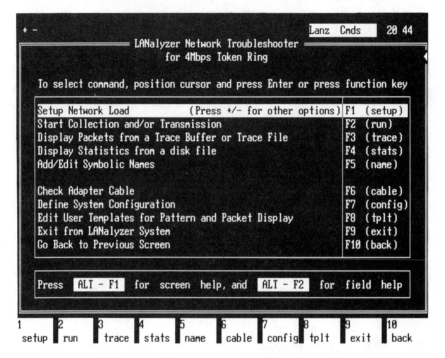

Figure 2-13
Novell, Inc. LANalyzer Monitor Network screen

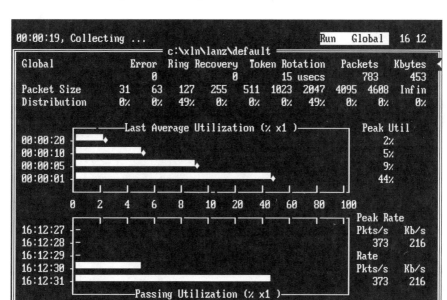

Figure 2-14
Novell, Inc. LANalyzer Station Monitor screen

```
00:00:29, Collecting ...                          Run   Station  16 35
═══════════════════════ c:\xln\lanz\default ═══════════════════════
142  Stations
                                   Packets:            Avg Size:   Errors:
No.   In Station Address    Out   Receive  Transmit   Rcv   Xmt    Rcv   Xmt
‡49    5> utah               4>    119*      82*       64    91
 50    4> 08 00 14 50 70 06  5>     83*     120*       90    64
 51       08 00 14 51 01 14          0        5*             92
 52       08 00 14 13 03 04          1*       1*       64    64
 53       08 00 14 70 01 75          1*       1*       64    64
 54       08 00 14 55 34 60          0        5*             92
 55       08 00 14 56 36 36          1*       6*       74    98
 56       qa1                        1*       6*       74    94
 57       08 00 14 51 02 46          1*       6*       74   102
 58       08 00 14 51 17 55          0        5*             92
 59       08 00 14 51 27 92          0        4*             92
 60       08 00 14 56 01 44          1*       5*       74    99
 61       08 00 14 61 00 05          0        5*             92
 62       08 00 14 50 80 10          0        5*             92
 63       cisloan_pc         1>      0        5*             92
 64       sco286_pc          1>      2*       7*       69    96

1       2       3       4       5       6       7       8       9       10
start   stop    globl   ctrs            stn     config          more    abort
```

Figure 2-15
Novell, Inc. LANalyzer Packet Slice screen

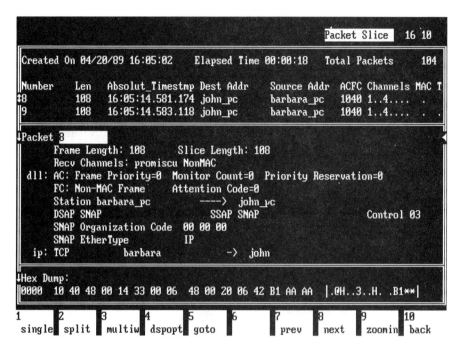

Protocol interpreters are available for TCP/IP, DECnet, XNS, AppleTalk, and OSI. An application library containing more than 45 pre-defined setups for performing many useful network tests is also supplied. The strengths of the LANalyzer include its specialized high-performance hardware, its ability to simultaneously transmit and receive, and its time-saving library (Reference [2-7] provides additional details.)

Spider Systems, Inc.'s SpiderAnalyzer

Spider Systems, Inc., is a subsidiary of Spider Systems, Ltd., of the United Kingdom and a relative newcomer to the United States. The company's SpiderAnalyzers are available in either kit form or packaged within a Compaq Portable III (Figure 2-16). Ethernet/IEEE 802.3 and IEEE 802.5 models are available and the unit has decoding packages for TCP/IP, XNS, ISO, DECnet, AppleTalk, SNA, and IPX. Higher layer protocol interpreters are also available for DoD (Department of Defense), NetWare, and DECnet suites.

Figure 2-16
Spider Systems, Inc. Spider Analyzer

The SpiderAnalyzer has seven modes of operation for Ethernet/IEEE 802.3 networks and nine modes for IEEE 802.5. The Alarms mode can log network errors (Figure 2-17) and trigger audible or visual alarms when specified errors occur. The Development mode is used for protocol filtering and decoding. The Trace listings (Figure 2-18) provide details of the captured frames. The Performance mode plots a histogram of network loads and utilization. The Statistics mode (Figure 2-19) tabulates or graphs network utilization over time. The Test mode provides a TDR. The Traffic Generation mode measures the impact of additional loads on the network. Token ring network analyzers add the Open Mode, which opens the SpiderMonitor as an active workstation; ands the Error mode, which logs the MAC error frames.

Figure 2-17
Spider Systems, Inc. Spider Analyzer Alarms Log Screen

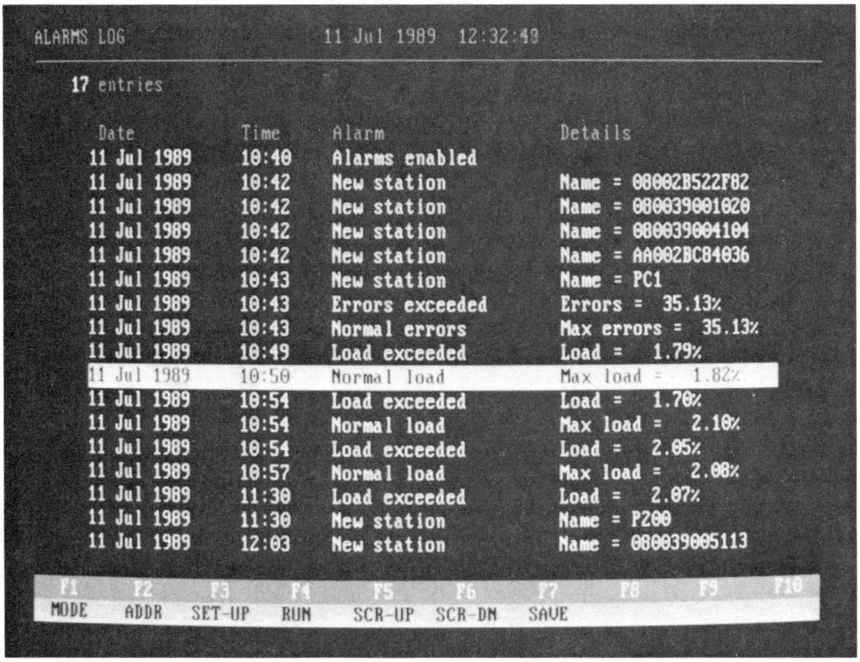

Figure 2-18
Spider Systems, Inc. Spider Analyzer Trace Listing Screen

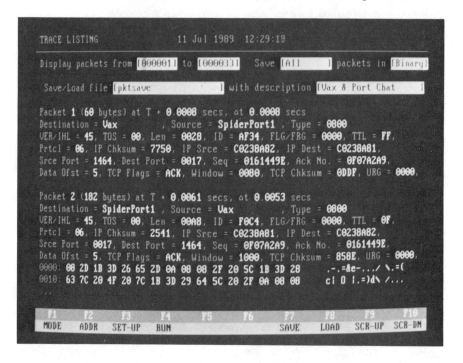

Figure 2-19
Spider Systems, Inc. Spider Analyzer Statistics Screen

```
STATISTICS SCREEN              11 Jul 1989  12:34:38

Statistics collected over a period of  1 hours 54 mins 26 secs
Number of collisions =      283       Number of short pkts = 70
Packets not analysed =       0        Display is in  Activity order
Number of table entries  = 11
```

Station name	Packets sent	Packets in error	Packets received	Bytes transmitted	Bytes received
TOTAL	708134	13	708121	121103016	121100650
080039004104	310335	13	1	56479750	60
P200	247712	0	0	45083584	0
Vax	86513	0	63508	15722680	3810400
SpiderPort1	37312	0	50742	2238720	9210537
SpiderPort2	26261	0	35734	1578100	6501939
Broadcast	0	0	97	0	16240
PC1	0	0	558021	0	101559822
AA002BC84036	0	0	3	0	180
08002B522F82	0	0	3	0	180
080039005113	0	0	5	0	304
080039001020	0	0	3	0	180

```
 F1    F2    F3    F4    F5    F6    F7   F8    F9    F10
MODE  ADDR  SET-UP RUN  SCR-UP SCR-DN SAVE           FIND
```

What is unique about the SpiderMonitor and SpiderAnalyzer are their multi-tasking characteristics, which allows DOS applications and network monitoring functions to operate simultaneously. (See reference [2-8] for further information.)

2.5.5 | Hewlett-Packard Co.'s HP4972A

Hewlett-Packard's 4972A protocol analyzer is a piece of test equipment developed in H-P's inimitable style, rugged and durable (see Figure 2-20). This is also evident in the architecture of the machine; it was designed as a piece of test equipment rather than a PC, is based upon the Motorola 68010 CPU, and has its own proprietary file and disk formats. The HP4972A currently supports Ethernet/IEEE 802.3 networks, and also StarLAN (IEEE 802.5 1BASE5) with a factory-installed optional interface module. Protocol interpreters are available for TCP/IP and various DoD protocols, as well as NFS, XNS, DECnet, and ISO.

Figure 2-20
Hewlett-Packard, Inc. HP-4972A Protocol Analyzer

The strength of H-P's test equipment heritage is evident when the various analysis and statistics packages are examined. The Network Summary Screen (Figure 2-21) displays a variety of network statistics averaged over variable sample times. Collisions, Network Utilization, and Average Frame lengths (Figure 2-22) can be graphically displayed. Network traffic can be characterized in several ways, including Node Lists and Connections in both tabular and graphical formats (Figure 2-23). Similar statistical analyses are available for each available protocol interpreter (Figure 2-24), and frame decodes are straightforward and easy to read (Figure 2-25).

Figure 2-21
Hewlett-Packard, Inc. HP-4972A Network Summary screen

```
========================= NETWORK SUMMARY ========================
16 Mar 90                                                03:42:28

=== Utilization and Throughput ===    ===== Frame Parameters =====

Current  Average   Peak                 Average Size     167 bytes
-------  -------   -------               Maximum Size   1,580 bytes
  20.44    14.87    68.08 %              Minimum Size      60 bytes
  2,028    1,475    6,755 kbits/s        Total Frames    65,129
  1,310    1,092    2,043 frms/s         Total Bytes   1.166E+7

======================= Errors and Collisions =======================
                Bad FCS/Misalign  Runts     Jabbers    Collisions
                  --------      --------   --------    --------
Total Count        7,117             0         11         146
Average          1.095E-1      0.000E+0   0.000E+0   1.465E-3 Cnt/frm
Peak             1.218E-1      0.000E+0   1.004E-3   1.267E-2 Cnt/frm

Start time = 15 Mar 90  07:02:00      Stop time = 15 Mar 90  07:03:00
Measurement time = 60 Seconds         Sample time =  1 Second
```

Figure 2-22
Hewlett-Packard, Inc. HP-4972A Collisions screen

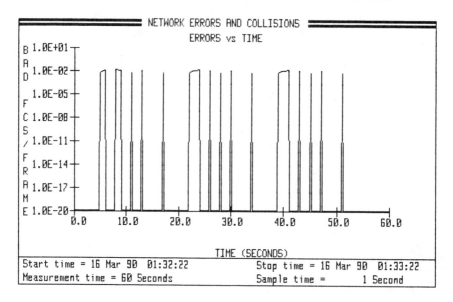

Figure 2-23
Hewlett-Packard, Inc. HP-4972A Connection Summary screen

```
══════════════════════ CONNECTION SUMMARY ══════════════════════
16 Mar 90                                                    03:30:56
   Connection Node    Last Sample   Frame    KByte    Error   Error   Avg. Frm
   Name or Address    Frame Cnt.    Count    Count    Count   Rate    Size
   ----------------   -----------   -------  -------  ------  -------  -----
   CHRIS_WKSTN        XMT    12      105        8       0    0.00E+0    69
   MARCOM_SERVER      XMT    14      149       25       0    0.00E+0   156

   LARRY_PC           XMT     0       47        4       0    0.00E+0    66
   MARCOM_SERVER      XMT     0       60       11       0    0.00E+0   174

   ZETA_B4/102        XMT     4       46        7       0    0.00E+0   141
   WANDA_PC           XMT     5       45        3       0    0.00E+0    60

   KEN_WKSTN          XMT     0       33        3       0    0.00E+0    66
   OMEGA_B4/104       XMT     0       46        7       0    0.00E+0   143


Start time = 16 Mar 90  03:23:34        Stop time = 16 Mar 90  03:24:34
Measurement time = 60 Seconds           Sample time =  5 Seconds
```

Figure 2-24
Hewlett-Packard, Inc. HP-4972A TCP/IP
Network Summary screen

```
══════════════════════════ TCP/IP NETWORK SUMMARY ══════════════
16 Mar 90                                              03:19:58

══════ Utilization ══════        ══════ TCP/UDP Port Activity ══════

Current  Average  Peak                    Current  Average   Peak
-------  -------  -------                  -------  -------   ------
    473      744    2,367  total f/s  FTP     20.22    20.01   20.44 %
    220      344    1,093     IP f/s  FTP_DATA 0.0000  0.0000  0.0000 %
 15,211   23,875   75,935 IP bytes/s  TELNET   20.22   20.01   20.33 %
                                      SMTP     20.22   20.01   20.33 %
══════ IP Frame Parameters ══════     SUN_NFS  39.34   39.96   40.66 %
                                      SUN_PC_N 0.0000  0.0000  0.0000 %
Total data bytes       1.907E+6       RWHO_RLO 0.0000  0.0000  0.0000 %
Total frames             27,438       OTHER    0.0000  0.0000  0.0000 %
Total fragments               0
Header overhead          22.35 %

Network = 10 Mbps
```

Figure 2-25
Hewlett-Packard, Inc. HP-4972A FTP Decode Data screen

```
#47        Elapsed  0:00:00.04611 Len    69 Filters xxx3xxx.xx......      No error
Ether: Dst 08-00-09-01-E6-5B  Src 02-60-8C-67-78-14      Type          DOD_IP
IP   : Version              4 Header Len Bytes  20 Type of Ser         Routine
     : Total Len           55 Ident            21 Flags      May Frag Last Frag
     : Frag Offset          0 Time to Live    255 Next Protocol            TCP
     : Cksum    Good 0D-03 Src       15.6.72.55 Dest             15.6.72.102
TCP  : Src           9227 Dest           FTP Sequence Number       169157752
     : Ack      29719294 Data Offset      20 Flags                  ACK PSH
     : Window        1000 Cksum    Good B2-AE Urgent Pointer   Not Used    0
     : Direction     Client --------------> Server    ( 15 bytes )
FTP  : STOR gaby.gal..

#48        Elapsed  0:00:00.10253 Len   115 Filters xx2xxxx.xx......      No error
Ether: Dst 02-60-8C-67-78-14  Src 08-00-09-01-E6-5B      Type          DOD_IP
IP   : Version              4 Header Len Bytes  20 Type of Ser         Routine
     : Total Len          101 Ident         21902 Flags      May Frag Last Frag
     : Frag Offset          0 Time to Live     60 Next Protocol            TCP
     : Cksum    Good 7A-5C Src      15.6.72.102 Dest              15.6.72.55
TCP  : Src            FTP Dest          9227 Sequence Number        29719294
     : Ack     169157767 Data Offset      20 Flags                  ACK PSH
     : Window        4096 Cksum    Good 0D-98 Urgent Pointer   Not Used    0
     : Direction     Server --------------> Client    ( 61 bytes )
FTP  : 150 Opening data connection for gaby.gal (15.6.72.55,7748)...

#49        Elapsed  0:00:00.00147 Len    60 Filters xx2xxxx.xx......      No error
Ether: Dst 02-60-8C-67-78-14  Src 08-00-09-01-E6-5B      Type          DOD_IP
IP   : Version              4 Header Len Bytes  20 Type of Ser         Routine
     : Total Len           44 Ident         21903 Flags      May Frag Last Frag
     : Frag Offset          0 Time to Live     60 Next Protocol            TCP
     : Cksum    Good 7A-94 Src      15.6.72.102 Dest              15.6.72.55
TCP  : Src       FTP_DATA Dest          7748 Sequence Number        29733697
     : Ack             0 Data Offset      24 Flags                      SYN
     : Window        8192 Cksum    Good F6-21 Urgent Pointer   Not Used    0
opt  : Max. Segment Size  Length            4 Max Seg Size             1457
     : Direction     Server --------------> Client    (  0 bytes )
```

The strength of the HP4972A is in the numerous (and fascinating) ways in which network data can be characterized, analyzed, graphed and displayed (see reference [2-9]). Unfortunately for some, that can also be a disadvantage; since it is not a PC, it cannot be used as a DOS workstation when the network is functioning properly.

| 2.5.6 | **Network General Corp.'s Sniffer** |

The Sniffer protocol analyzer is available in either a Toshiba laptop or Compaq Portable 386 computer (Figure 2-26). One obvious advantage offered by the Sniffer is immediately evident when you consider the number of options. Hardware interfaces are available for Ethernet/IEEE 802.3, StarLAN, IEEE 802.5, IBM PC Network, ARCNET and LocalTalk. Eleven different protocol interpreter suites cover IBM, NetWare, XNS, TCP/IP, Sun, ISO, DECnet, Nestar PLAN, Banyan VINES, AppleTalk, and XWindows. In all, an impressive list of over 120 protocols can be interpreted. It's fairly safe to bet that Network General has a hardware interface and protocol interpreter for your LAN.

Figure 2-26
Network General Corp. Sniffer Protocol Analyzer family

The main menu (Figure 2-27) has an extremely intuitive user interface that offers cable testing, traffic generation, data capture, filtering, and display options. Selecting one option, such as Protocol Filters, on one menu opens another window displaying another set of available options (Figure 2-28). Captured data can be displayed in one of three formats: Summary, Detail, or Hexadecimal (Figure 2-29).

Figure 2-27
Network General Corp. Sniffer Main Menu screen

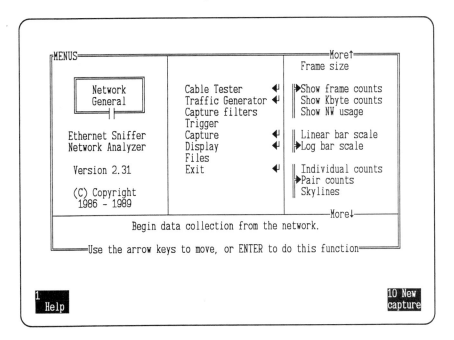

Figure 2-28
Network General Corp. Sniffer Protocol Filters screen

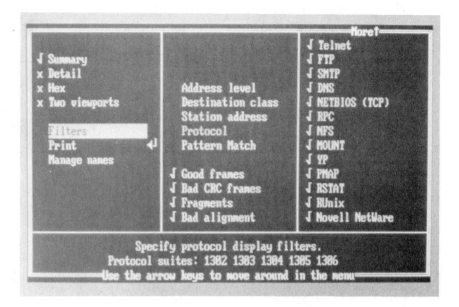

Figure 2-29
Network General Corp. Sniffer Decoded Data screen

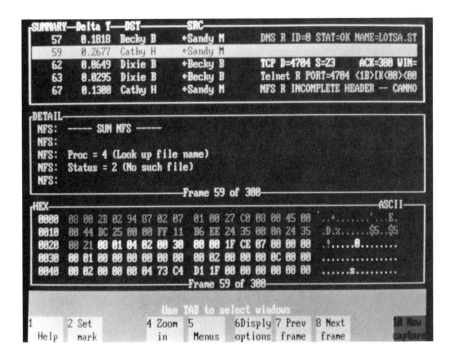

Expansion of the Detail window (Figure 2-30) reveals details of the seven-layer decodes (available in color) that delineate each field and subfield of the captured frame. Network Statistics show utilization, fragments, invalid frames, or CRC errors, and can be displayed in bar charts (Figure 2-31).

Figure 2-30
Network General Corp. Sniffer Detailed Protocol Decodes screen

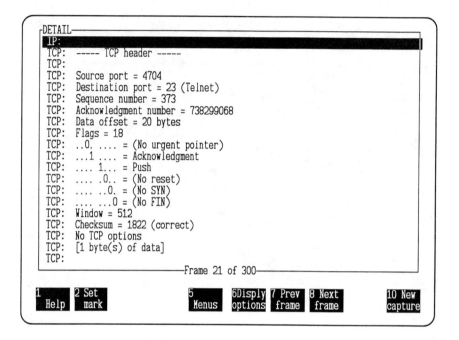

```
┌DETAIL
│ IP:
│ TCP:  ----- TCP header -----
│ TCP:
│ TCP:  Source port = 4704
│ TCP:  Destination port = 23 (Telnet)
│ TCP:  Sequence number = 373
│ TCP:  Acknowledgment number = 738299068
│ TCP:  Data offset = 20 bytes
│ TCP:  Flags = 18
│ TCP:  ..0. .... = (No urgent pointer)
│ TCP:  ...1 .... = Acknowledgment
│ TCP:  .... 1... = Push
│ TCP:  .... .0.. = (No reset)
│ TCP:  .... ..0. = (No SYN)
│ TCP:  .... ...0 = (No FIN)
│ TCP:  Window = 512
│ TCP:  Checksum = 1822 (correct)
│ TCP:  No TCP options
│ TCP:  [1 byte(s) of data]
│ TCP:
                    Frame 21 of 300

 1        2 Set            5       6Display 7 Prev  8 Next         10 New
  Help     mark            Menus   options   frame   frame        capture
```

Figure 2-31
Network General Corp. Sniffer Network Statistics screen

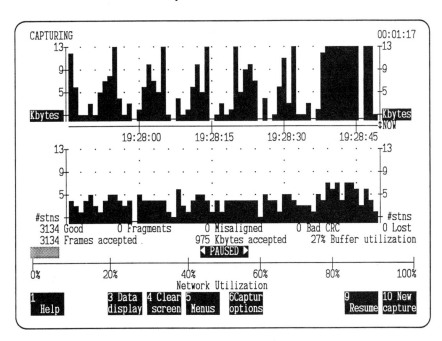

Network General has recently added an Advanced Monitoring capability to the Sniffer including a Report Writer and Screen Editor to customize tabular or graphical reports that summarize the captured data. Another feature is active station testing, which determines if a given station is functional or non-functional by testing its response using four different LAN echo protocols. These new features are also available in a distributed environment using Sniffmaster I, which provides a point of central control for multiple Sniffer units from a single Sun workstation.

The Sniffer's greatest strength is that it covers almost every possible LAN hardware and software combination (see reference [2-10]. For this reason, and to allow the reader to see consistent information, the decoded protocol offered in Chapters 3 through 7 will be derived from data captured with the Network General Sniffer.

2.6 | Selecting a Protocol Analyzer

With so many protocol analyzers to choose from, making a selection for analyzing your network could be difficult. Here are some guidelines:

First, eliminate analyzers that do not support the hardware architecture (token ring, ARCNET, etc.) that you currently support. More importantly, look at other areas of your enterprise-wide network and make sure that the analysis tool you pick can interface to the hardware of other departments or divisions within your company. After all, your expertise may be required at some remote facility.

Next, be certain that your analyzer can handle the LAN Operating System(s) in use, such as NetWare, VINES, or AppleTalk. Assure that your version of the operating system is supported as well. For example, 3Com's 3+Open contains the NetBIOS protocol (NBP) which cannot be decoded by analyzers supporting only the XNS protocol suite used with 3Com's 3+. Ask these questions before you buy.

Third, look at any mid-layer protocols, such as TCP/IP that might be used within your internet.

Fourth, consider all the higher layer protocols, such as electronic mail or file transfer applications, that are used on your network. Having only a hexadecimal decode of a higher layer application available can be very frustrating.

Finally, consider the reputation of the vendor, and the local and national support available through the dealer or manufacturer. Protocol analyzers can be a challenge to use at times, and its reassuring to know that the manufacturer is standing behind the product with protocol experts that can assist with difficult analyses.

To get you started towards understanding and analyzing the specific protocols running on your network, we'll now look in detail at the architecture and internals of Novell's NetWare, 3Com's 3+ and 3+Open, the IBM Token-Ring related protocols, Banyan VINES, and Apple Computer's AppleTalk. Roll up your sleeves and get ready to dig in!

2.7 | References

[2-1] International Organization for Standardization, Information Processing Systems - Open Systems Interconnection - Basic Reference Model, ISO 7498-1984.

[2-2] Spider Systems, Inc., Spider Application Note "Hardware and Software Faults," document number 200.4.

[2-3] Spider Systems, Inc., Packets and Protocols, 1989.

[2-4] Hewlett-Packard Company, LAN Performance Analysis Product Note, document 5952-5103, 1986.

[2-5] FTP Software, Inc., LANWatch User's Guide, version 2.0, January 1990.

[2-6] Digilog, Inc., LANVista Guide to Operations, 1989.

[2-7] Excelan, Inc., LANalyzer Reference Manual, 1989.

[2-8] Spider Systems, Inc., SpiderAnalyzer User Guide, 1989.

[2-9] Hewlett-Packard Co., HP-4972A LAN Protocol Analyzer Reference Manual, November 1988.

[2-10] Network General Corporation, Sniffer Operation and Reference Manual, 1986-1989.

Manufacturers of LAN Analysis Tools

Digilog, Inc.
1370 Welsh Road
Montgomeryville, PA 18936
Phone: (215) 628-4530 or
(800) DIGILOG
Fax: (215) 628-3935

FTP Software, Inc.
26 Princess Street
Wakefield, MA 01880
Phone: (617) 246-0900
Fax: (617) 246-0901

Hewlett-Packard Co.
5070 Centennial Blvd.
Colorado Springs, CO 80919
Phone: (719) 531-4000
Fax: (719) 531-4505

Network General Corporation
4200 Bohannan Drive
Menlo Park, CA 94025
Phone: (415) 688-2700
Fax: (415) 321-0855

Novell, Inc.
2180 Fortune Drive
San Jose, CA 95131
Phone: (408) 434-2300 or
(800) EXCELAN
Fax: (408) 954-9930

Spider Systems, Inc.
12 New England Executive Park
Burlington, MA 01803
Phone: (617) 270-3510 or
(800) 447-7807
Fax: (617) 270-9818

CHAPTER THREE

Analyzing Novell's NetWare

According to market research quoted by Novell, Inc. (see reference [3-1]), more workstations are connected to NetWare than any other Network Operating System (NOS). NetWare is based on the Xerox Network Systems (XNS) protocols, which were developed at the Xerox Corporation's Palo Alto Research Center. XNS has a layered architecture with well-defined functions at each layer. Some believe this approach had a considerable influence on the OSI model we have today (see reference [3-2]). Since XNS uses a straightforward approach to addressing networking and internetworking issues, the adaptation of XNS to local area networks seemed a logical next step. Other companies, including Ungermann-Bass, Inc. and 3Com Corporation, have also used XNS in their products. (Further historical details on XNS are given in reference [3-3].)

One of the reasons for the strong acceptance of NetWare by the LAN marketplace is the number of different versions available, each addressing specific networking requirements. For example, Entry Level System (ELS) levels I and II are designed for the small user, supporting either four or eight workstations, respectively. Larger networks would use Advanced NetWare Version 2.15, which supports up to 100 concurrent users and interfaces with NetWare for the Macintosh and the NetWare Requester for OS/2 workstations. System Fault Tolerant (SFT) NetWare Version 2.15 includes disk mirroring and duplexing, uninterruptible power supply (UPS) monitoring, and the Transaction Tracking System (TTS) which is used to prevent database record corruption. NetWare 386 Version 3.0 is designed for the 32-bit 80386 microprocessor and permits up to 250 concurrent users. NetWare VMS allows a Digital Equipment Corporation VAX computers to act as a server on a PC-based LAN.

Because of its great acceptance within the user as well as software development community, we will focus on Advanced NetWare Version 2.15 in this chapter.

3.1 | NetWare and the OSI Model

NetWare's components can be easily matched with the OSI model. At the Physical and Data Link layers, NetWare supports Ethernet, IEEE 802.3, IEEE 802.5, as well as ARCNET and a variety of other network architectures. Network and Transport layer functions are handled by the Internetwork Packet Exchange (IPX) and Sequenced Packet Exchange (SPX) protocols, respectively, both which are derivatives of XNS. At the Session layer, the Network Basic Input Output System (NetBIOS) interface, developed by IBM and Sytek, Inc., is available. The Presentation and Application Layers encompass the NetWare Core Protocols (NCP), NetWare Core and Value-Added Services, DOS, and various user applications (see Figure 3-1 and reference [3-4]).

Applications can access the NetWare protocols at four distinct interfaces, as shown in Figure 3-2. The Network layer interface is IPX, which provides a connectionless communications link between workstations. Neither packet delivery nor packet sequence is assured. This interface is referred to be the Datagram Interface.

Figure 3-1
Advanced NetWare's relationship to the OSI model

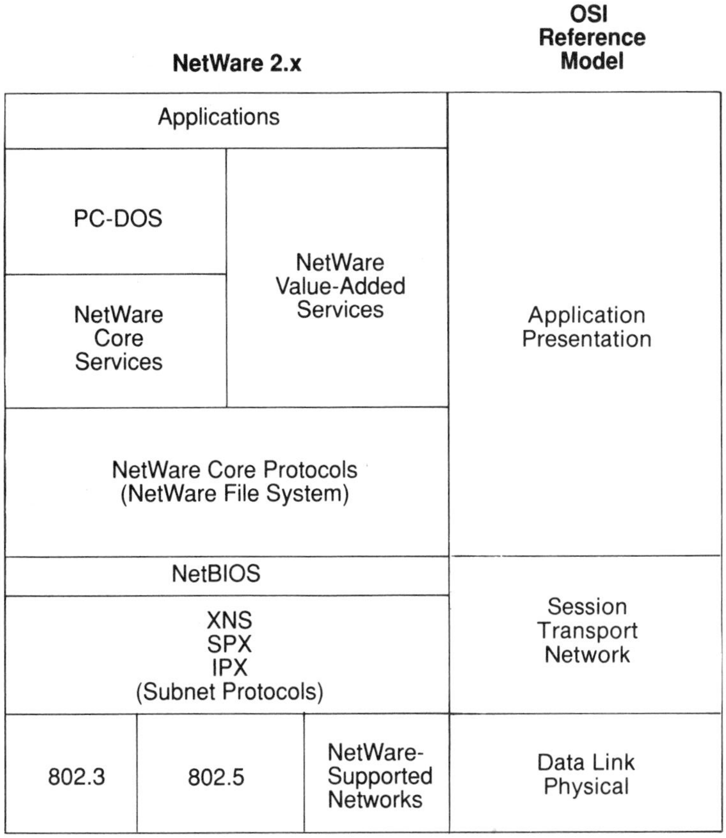

NetWare 2.x			OSI Reference Model
Applications			Application Presentation
PC-DOS	NetWare Value-Added Services		
NetWare Core Services			
NetWare Core Protocols (NetWare File System)			
NetBIOS			Session Transport Network
XNS SPX IPX (Subnet Protocols)			
802.3	802.5	NetWare-Supported Networks	Data Link Physical

The Transport Layer interface is SPX, which provides a connection-oriented path between workstations. The connection must be established prior to any data transmission. SPX provides guaranteed delivery of the packets, in sequence, and without errors or duplications. The Transport Layer interface is called the Virtual-Connection Interface.

The Session Layer interface is a NetBIOS emulator. (We will discuss NetBIOS further in Chapter 5.) Network applications that are

NetBIOS-compatible can access the network through this interface, which is called the Session Interface.

Figure 3-2
Advanced NetWare network interfaces

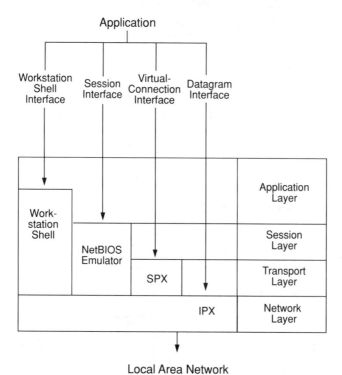

Local Area Network

Finally, the Workstation Shell provides DOS file service compatibility. The Shell provides a connection between the DOS requests and the IPX protocol for transmission over the network. Programs use this interface to communicate from the workstation to the server to perform network-related functions, such as to access a file on the server or print to the shared laser printer. This interface is called the Workstation Shell Interface.

3.2 | NetWare Architecture

NetWare 2.1x has several major components that facilitate its operation. Starting at the Physical Layer, the Network Interface Cards (NIC) in both the workstation and server communicate via the appropriate transmission medium such as unshielded twisted pair or coax. A software driver, specific to that particular NIC, provides a direct interface between the IPX protocol and hardware for network communication.

Figure 3-3
NetWare workstation/server interaction

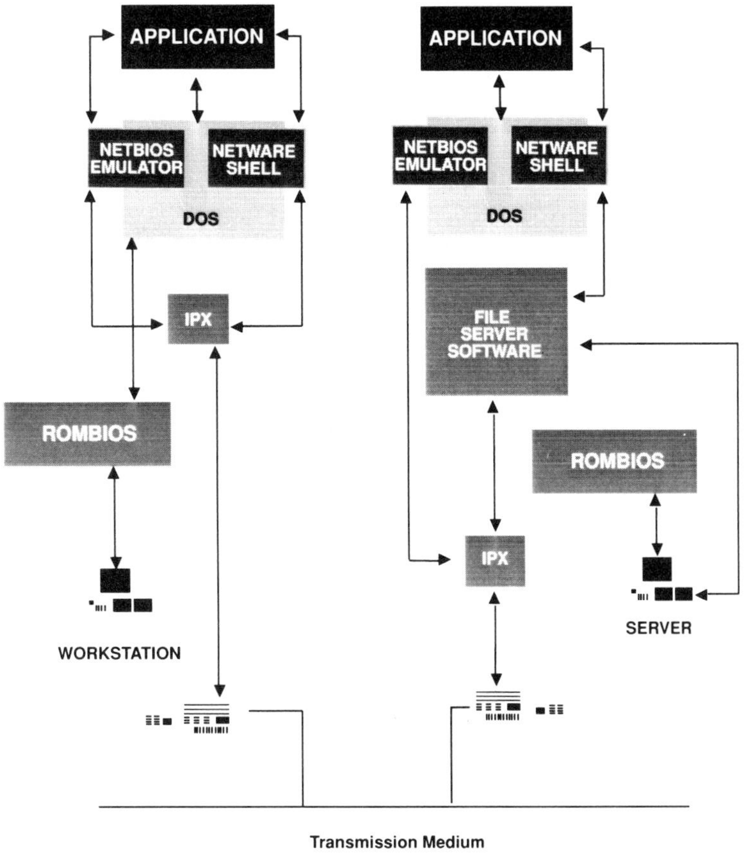

Application programs can access IPX in two ways: via a NetBIOS emulator (for NetBIOS-compatible applications); or via the NetWare Shell for DOS calls. Local DOS calls are passed to the ROMBIOS and local hardware; network calls are passed to IPX, the network hardware, and finally to the file server software. These interactions are shown in Figure 3-3, taken from reference [3-5]. We'll look at the individual NetWare layers, beginning with the Data Link Layer.

3.3 NetWare Data Link Layer Protocols

We'll begin our investigation of the NetWare protocols by looking at the Data Link Layer frame transmitted between workstation and server. The ARCNET frame (Figure 3-4a) contains one field unique to the ARCNET implementation. The fragmentation header consists of a one-octet fragment number (non-fragmented, fragment 1 of 2, or fragment 2 of 2) plus a two-octet sequence number. This field is necessary since the largest ARCNET frame can contain 508 octets of data, whereas the IPX packet can contain a maximum of 576 octets. When a maximum-length IPX packet is transmitted, two ARCNET fragments will inevitably result; the first ARCNET frame will contain 508 octets of the IPX packet and the second will contain up to 68 octets.

The Ethernet frame (Figure 3-4b) contains the Ethertype (8137H), thus specifying that NetWare is the protocol used within the data field. The NetWare IPX packet would be contained within the Data field and does not require fragmentation.

For IEEE 802.3 and 802.5 frames (Figures 3-4c and d, respectively), the NetWare Service Access Point Addresses (DSAP and SSAP) are defined to be E0H. These are contained within the 802.2 LLC header, which is the first part of the Data fields. The IPX packet then follows. As with the Ethernet frame, no fragmentation is required.

A recent trend in LAN performance analysis has been to evaluate a number of different types and brands of NICs to compare their speed. Not only is this type of study useful for determining the preferred architecture (for example, Ethernet or Token-Ring), but it can also give insight into the transmission speed requirements (for example, 4 Mbps vs. 16 Mbps for Token-Ring) as well. A recent article (reference [3-6]) described such an analysis of 47 different NICs running SFT NetWare version 2.15. Of interest to protocol analysts was the fact that the frame size had an impact on performance. In addition, the NetWare frames transmit more than the IPX packet sizes (576 octets) at a time, even though this is not evident from the Novell literature. For example, one of the NetWare examples in this chapter (Figure 3-11) shows NetWare 802.3 frames with 1024 octets of data, not 576. Apparently, the NetWare drivers for each type of NIC have been optimized by Novell for higher throughput, even though they may not strictly adhere to the IPX packet sizes.

The IPX and SPX protocols are unique to NetWare and are used for communication between a workstation and the NetWare Server. (For details see reference [3-7], Chapter 4, and reference [3-8].) We will discuss the IPX and SPX protocols individually in the next two sections.

Figure 3-4a
Novell's NetWare core protocol packet encapsulated within an ARCNET frame

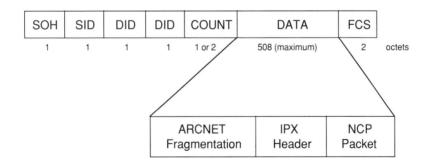

Figure 3-4b
Novell NetWare core protocol packet encapsulated within an Ethernet frame

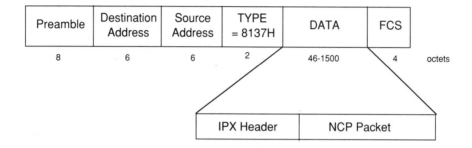

Figure 3-4c
Novell NetWare core protocol packet encapsulated within an IEEE 802.3 frame

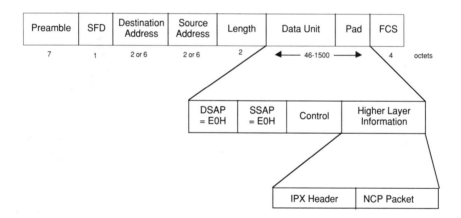

Figure 3-4d
Novell NetWare Core Protocol packet encapsulated
within an IEEE 802.5 frame

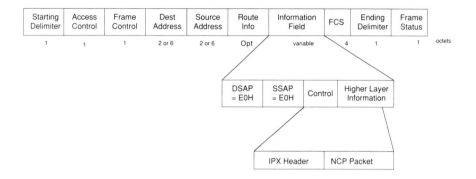

3.4 NetWare Network Layer Protocol

The IPX protocol provides the Network Layer functions of addressing, routing, and switching packets from the source workstation to the destination, as we saw in Figure 3-3. Since it is a connectionless protocol, it lacks the reliable delivery obtained from the Sequence and Acknowledgement number counters included as part of the SPX header (see section 3.5).

The IPX packet is identical in syntax to the XNS Internetwork Datagram Packet protocol (IDP) described in reference [3-9]. The maximum packet size is 576 octets, which includes 30 octets of header information and defined for a maximum of 546 octets of data (see Figure 3-5).

Figure 3-5
Internetwork Packet Exchange (IPX) protocol packet

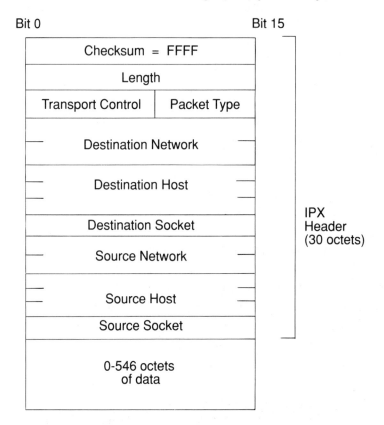

The checksum field is set to FFFFH by IPX. The checksum field is included for conformance with the original XNS header, but is not necessary since the LAN frame provides a cyclic redundancy check (CRC) at the Data Link Layer. The Length field gives the length in octets of the IPX datagram, with allowable values of 30 – 576 octets. The Transport Control field is used by NetWare Internetwork routers and set to zero by IPX prior to sending the packet. The first four bits are reserved (undefined), and the last four octets give the hop count, which is used for internetworking to define the total number of routers that this packet has passed through on its way from source to destination. Each time this packet goes through a router, the hop count is incremented by one.

The Packet Type field defines the type of service offered or defined by that packet. Xerox has defined the following values (shown in decimal):

0 Unknown Packet Type
1 Routing Information Packet (RIP)
2 Echo Packet
3 Error Packet
4 Packet Exchange Packet (PEP)
5 Sequenced Packet Protocol (SPP)
16 – 31 Experimental Protocols
17 NetWare Core Protocol (NCP)

Of these options, four are of interest to NetWare users: IPX uses packet types 0 or 4, SPX uses packet type 5, and NCP uses packet type 17.

The Destination Network field is a four-octet number assigned by the network administrator to identify the unique network within the sub-network. A value of 0 indicates that source and destination nodes are on the same LAN (also known as the "local net"), and that the packet will not be processed by the NetWare internetwork router. Any other value indicates that internetworking to another LAN may be required.

The Destination Host field specifies the physical hardware address, such as the NIC, for the destination node. All six octets are used when IEEE 802.3 and 802.5 destination addresses are specified. If fewer octets are required, such as the one-octet address used with ARCNET, the most significant octets are then filled with zeros. Broadcast packets contain a Destination Host value of FFFFFFFFFFFFH.

The Destination Socket field specifies the process within the destination node. Xerox has defined the following values:

0001:   Routing Information Packet
0002:   Echo Protocol Packet
0003:   Error Handler Packet
0020H – 003FH: Experimental
0001H – 0BB8H: Registered with Xerox
0BB9H and higher: Dynamically assignable

Xerox has assigned a set of sockets to Novell for use by NetWare:

0451H: File Service Packet
0452H: Service Advertising Packet
0453H: Routing Information Packet
0455H: NetBIOS Packet
0456H: Diagnostic Packet

NetWare file servers use socket number 0451H (1105 decimal). Novell assigns dynamic socket numbers beginning at 4000H for value-added NetWare packages, and well-known sockets begin at 8000H.

The Source Network field is next. These four octets are assigned by the network administrator, similar to the Destination Network field, and set by IPX to that network number. A value of zero indicates an unknown network.

Source Node and Source Socket addresses follow the same convention as their Destination counterparts.

The Data field can contain up to 546 octets of information from the higher layers, such as NCP. We'll look at these in greater detail in section 3.6.

3.5 | NetWare Transport Layer Protocol

SPX adds the Transport Layer functions to the IPX packet, providing a connection-oriented, guaranteed delivery link between workstations. According to Novell's NetWare System Interface Technical Overview (reference [3-7]), one disadvantage to this connection-oriented service provided with the SPX protocol is that broadcast packets require an individual connection be established between the source and each destination before the message can be sent. For a large number of destinations, this process could be very lengthy and is therefore not worth the reliability that SPX provides. For this reason, Application and Presentation Layer (NetWare Core) protocols interface directly to the Network Layer (IPX) protocol for workstation/server interaction. The SPX (Transport Layer) protocols are thus bypassed in this case. Third-party applications may utilize the SPX protocol.

The SPX packet structure is identical to that of the IPX packet, except that it includes 12 additional octets in the header. Since the packet length is fixed at 576 octets, the maximum SPX data field is reduced to 534 octets (see Figure 3-6).

The first 30 octets are the same as the IPX header fields with two exceptions: the Packet Type field (octet 6) is set to a decimal 5 (a Packet Exchange Protocol or PEP packet) and the Destination Host address of FFFFFFFFFFFFH (broadcast) is not allowed.

Figure 3-6
Sequenced Packet Exchange (SPX) protocol packet

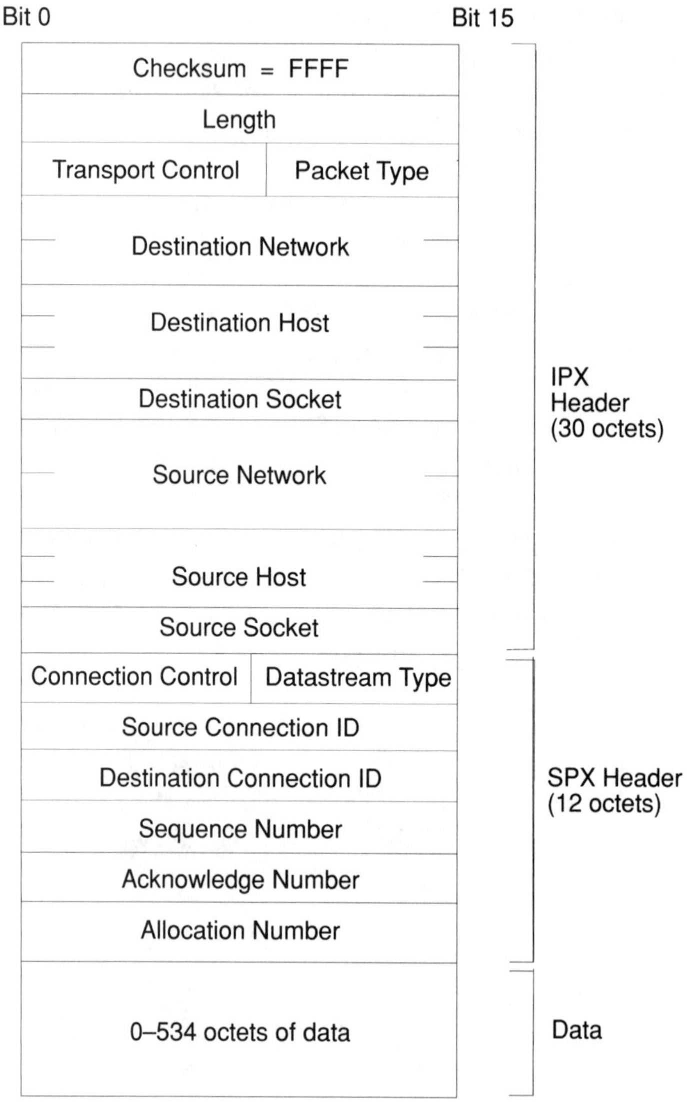

Bit 0   Bit 15

Checksum = FFFF	
Length	
Transport Control	Packet Type

Destination Network

Destination Host

Destination Socket

Source Network

Source Host

Source Socket

IPX Header (30 octets)

Connection Control	Datastream Type
Source Connection ID	
Destination Connection ID	
Sequence Number	
Acknowledge Number	
Allocation Number	

SPX Header (12 octets)

0–534 octets of data

Data

The first octet of the SPX header is the Connection Control field that contains four, one-bit flags that control the data flow between end-points:

01H – 08H: Undefined
10H: End of message
20H: Attention
40H: Acknowledgement required
80H: System packet

The second octet is the Datastream Type field, which identifies the data within the packet, similar to the Ethernet Type field. These include:

00H – FDH: Client defined
FEH: End of connection
FFH: End of connection acknowledgement

Next is the Source Connection ID, a one-octet field assigned by SPX at the packet source, and the Destination Connection ID, which is used to demultiplexing multiple connections into the same socket, as is the case with the server.

The Sequence Number and Acknowledgement Number fields (two octets each) provide the packet numbers for the sending and next expected receiving packets, thus assuring reliable packet delivery.

The Allocation Number is used for end-to-end flow control. The field indicates the number of receiver buffers available for that connection. The transmitter may send packets until the Sequence and Allocation numbers are equal.

The last field is the Data field, which is defined to contain up to 534 octets.

3.6 | NetWare Higher Layers

The NetWare Core Protocols (NCP) provide a mechanism for client/server-like interaction between the workstation and the server. As mentioned previously, a NCP packet follows the IPX header, and is encapsulated within an ARCNET, Ethernet, token ring, and other frames.

Following the IPX header is a two-octet Request Type field which is defined as follows:

1111H: Create service connection
2222H: Request (to server)
3333H: Reply (from server)
5555H: Destroy service connection
9999H: Request being processed response

The Sequence number, Connection number, and Task number (each one octet in length) uniquely identify the client/server connection. The Code field indicates the specific packet type. Depending upon the success or failure of the client request (type 2222), an appropriate server response (type 3333) is generated. For additional details, see reference [3-8].

3.7 | NetWare System Calls

System calls are the mechanisms that NetWare provides so that a DOS application can operate and communicate over a NetWare network (see reference [3-10). Many categories exist for these system calls. In summary form, they are:

• Accounting services, which allow the server to charge for the use of its services.

• AppleTalk Filing Protocol (AFP) services, which allow both DOS and Apple data files to be stored on a NetWare file server. The AFP services are used to create, access, and delete Macintosh-format directories and files on a NetWare file server.

• Bindery services, which is the database within the file server that relates resources, such as a print server, to a client or user.

• Communication services, which allow application programs to access the IPX and SPX protocols.

• Connection services, which are used to create the logical connection between the user and the file server. The user records the file server name and internetwork address in its memory, then asks the file server to assign a connection number (between 1 and 100 for NetWare 2.1x or up to 250 for NetWare 3.X) to the workstation.

• Diagnostic services, which use the IPX and SPX protocols to study a network's configuration and performance.

• Directory services, which allow an application program to create, destroy, rename, and otherwise manage volumes and directories.

• File server environment services, which allow the applications to set file server parameters and obtain information about the file server.

• File services, which allow applications to open, read, write, close, and delete files on the file server.

• Message services, which permit applications to send broadcast messages (1 – 55 octets in length) or pipe messages (1 – 126 octets in length) to a specified target connection. Broadcast messages are transmitted from a user to the file server or a number of other workstations. Piped messages are sent between two distinct workstations.

• Print services, which allow an application's print job to be redirected to a particular file server.

• Queue services, which organize request made to a job server by a workstation. The job server provides a specific service, such as printing, compilation, messaging, etc.

• Service Advertising Protocol (SAP) services, which allow NetWare servers to advertise their services by name and type. SAP uses the IPX protocol to transmit and defines two packet types. The Service Query Packet is used to discover the identity of servers on the internetwork. The Service Identification Packet is broadcast from each server every 60 seconds to inform bridges and all other servers of its identity.

• Synchronization services, which coordinate access to network files and resources between various applications, such as file and record locking.

• Transaction tracking services, which provide database integrity by assuring that all transaction operations transaction are completed or, in the event a failure such as a power outage, no transactions are completed.

• Value-Added Process (VAP) services, which are programs that reside in a NetWare file server or bridge to offer enhanced services to the network.

• Workstation services, which enable applications to interact with the file server.

3.8 | Protocol Analysis With NetWare

Now that we have a background in the IPX, SPX, and NCP protocols, let's take a look at several examples of NetWare protocols in use.

To begin, let's investigate a request from one host to another host to create a connection (Figure 3-7a). The abbreviations (DLC, NOV, XNS, etc.) indicate which protocol layer is being decoded. At the Data Link Control (DLC) Layer, destination and source hosts are identified as stations 44 and 20, respectively. The ARCNET fragmentation header comes next indicating an unfragmented frame. The XNS (IPX) header further identifies the destination and source workstations, and we now know that the ultimate destination (10005A0033BFH) is a NetWare server on another network. The NCP packet (request type 1111) is identified by the Sniffer as a "Create Service Connection" packet. The response packet (request type 3333), a "Create Service Connection Reply," is seen in Figure 3-7b. The completion code and connection status flags indicate that a connection has been successfully established with the server on the remote network.

Figure 3-7a
Novell NetWare "Create Service Connection" packet

```
DLC:  ----- DLC Header -----
DLC:
DLC:  Frame 1 arrived at  13:39:34.0195 ; frame size is 45 (002D hex) bytes.
DLC:  Destination: Station 44
DLC:  Source     : Station 20
DLC:  ARCNET system code = FA
DLC:
NOV:  ----- Novell ARCNET fragmentation header -----
NOV:
NOV:  Unfragmented frame
NOV:  Sequence number = 3
NOV:
XNS:  ----- XNS Header -----
XNS:
XNS:  Checksum = FFFF
XNS:  Length = 37
XNS:  Transport control = 00
XNS:          0000 .... = Reserved
```

Figure 3-7a (continued)

```
XNS:          .... 0000 = Hop count
XNS: Packet type = 17 (Novell Netware)
XNS:
XNS: Dest   net = 00001111, host = 10005A0033BF, socket = 1105 (NetWare Server)
XNS: Source net = 00002222, host = 000000000020, socket = 4001 (16385)
XNS:
XNS: ----- Novell Advanced NetWare -----
XNS:
XNS: Request type = 1111 (Create Connection)
XNS: Seq no=0    Connection no=255   Task no=0
XNS:
NCP: ----- Create Service Connection -----
NCP:
NCP: [Normal end of Netware "Create Service Connection" packet.]
NCP:
```

Figure 3-7b
Novell NetWare "Create Service Connection Reply" packet

```
DLC: ----- DLC Header -----
DLC:
DLC: Frame 2 arrived at  13:39:34.0611 ; frame size is 46 (002E hex) bytes.
DLC: Destination: Station 20
DLC: Source     : Station 44
DLC: ARCNET system code = FA
DLC:
NOV: ----- Novell ARCNET fragmentation header -----
NOV:
NOV: Unfragmented frame
NOV: Sequence number = 28628
NOV:
XNS: ----- XNS Header -----
XNS:
XNS: Checksum = FFFF
XNS: Length = 38
XNS: Transport control = 00
XNS:          0000 .... = Reserved
XNS:          .... 0000 = Hop count
XNS: Packet type = 17 (Novell Netware)
XNS:
XNS: Dest   net = 00002222, host = 000000000020, socket = 4001 (16385)
XNS: Source net = 00001111, host = 10005A0033BF, socket = 1105 (NetWare Server)
XNS:
XNS: ----- Novell Advanced NetWare -----
```

Figure 3-7b (continued)

```
XNS:
XNS:    Request type = 3333 (Reply)
XNS:    Seq no=0    Connection no=1    Task no=0
XNS:
NCP:    ----- Create Service Connection Reply -----
NCP:
NCP:    Completion code = 00 (OK)
NCP:    Connection status flags = 00 (OK)
NCP:    [Normal end of Netware "Create Service Connection Reply" packet.]
NCP:
```

A second example (Figure 3-8a) shows the interaction between a work-station (Mark) and server (Dolchserver1) when a file (CI.EXE) is opened on the server. NetWare reads the file in 512-octet (or one-byte) increments and requires two transmission frames for each of these reads. (Recall that ARCNET can transmit 508 octets per frame, maximum.) After reading the 1,917 octets, the file is closed. Further details of the Open File Request (packet type 2222, code 76) are shown in Figure 3-8b. The desired access rights are defined as exclusive (single-user) and read-only. The Open File Reply packet confirms shareable, read-only file attributes. If a user had been denied access to this file, a check for a mismatch between the desired access rights and the existing file attributes would reveal the problem. When the complete file is read, NetWare issues a Close File Request packet (Figure 3-8c), code 66 in frame 31, which receives a reply with a Close File Reply packet in frame 32. The status flags in frame 32 indicate a successful operation.

Figure 3-8a
Novell NetWare File Retrieval Summary

Sniffer Network Analyzer data from 12-Jan-90 at 06:57:24,
file A:\NETWARE\XECUTECI.ARC, Page 1

SUMMARY		Delta T	Destination	Source	Summary
M	1		workstation	dolchserver	XNS NetWare Request Keep alive
	2	0.0008	dolchserver	workstation	XNS NetWare Reply Keep alive
	3	5.3799	Broadcast	dolchserver	XNS RIP response: 1 network,
	4	6.4166	dolchserver	workstation	NCP C Get dir path of handle
	5	0.0012	workstation	dolchserver	NCP R OK Path=SYS:PUBLIC/UTIL
	6	0.0015	dolchserver	workstation	NCP C Dir search parms for
	7	0.0009	workstation	dolchserver	NCP R OK Next=-1
	8	0.0010	dolchserver	workstation	NCP C Dir search CI.???
	9	0.0019	workstation	dolchserver	NCP R OK File=CI.DOC
	10	0.0012	dolchserver	workstation	NCP C Dir search CI.???
	11	0.0015	workstation	dolchserver	NCP R OK File=CI.EXE
	12	0.0012	dolchserver	workstation	NCP C Dir search CI.???
	13	0.0021	workstation	dolchserver	NCP R File not found
	14	0.0011	dolchserver	workstation	NCP C Dir search CI.???
	15	0.0021	workstation	dolchserver	NCP R File not found
	16	0.0013	dolchserver	workstation	NCP C Get dir path of handle
	17	0.0013	workstation	dolchserver	NCP R OK Path=SYS:PUBLIC/UTIL
	18	0.0025	dolchserver	workstation	NCP C Open file /PUBLIC/UTIL/C
	19	0.0040	workstation	dolchserver	NCP R F=190E OK Opened
	20	0.0018	dolchserver	workstation	NCP C F=190E Read 512 at 0
	21	0.0521	workstation	dolchserver	NCP R OK 512 bytes read
	22	0.0006	workstation	dolchserver	NCP Frag F=02 (2nd half), Seq=
	23	0.0023	dolchserver	workstation	NCP C F=190E Read 512 at 512
	24	0.0039	workstation	dolchserver	NCP R OK 512 bytes read
	25	0.0004	workstation	dolchserver	NCP Frag F=02 (2nd half), Seq=
	26	0.0014	dolchserver	workstation	NCP C F=190E Read 512 at 1024
	27	0.0038	workstation	dolchserver	NCP R OK 512 bytes read
	28	0.0006	workstation	dolchserver	NCP Frag F=02 (2nd half), Seq=
	29	0.0013	dolchserver	workstation	NCP C F=190E Read 512 at 1536
	30	0.0034	workstation	dolchserver	NCP R OK 381 bytes read
	31	0.0019	dolchserver	workstation	NCP C F=190E Close file
	32	0.0016	workstation	dolchserver	NCP R OK
	33	5.2966	dolchserver	workstation	NCP C End of task
	34	0.0010	workstation	dolchserver	NCP R OK
	35	0.0411	dolchserver	workstation	NCP C End of task
	36	0.0015	workstation	dolchserver	NCP R OK
	37	0.0016	dolchserver	workstation	NCP C Get dir path of handle
	38	0.0013	workstation	dolchserver	NCP R OK Path=SYS:PUBLIC/UTIL

Figure 3-8b
Novell NetWare Open File Request and Reply Packets

```
Sniffer Network Analyzer data from 12-Jan-90 at 06:57:24,
file A:\NETWARE\XECUTECI.ARC, Page 1


- - - - - - - - - - - - - - - - Frame 18 - - - - - - - - - - - - - - - - -

DLC:   ----- DLC Header -----
DLC:
DLC:   Frame 18 arrived at  06:57:38.4805 ; frame size is 71 (0047 hex)
DLC:   Destination: Station 07, dolchserver
DLC:   Source     : Station 0F, workstation
DLC:   ARCNET system code = FA
DLC:
FRAG:  ----- NCP ARCNET fragmentation header -----
FRAG:
FRAG:  Split flags = 00 (Complete)
FRAG:  Sequence number = 703
FRAG:
XNS:   ----- XNS Header -----
XNS:
XNS:   Checksum = FFFF
XNS:   Length = 63
XNS:   Transport control = 00
XNS:        0000 .... = Reserved
XNS:        .... 0000 = Hop count
XNS:   Packet type = 17 (Novell NetWare)
XNS:
XNS:   Dest   net = 00000001, host = 000000000007, socket = 1105 (NetWare Server)
XNS:   Source net = 00000001, host = 00000000000F, socket = 16387 (4003)
XNS:
XNS:   ----- Novell Advanced NetWare -----
XNS:
XNS:   Request type = 2222 (Request)
XNS:   Seq no=186  Connection no=2    Task no=1
XNS:
NCP:   ----- Open File Request -----
NCP:
NCP:   Request code = 76
NCP:
NCP:   Dir handle = 07
NCP:   Search attribute flags = 4E
NCP:             .... .1.. = System files allowed
NCP:             .... ..1. = Hidden files allowed
NCP:   Desired access rights = 11
NCP:             000. .... = Not defined
NCP:             ...1 .... = Exclusive (single-user mode)
NCP:             .... 0... = Allow others to open for writing
NCP:             .... .0.. = Allow others to open for reading
```

Figure 3-8b (continued)

```
NCP:                .... ..0. = Open for writing disallowed
NCP:                .... ...1 = Open for reading
NCP:  File name = "/PUBLIC/UTILITY/CI.EXE"
NCP:  [Normal end of NetWare "Open File Request" packet.]


- - - - - - - - - - - - - - - Frame 19 - - - - - - - - - - - - - - - - -

DLC:  ----- DLC Header -----
DLC:
DLC:  Frame 19 arrived at  06:57:38.4845 ; frame size is 82 (0052 hex)
DLC:  Destination: Station 0F, workstation
DLC:  Source     : Station 07, dolchserver
DLC:  ARCNET system code = FA
DLC:
FRAG: ----- NCP ARCNET fragmentation header -----
FRAG:
FRAG: Split flags = 00 (Complete)
FRAG: Sequence number = 744
FRAG:
XNS:  ----- XNS Header -----
XNS:
XNS:  Checksum = FFFF
XNS:  Length = 74
XNS:  Transport control = 00
XNS:         0000 .... = Reserved
XNS:         .... 0000 = Hop count
XNS:  Packet type = 17 (Novell NetWare)
XNS:
XNS:  Dest   net = 00000001, host = 00000000000F, socket = 16387 (4003)
XNS:  Source net = 00000001, host = 000000000007, socket = 1105 (NetWare Server)
XNS:
XNS:  ----- Novell Advanced NetWare -----
XNS:
XNS:  Request type = 3333 (Reply)
XNS:  Seq no=186  Connection no=2     Task no=0
XNS:
NCP:  ----- Open File Reply -----
NCP:
NCP:  Request code = 76 (reply to frame 18)
NCP:
NCP:  Completion code = 00 (OK)
NCP:  Connection status flags = 00 (OK)
NCP:  File handle = 0000 0A0E 1300
NCP:  File name = "CI.EXE"
NCP:  File attribute flags = 21
NCP:          0... .... = File is not sharable
NCP:          .0.. .... = Not defined
NCP:          ..1. .... = Changed since last archive
```

Figure 3-8b (continued)

```
NCP:               ...0 .... = Not a subdirectory
NCP:               .... 0... = Not execute-only file
NCP:               .... .0.. = Not a system file
NCP:               .... ..0. = Not a hidden file
NCP:               .... ...1 = Read-only
NCP:  File execute type = 00
NCP:  File length = 1917
NCP:  Creation date       = 22-Dec-89
NCP:  Last access date    =  8-Jan-90
NCP:  Last update date/time = 24-Jun-87 15:42:00
NCP:  [Normal end of NetWare "Open File Reply" packet.]
```

Figure 3-8c
Novell NetWare Close File Request and Reply Packets

```
Sniffer Network Analyzer data from 12-Jan-90 at 06:57:24,
file A:\NETWARE\XECUTECI.ARC, Page 1

- - - - - - - - - - - - - - - - Frame 31 - - - - - - - - - - - - - - - - - -

DLC:  ----- DLC Header -----
DLC:
DLC:  Frame 31 arrived at  06:57:38.5586 ; frame size is 52 (0034 hex)
DLC:  Destination: Station 07, dolchserver
DLC:  Source     : Station 0F, workstation
DLC:  ARCNET system code = FA
DLC:
FRAG: ----- NCP ARCNET fragmentation header -----
FRAG:
FRAG: Split flags = 00 (Complete)
FRAG: Sequence number = 708
FRAG:
XNS:  ----- XNS Header -----
XNS:
XNS:  Checksum = FFFF
XNS:  Length = 44
XNS:  Transport control = 00
XNS:        0000 .... = Reserved
XNS:        .... 0000 = Hop count
XNS:  Packet type = 17 (Novell NetWare)
XNS:
XNS:  Dest   net = 00000001, host = 000000000007, socket = 1105 (NetWare Server)
XNS:  Source net = 00000001, host = 00000000000F, socket = 16387 (4003)
XNS:
```

Figure 3-8c (continued)

```
XNS:  ----- Novell Advanced NetWare -----
XNS:
XNS:  Request type = 2222 (Request)
XNS:  Seq no=191  Connection no=2    Task no=1
XNS:
NCP:  ----- Close File Request -----
NCP:
NCP:  Request code = 66
NCP:
NCP:  File handle = 0000 0A0E 1300
NCP:
NCP:  [Normal end of NetWare "Close File Request" packet.]
NCP:


- - - - - - - - - - - - - - - - - - Frame 32 - - - - - - - - - - - - - - - - - -


DLC:  ----- DLC Header -----
DLC:
DLC:  Frame 32 arrived at  06:57:38.5603 ; frame size is 46 (002E hex) bytes.
DLC:  Destination: Station 0F, workstation
DLC:  Source     : Station 07, dolchserver
DLC:  ARCNET system code = FA
DLC:
FRAG: ----- NCP ARCNET fragmentation header -----
FRAG:
FRAG: Split flags = 00 (Complete)
FRAG: Sequence number = 749
FRAG:
XNS:  ----- XNS Header -----
XNS:
XNS:  Checksum = FFFF
XNS:  Length = 38
XNS:  Transport control = 00
XNS:        0000 .... = Reserved
XNS:        .... 0000 = Hop count
XNS:  Packet type = 17 (Novell NetWare)
XNS:
XNS:  Dest   net = 00000001, host = 00000000000F, socket = 16387 (4003)
XNS:  Source net = 00000001, host = 000000000007, socket = 1105 (NetWare Server)
XNS:
XNS:  ----- Novell Advanced NetWare -----
XNS:
XNS:  Request type = 3333 (Reply)
XNS:  Seq no=191  Connection no=2    Task no=0
XNS:
NCP:  ----- Close File Reply -----
NCP:
NCP:  Request code = 66 (reply to frame 31)
```

Figure 3-8c (continued)

```
NCP:
NCP:  Completion code = 00 (OK)
NCP:  Connection status flags = 00 (OK)
NCP:  [Normal end of NetWare "Close File Reply" packet.]
NCP:
```

A third NetWare example deals with network printing. The NetWare command NPRINT invokes the spooling/printing function on a server. In this case (Figure 3-9), the document file (CI.DOC) for the previously-executed program is printed. The NPRINT executable file is first located (frames 10 – 25), opened (frames 26 – 27), transferred to the workstation (frames 28 – 265), and then closed (frames 266 – 267). Note that the ARCNET frame format requires twice the number of transmissions because of the fragmentations. Next, the MAIL is checked (frames 274 – 283), the server's properties and workstation's properties are read (frames 288 – 308), and finally the file (CI.DOC) is located and printed (frames 309 – 334). See reference [3-11] for further details on the use of the NPRINT utility.

Figure 3-9
Novell NetWare printing example

```
Sniffer Network Analyzer data from 12-Jan-90 at 06:58:34,
file A:\NETWARE\NPRINTCI.ARC, Page 1


SUMMARY   Delta T     Destination    Source        Summary

M    1                 Broadcast     dolchserver   XNS RIP response: 1 network
     2      32.9565    Broadcast     dolchserver   NCP R DOLCHSERVER
     3      32.9409    Broadcast     dolchserver   XNS RIP response: 1 network,0000000
     4      32.9562    Broadcast     dolchserver   NCP R DOLCHSERVER
     5      32.9411    Broadcast     dolchserver   XNS RIP response: 1 network, 000000
     6       8.8633    dolchserver   workstation   NCP C Get dir path of handle 07
     7       0.0013    workstation   dolchserver   NCP R OK Path=SYS:PUBLIC/UTILITY
     8       0.0017    dolchserver   workstation   NCP C Dir search parms for [null]
     9       0.0010    workstation   dolchserver   NCP R OK Next=-1
    10       0.0011    dolchserver   workstation   NCP C Dir search NPRINT.???
    11       0.0026    workstation   dolchserver   NCP R File not found
    12       0.0010    dolchserver   workstation   NCP C Dir search NPRINT.???
    13       0.0024    workstation   dolchserver   NCP R File not found
    14       0.0012    dolchserver   workstation   NCP C Get dir path of handle 0D
```

Figure 3-9 (continued)

```
15    0.0012   workstation   dolchserver    NCP R OK Path=SYS:PUBLIC
16    0.0016   dolchserver   workstation    NCP C Dir search parms for ./
17    0.0023   workstation   dolchserver    NCP R OK Next=-1
18    0.0010   dolchserver   workstation    NCP C Dir search NPRINT.???
19    0.0036   dolchserver   workstation    NCP R OK File=NPRINT.EXE
20    0.0012   dolchserver   workstation    NCP C Dir search NPRINT.???
21    0.0094   workstation   dolchserver    NCP R File not found
22    0.0011   dolchserver   workstation    NCP C Dir search NPRINT.???
23    0.0096   workstation   dolchserver    NCP R File not found
24    0.0013   dolchserver   workstation    NCP C Get dir path of handle 0D
25    0.0010   workstation   dolchserver    NCP R OK Path=SYS:PUBLIC
26    0.0021   dolchserver   workstation    NCP C Open file /PUBLIC/NPRINT.EXE
27    0.0056   workstation   dolchserver    NCP R F=1E0E OK Opened
28    0.0019   dolchserver   workstation    NCP C F=1E0E Read 30 at 0
29    0.0010   workstation   dolchserver    NCP R OK 30 bytes read
30    0.0021   dolchserver   workstation    NCP C F=1E0E Read 512 at 512
31    0.0038   workstation   dolchserver    NCP R OK 512 bytes read
32    0.0005   workstation   dolchserver    NCP Frag F=02 (2nd half), Seq=771
33    0.0015   dolchserver   workstation    NCP C F=1E0E Read 512 at 1024
34    0.0038   workstation   dolchserver    NCP R OK 512 bytes read
35    0.0005   workstation   dolchserver    NCP Frag F=02 (2nd half), Seq=772
36    0.0014   dolchserver   workstation    NCP C F=1E0E Read 512 at 1536
37    0.0038   workstation   dolchserver    NCP R OK 512 bytes read
38    0.0005   workstation   dolchserver    NCP Frag F=02 (2nd half), Seq=773
         •
         •
         •
255   0.0014   dolchserver   workstation    NCP C F=1E0E Read 512 at 38912
256   0.0039   workstation   dolchserver    NCP R OK 512 bytes read
257   0.0005   workstation   dolchserver    NCP Frag F=02 (2nd half), Seq=846
258   0.0014   dolchserver   workstation    NCP C F=1E0E Read 512 at 39424
259   0.0039   workstation   dolchserver    NCP R OK 512 bytes read
260   0.0005   workstation   dolchserver    NCP Frag F=02 (2nd half), Seq=847
261   0.0013   dolchserver   workstation    NCP C F=1E0E Read 512 at 39936
262   0.0039   workstation   dolchserver    NCP R OK 512 bytes read
263   0.0005   workstation   dolchserver    NCP Frag F=02 (2nd half), Seq=848
264   0.0014   dolchserver   workstation    NCP C F=1E0E Read 512 at 40448
265   0.0016   workstation   dolchserver    NCP R OK 119 bytes read
266   0.0014   dolchserver   workstation    NCP C F=1E0E Close file
267   0.0012   workstation   dolchserver    NCP R OK
268   0.0264   dolchserver   workstation    NCP C Check server version
269   0.0016   workstation   dolchserver    NCP R OK
270   0.0055   dolchserver   workstation    NCP C Get station number
271   0.0008   workstation   dolchserver    NCP R OK Station is 02
272   0.0011   dolchserver   workstation    NCP C Get connection info
273   0.0036   workstation   dolchserver    NCP R OK
274   0.0031   dolchserver   workstation    NCP C Open file SYS:MAIL/9003D
275   0.0049   workstation   dolchserver    NCP R File not found
```

Figure 3-9 (continued)

```
276   0.5574   dolchserver   workstation    NCP C Open file SYS:MAIL/9003D
277   0.0053   workstation   dolchserver    NCP R File not found
278   0.9980   dolchserver   workstation    NCP C Open file SYS:MAIL/9003D/
279   0.0053   workstation   dolchserver    NCP R File not found
280   0.9829   dolchserver   workstation    NCP C Open file SYS:MAIL/9003D/
281   0.0052   workstation   dolchserver    NCP R File not found
282   0.9832   dolchserver   workstation    NCP C Open file SYS:MAIL/9003D/
283   0.0050   workstation   dolchserver    NCP R File not found
284   0.9825   dolchserver   workstation    NCP C Get station number
285   0.0008   workstation   dolchserver    NCP R OK Station is 02
286   0.0010   dolchserver   workstation    NCP C Get connection info
287   0.0034   workstation   dolchserver    NCP R OK
288   0.0014   dolchserver   workstation    NCP C Read DOLCHSERVER's properties
289   0.0045   workstation   dolchserver    NCP R OK
290   0.0046   dolchserver   workstation    NCP C Get spooler 0 mapping
291   0.0002   dolchserver   workstation    NCP Frag F=02 (2nd half), Seq=815
292   0.0012   workstation   dolchserver    NCP R OK Printer object 00150000
293   0.0011   dolchserver   workstation    NCP C Map Trustee to user
294   0.0029   workstation   dolchserver    NCP R OK Mapped: PRINTQ_0
295   0.0012   dolchserver   workstation    NCP C Get station number
296   0.0007   workstation   dolchserver    NCP R OK Station is 02
297   0.0011   dolchserver   workstation    NCP C Get connection info
298   0.0032   workstation   dolchserver    NCP R OK
299   0.0014   dolchserver   workstation    NCP C Search bindery for PRINTQ_0
300   0.0035   workstation   dolchserver    NCP R OK Found PRINTQ_0
301   0.0014   dolchserver   workstation    NCP C Check PRINTQ_0's membership
302   0.0068   workstation   dolchserver    NCP R Non-existent member
303   0.0012   dolchserver   workstation    NCP C Read MARK's properties
304   0.0048   workstation   dolchserver    NCP R OK
305   0.0014   dolchserver   workstation    NCP C Map Trustee to user
306   0.0024   workstation   dolchserver    NCP R OK Mapped: EVERYONE
307   0.0015   dolchserver   workstation    NCP C Check PRINTQ_0's membership
308   0.0060   workstation   dolchserver    NCP R OK
309   0.0492   dolchserver   workstation    NCP C Create handle for
310   0.0026   workstation   dolchserver    NCP R OK Handle=03
311   0.0013   dolchserver   workstation    NCP C Get dir path of handle 03
312   0.0014   workstation   dolchserver    NCP R OK Path=SYS:PUBLIC/UTILITY
313   0.0323   dolchserver   workstation    NCP C Dir search parms for [null]
314   0.0008   workstation   dolchserver    NCP R OK Next=-1
315   0.0011   dolchserver   workstation    NCP C Dir search CI.DOC
316   0.0017   workstation   dolchserver    NCP R OK File=CI.DOC
317   0.0030   dolchserver   workstation    NCP C Create queue 00040015 job
318   0.0102   workstation   dolchserver    NCP R OK F=1F0E Job=14
319   0.0019   dolchserver   workstation    NCP C Open file CI.DOC
320   0.0019   workstation   dolchserver    NCP R F=3D0E OK Opened
321   0.0017   dolchserver   workstation    NCP C F=3D0E Get file current size
322   0.0007   workstation   dolchserver    NCP R OK
323   0.0012   dolchserver   workstation    NCP C F=3D0E Read 512 at 0
```

Figure 3-9 (continued)

```
324    0.0036   workstation   dolchserver    NCP R OK 403 bytes read
325    0.0018   dolchserver   workstation    NCP C Copy file to file
326    0.0012   workstation   dolchserver    NCP R OK
327    0.0010   dolchserver   workstation    NCP C F=1FOE Close file
328    0.0008   workstation   dolchserver    NCP R OK
329    0.0011   dolchserver   workstation    NCP C F=3DOE Close file
330    0.0009   workstation   dolchserver    NCP R OK
331    0.0329   dolchserver   workstation    NCP C Start queue job 14
332    0.0024   workstation   dolchserver    NCP R OK
333    0.0044   dolchserver   workstation    NCP C End of task
334    0.0011   workstation   dolchserver    NCP R OK
```

Our fourth example (taken from reference [3-12]) shows the subtleties of workstation caching under NetWare. The CONFIG.SYS file establishes a cache buffer is established at each workstation, which sets aside a portion of that workstation's RAM for a cache buffer. This cache buffer is designed to speed up the process of reading data from the network server. When the workstation requests the server to send a portion of a file, the server sends the data requested and a little bit more. In other words, the server assumes that the workstation will issue a subsequent read command, and if the data is already in the cache buffer, additional transmission of data over the network will not be required. Caching can also be accomplished at the server by reserving some of the server's RAM for a cache, thus eliminating some server disk I/O when reading smaller files.

There is a downside to caching as well. A portion of the workstation's RAM is lost to the cache, and in some cases the server bets that the workstation will request additional data when in fact it does not. In most cases, however, the concept of caching improves system performance. In this example, a workstation cache buffer of 512 bytes was established, but the buffer was only used when the file attributes were defined for "not shareable." Let's see exactly what impact this has on the performance of the network.

The problem presented in Figure 3-10a is that there are numerous READ requests from the workstation (HarrysPC) to the server (BIZ-

ONE) for a relatively small file (301 octets) with a file handle of F=1B91. Note that the file requests are in increments of 70 octets, and that some are overlapping, such as frame 183 which reads 70 at 94, but frame 185 reads 70 at 113, not 164.

Investigating the file access rights requested with the workstation's Open File Request (Figure 3-10b) indicates that the file is Open for Reading but not for Writing, which seems appropriate for the application. The server's Open File Reply (Figure 3-10c) defines the file as Shareable and Read-only, both of which also seem correct. Unfortunately, NetWare enables the workstation cache to accept only nonshared files, working on the premise that any information left in the cache buffer may be corrupted if a subsequent file modification is made by another workstation.

Figure 3-10a
Novell NetWare caching example summary

```
Sniffer Network Analyzer data from 18-Oct-88 at 18:49:46, file
NETWARE\SHARED.ENC, Page 1

SUMMARY  Delta T     Destination   Source        Summary

    181   0.0014  BIZ-ONE      HarrysPC      NCP C F=1B91 Read 70 at 74
    182   0.0012  HarrysPC     BIZ-ONE       NCP R OK 70 bytes read
    183   0.0020  BIZ-ONE      HarrysPC      NCP C F=1B91 Read 70 at 94
    184   0.0013  HarrysPC     BIZ-ONE       NCP R OK 70 bytes read
    185   0.0015  BIZ-ONE      HarrysPC      NCP C F=1B91 Read 70 at 113
    186   0.0013  HarrysPC     BIZ-ONE       NCP R OK 70 bytes read
    187   0.0020  BIZ-ONE      HarrysPC      NCP C F=1B91 Read 70 at 135
    188   0.0012  HarrysPC     BIZ-ONE       NCP R OK 70 bytes read
    189   0.0014  BIZ-ONE      HarrysPC      NCP C F=1B91 Read 70 at 145
    190   0.0013  HarrysPC     BIZ-ONE       NCP R OK 70 bytes read
    191   0.0019  BIZ-ONE      HarrysPC      NCP C F=1B91 Read 70 at 159
    192   0.0012  HarrysPC     BIZ-ONE       NCP R OK 70 bytes read
    193   0.0014  BIZ-ONE      HarrysPC      NCP C F=1B91 Read 70 at 170
    194   0.0012  HarrysPC     BIZ-ONE       NCP R OK 70 bytes read
    195   0.0016  BIZ-ONE      HarrysPC      NCP C F=1B91 Read 70 at 179
    196   0.0012  HarrysPC     BIZ-ONE       NCP R OK 70 bytes read
    197   0.0014  BIZ-ONE      HarrysPC      NCP C F=1B91 Read 70 at 188
    198   0.0012  HarrysPC     BIZ-ONE       NCP R OK 70 bytes read
    199   0.0026  BIZ-ONE      HarrysPC      NCP C F=1B91 Read 70 at 220
    200   0.0012  HarrysPC     BIZ-ONE       NCP R OK 70 bytes read
    201   0.0014  BIZ-ONE      HarrysPC      NCP C F=1B91 Read 70 at 226
```

Figure 3-10a (continued)

```
202   0.0012  HarrysPC    BIZ-ONE      NCP R OK 70 bytes read
203   0.0016  BIZ-ONE     HarrysPC     NCP C F=5460 Read 512 at 0
204   0.0010  HarrysPC    BIZ-ONE      NCP R OK 0 bytes read
205   0.0012  BIZ-ONE     HarrysPC     NCP C F=5460 Read 512 at 0
206   0.0010  HarrysPC    BIZ-ONE      NCP R OK 0 bytes read
207   0.0012  BIZ-ONE     HarrysPC     NCP C F=5460 Write 0 at 0
208   0.0011  HarrysPC    BIZ-ONE      NCP R OK
```

Figure 3-10b
Novell NetWare Open File Request Packet

```
Sniffer Network Analyzer data from 18-Oct-88 at 18:49:46,
file A:\NETWARE\SHARED.ENC, Page 1

- - - - - - - - - - - - - - - Frame 1 - - - - - - - - - - - - - - - -

NCP:    ----- Open File Request -----
NCP:
NCP:    Request code = 76
NCP:
NCP:    Dir handle = 05
NCP:    Search attribute flags = 06
NCP:                .... .1.. = System files allowed
NCP:                .... ..1. = Hidden files allowed
NCP:    Desired access rights = 11
NCP:            000. .... = Not defined
NCP:            ...1 .... = Exclusive (single-user mode)
NCP:            .... 0... = Allow others to open for writing
NCP:            .... .0.. = Allow others to open for reading
NCP:            .... ..0. = Open for writing disallowed
NCP:            .... ...1 = Open for reading
NCP:    File name = "SAMPLE.MNU"
NCP:
NCP:    [Normal end of NetWare "Open File Request" packet.]
NCP:
```

Figure 3-10c
Novell NetWare Original Open File Reply Packet

```
Sniffer Network Analyzer data from 18-Oct-88 at 18:49:46,
file A:\NETWARE\SHARED.ENC, Page 1

- - - - - - - - - - - - - - - - Frame 2 - - - - - - - - - - - - - - - -

NCP:    ----- Open File Reply -----
NCP:
NCP:    Request code = 76 (reply to frame 1)
NCP:
NCP:    Completion code = 00 (OK)
NCP:    Connection status flags = 00 (OK)
NCP:    File handle = 2E97 D416 E110
NCP:    File name = "SAMPLE.MNU"
NCP:    File attribute flags = A1
NCP:                1... .... = File is sharable
NCP:                .0.. .... = Not defined
NCP:                ..1. .... = Changed since last archive
NCP:                ...0 .... = Not a subdirectory
NCP:                .... 0... = Not execute-only file
NCP:                .... .0.. = Not a system file
NCP:                .... ..0. = Not a hidden file
NCP:                .... ...1 = Read-only
NCP:    File execute type = 00
NCP:    File length = 301
NCP:    Creation date       = 20-Oct-88
NCP:    Last access date    = 20-Oct-88
NCP:    Last update date/time = 31-Aug-88 18:04:46
NCP:
NCP:    [Normal end of NetWare "Open File Reply" packet.]
NCP:
```

Figure 3-10d
Novell NetWare Revised Open File Reply Packet

```
Sniffer Network Analyzer data from 18-Oct-88 at 18:55:38,
file A:\NETWARE\UNSHARED.ENC, Page 1

- - - - - - - - - - - - - - - - Frame 2 - - - - - - - - - - - - - - - -

NCP:    ----- Open File Reply -----
NCP:
NCP:    Request code = 76 (reply to frame 1)
NCP:
```

Figure 3-10d (continued)

```
NCP:    Completion code = 00 (OK)
NCP:    Connection status flags = 00 (OK)
NCP:    File handle = 2E97 0E1E ED18
NCP:    File name = "SAMPLE.MNU"
NCP:    File attribute flags = 21
NCP:                0... .... = File is not sharable
NCP:                .0.. .... = Not defined
NCP:                ..1. .... = Changed since last archive
NCP:                ...0 .... = Not a subdirectory
NCP:                .... 0... = Not execute-only file
NCP:                .... .0.. = Not a system file
NCP:                .... ..0. = Not a hidden file
NCP:                .... ...1 = Read-only
NCP:    File execute type = 00
NCP:    File length = 301
NCP:    Creation date       = 20-Oct-88
NCP:    Last access date    = 20-Oct-88
NCP:    Last update date/time = 31-Aug-88 18:04:46
NCP:
NCP:    [Normal end of NetWare "Open File Reply" packet.]
NCP:
```

Figure 3-10e
Novell NetWare Revised Cache Example Summary

```
Sniffer Network Analyzer data from 18-Oct-88 at 18:55:38,
file A:\NETWARE\UNSHARED.ENC, Page 1
```

SUMMARY	Delta T	Destination	Source	Summary
167	0.0081	BIZ-ONE	HarrysPC	NCP C Open file MENUPARZ.HLP
168	0.0047	HarrysPC	BIZ-ONE	NCP R F=3733 OK Opened
169	0.0009	BIZ-ONE	HarrysPC	NCP C F=3733 Read 410 at 0
170	0.0019	HarrysPC	BIZ-ONE	NCP R OK 410 bytes read
171	0.0018	BIZ-ONE	HarrysPC	NCP C F=3733 Read 512 at 0
172	0.0020	HarrysPC	BIZ-ONE	NCP R OK 512 bytes read
173	0.0020	BIZ-ONE	HarrysPC	NCP C F=CD91 Read 512 at 0
174	0.0016	HarrysPC	BIZ-ONE	NCP R OK 301 bytes read
175	0.0167	BIZ-ONE	HarrysPC	NCP C F=8460 Read 512 at 0
176	0.0011	HarrysPC	BIZ-ONE	NCP R OK 0 bytes read
177	0.0012	BIZ-ONE	HarrysPC	NCP C F=8460 Read 512 at 0
178	0.0010	HarrysPC	BIZ-ONE	NCP R OK 0 bytes read
179	0.0011	BIZ-ONE	HarrysPC	NCP C F=8460 Write 0 at 0
180	0.0011	HarrysPC	BIZ-ONE	NCP R OK

Changing the file attributes to Not Shareable and Read Only (Figure 3-10d) produces a dramatic improvement in performance. Now the entire 301-octet file is read in one frame (frame 174 of Figure 3-10e), and the multiple reads and overlaps are eliminated. This example demonstrates the importance of understanding the intricacies of the network operating system, and how the various file attributes can affect the transmission of data. While multiple transmissions of small amounts of data would not have a significant effect on a lightly loaded network, a more active network would experience degradations from collisions or other transmission delays when these parameters are not properly administered (see reference [3-13]).

The final example shows how NetWare handles a workstation that has a defective NIC. In this case, an Ethernet network has one file server (DCSP1) and 16 users (see Figure 3-11a). Deloris is on the network and reading information from the server in frames 1 – 37. Gary then attempts to login (frame 38), which is decoded as a BAD FRAME. Details of that frame (Figure 3-11b) show the reason. Gary's NIC only transmitted 12 octets when the minimum frame size is 64 octets. This resulted in both a fragment, or short frame, and a bad alignment, indicating that the number of bits of data was not evenly divisible by eight. These bad frames continue until frame 95 (not shown). Beginning in frame 96, the analyzer again captures Deloris's transmission, with everything appearing normal. The problem points to Gary's NIC. When he replaced it, he was able to login successfully.

Figure 3-11a
Novell NetWare Defective NIC Example

```
Sniffer Network Analyzer data from 23-Feb-90 at 08:15:36,
file A:DCSP2.ENC, Page 1


SUMMARY  Delta T    Destination   Source       Summary

M   1                dcspserver    deloris      NCP C F=2A11 Read 1024 at 3072
    2     0.0047     deloris       dcspserver   NCP R OK 1024 bytes read
    3     0.0032     dcspserver    deloris      NCP C F=2A11 Read 1024 at 4096
    4     0.0048     deloris       dcspserver   NCP R OK 1024 bytes read
    5     0.0031     dcspserver    deloris      NCP C F=2A11 Read 1024 at 5120
    6     0.0047     deloris       dcspserver   NCP R OK 1024 bytes read
    7     0.6933     dcspserver    deloris      NCP C F=2A11 Read 1024 at 5120
    8     0.0046     deloris       dcspserver   NCP R OK 1024 bytes read
    9     0.0031     dcspserver    deloris      NCP C F=2A11 Read 1024 at 6144
   10     0.0048     deloris       dcspserver   NCP R OK 1024 bytes read
   11     1.0309     dcspserver    deloris      NCP C F=2A11 Read 1024 at 6144
   12     0.0047     deloris       dcspserver   NCP R OK 1024 bytes read
   13     1.4782     dcspserver    deloris      NCP C F=2A11 Read 1024 at 6144
   14     0.0046     deloris       dcspserver   NCP R OK 1024 bytes read
   15     1.4782     dcspserver    deloris      NCP C F=2A11 Read 1024 at 6144
   16     0.0046     deloris       dcspserver   NCP R OK 1024 bytes read
   17     0.0031     dcspserver    deloris      NCP C F=2A11 Read 1024 at 7168
   18     0.0047     deloris       dcspserver   NCP R OK 1024 bytes read
   19     1.4704     dcspserver    deloris      NCP C F=2A11 Read 1024 at 7168
   20     0.0047     deloris       dcspserver   NCP R OK 1024 bytes read
   21     1.4781     dcspserver    deloris      NCP C F=2A11 Read 1024 at 7168
   22     0.0047     deloris       dcspserver   NCP R OK 1024 bytes read
   23     1.4781     dcspserver    deloris      NCP C F=2A11 Read 1024 at 7168
   24     0.0047     deloris       dcspserver   NCP R OK 1024 bytes read
   25     1.4783     dcspserver    deloris      NCP C F=2A11 Read 1024 at 7168
   26     0.0046     deloris       dcspserver   NCP R OK 1024 bytes read
   27     1.4781     dcspserver    deloris      NCP C F=2A11 Read 1024 at 7168
   28     0.0047     deloris       dcspserver   NCP R OK 1024 bytes read
   29     0.0032     dcspserver    deloris      NCP C F=2A11 Read 1024 at 8192
   30     0.0047     deloris       dcspserver   NCP R OK 1024 bytes read
   31     1.4702     dcspserver    deloris      NCP C F=2A11 Read 1024 at 8192
   32     0.0046     deloris       dcspserver   NCP R OK 1024 bytes read
   33     0.0031     dcspserver    deloris      NCP C F=2A11 Read 1024 at 9216
   34     0.0047     deloris       dcspserver   NCP R OK 1024 bytes read
   35     0.0031     dcspserver    deloris      NCP C F=2A11 Read 1024 at 10240
   36     1.0279     dcspserver    deloris      NCP C F=2A11 Read 1024 at 10240
   37     0.0047     deloris       dcspserver   NCP R OK 1024 bytes read
   38     0.5199     dcspserver    gary         DLC, BAD FRAME, size=12 bytes
```

Figure 3-11a (continued)

```
39    0.0014   gary          dcspserver    NCP R OK
40    0.0158   dcspserver    gary          DLC, BAD FRAME, size=12 bytes
41    0.0014   gary          dcspserver    NCP R OK
42    0.0009   dcspserver    gary          DLC, BAD FRAME, size=12 bytes
43    0.0013   gary          dcspserver    NCP R OK
```

Figure 3-11b
Novell NetWare Defective NIC Details

```
Sniffer Network Analyzer data from 23-Feb-90 at 08:15:36,
file A:DCSP2.ENC, Page 1


- - - - - - - - - - - - - - - Frame 38 - - - - - - - - - - - - - - - -

DLC:   ----- DLC Header -----
DLC:
DLC:   Frame 38 arrived at  08:15:53.3442 ; frame size is 12 (000C hex)
DLC:   FRAME ERROR: Fragment    Bad alignment
DLC:   Destination: Station Novell20BD3C, dcspserver
DLC:   Source     : Station Novell20E1B3, gary
DLC:

- - - - - - - - - - - - - - - Frame 39 - - - - - - - - - - - - - - - -

NCP:   ----- Unknown Command Code Reply -----
NCP:
NCP:   *** Original request packet not available. ***
NCP:
NCP:   Completion code = 00 (OK)
NCP:   Connection status flags = 00 (OK)
NCP:   Padded with 28 byte(s) of additional data.
NCP:
NCP:   [Normal end of NetWare "Unknown Command Code Reply" packet.]
NCP:
```

Reference [3-14] provides additional details on how to effectively use
Network General Corp.'s Sniffer Protocol Analyzer.

3.9 | References

[3-1] NetWare Buyer's Guide, Document 482-000020-002, Winter 1990.

[3-2] Dale Neibaur, "Understanding XNS: The Prototypical Internetwork Protocol," *Data Communications*, Volume 18, Number 12, September 21, 1989, pp. 43-51.

[3-3] Xerox Network System Architecture General Information Manual, Document XNSG068504, Xerox Corporation, April 1985.

[3-4] Advanced NetWare Theory of Operations Version 2.1, Novell, Inc., 1987.

[3-5] LAN Operating System Report, Novell, Inc., 1986.

[3-6] David W. White and Tom Henderson, "LAN Grand Prix," *LAN Magazine*, January 1990, pp. 48–56.

[3-7] NetWare System Interface Technical Overview, Document 100-00569-001, Novell, Inc. 1989.

[3-8] Advanced NetWare v2.0 File Service Core Protocols, Novell, Inc., 1986.

[3-9] Xerox Corporation, Internet Transport Protocols, document XNSS 028112, 1981.

[3-10] NetWare System Calls – DOS, Document 100-000571-001, Novell, Inc. 1989.

[3-11] NetWare User Reference, Part III: Command Line Utilities, document number 100-000231-001, Novell, Inc., 1986.

[3-12] Network General Corporation, "Real Networks Real Problems. A Tutorial," document number 24101-001, January 1990.

[3-13]   Novell, Inc., NetWare reference for ELS-II, document number 100-000556-001, 1989.

[3-14]   ARCNET Network Portable Protocol Analyzer Operation and Reference Manual, Network General Corporation, 1986-1988.

CHAPTER FOUR

Analyzing 3Com's 3+ and 3+Open

3+ is 3Com Corp.'s Network Operating System for DOS workstations and servers. It is a unique blend of the Xerox Network Systems (XNS) protocols, Microsoft Corp.'s Server/Redirector File Sharing Protocol, plus an emulation of IBM's NetBIOS which is also used in both Novell's NetWare (see Chapter 3) and Banyan VINES (see Chapter 6). The Server/Redirector and NetBIOS are heavily used by the IBM Token-Ring protocols (see Chapter 5). 3+ is able to capitalize on the strengths of each of its components: the well-accepted DOS and Redirector elements for application programs, the workstation/server communication strength of NetBIOS, and the rigors of the XNS protocols for internetworking.

3+Open, on the other hand, uses OS/2-based servers, and supports DOS, Macintosh, and OS/2 workstations. One of the fundamental differences between these two operating systems is that 3+ is very tightly tied to the XNS protocols, whereas 3+Open is based upon the NetBIOS programming interface. Another significant difference is in the device drivers that support various protocol stacks. Where 3+ supports Ethernet and token-ring hardware with the XNS protocols, 3+Open supports a number of hardware and protocol suite options in an interoperable manner.

As one would expect, there are also similarities. Both 3+ and 3+Open use the Microsoft Server Message Block (SMB) protocol for file and print services. Both support the NetBIOS interface. Applications, such as 3+Mail and 3+Open/Mail, are also designed for compatibility.

Since the internal protocols of the two operating systems demonstrate the most significant differences between 3+ and 3+Open, we will study the two operating systems individually. We'll begin with 3+, comparing it with the OSI Reference Model. Our discussion of 3+Open will begin in section 4.6.

4.1 | 3+ Architecture and the OSI Model

The 3+ operating system provides a network environment with four major components: the Process Manager, MINDS (MS-DOS Internal Network Driver Scheme), CIOSYS (Concurrent I/O system), and the Application Program Interfaces (APIs) (see Figure 4-1). Together they provide the interfaces between Application programs and network adapters. Network adapters that are currently supported by 3+ include IEEE 802.3/Ethernet and IEEE 802.5/token ring.

Figure 4-1
3Com 3+ architecture

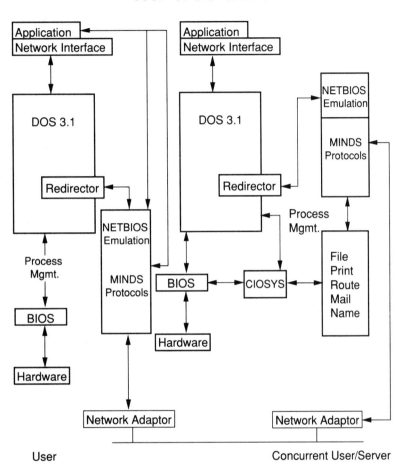

User   Concurrent User/Server

3+ Components

The first of the 3+ components is the Process Manager (shown as Process Management in Figure 4-1), a multi-tasking kernel which provides communication between the various 3+ elements. The Process Manager keeps track of up to 64 processes simultaneously, and exists on both workstations and servers. The MINDS Protocols are 3Com's implementation of XNS to provide network communication between

131

workstations and servers. CIOSYS is a DOS-compatible, multi-threaded file system that allows the server to handle up to four DOS processes at one time. Finally, the Application programs on the workstations or servers interface with either DOS 3.1 and the Redirector, a NetBIOS emulation, or the MINDS protocols directly.

Several 3Com publications would be of interest to network designers and troubleshooters. Reference [4-1] is a high-level architectural overview of the 3+ operating system. The Developer's Guide (reference [4-2]) and NetProbe Utility Guide (reference [4-3]) provide further details on the 3+ protocols. Many of the 3+ components described above are derivatives of the Xerox Network Systems protocols that were developed in the 1970s, therefore reference [4-4] might be instructive since it provides an excellent historical summary of XNS. References [4-5] and [4-6] describe the protocols and formats in detail.

4.1.2 Comparing 3+ and the OSI Model

In view of the influence of XNS, we'll include a brief discussion of the various XNS protocols as we compare 3+ with the layers of the OSI Reference Model (see Figure 4-2).

At the lower layers (Physical and Data Link), 3+ supports Ethernet/IEEE 802.3, IEEE 802.5, Apple Computer's LocalTalk for Macintosh workstations, plus asynchronous line connections. The asynchronous protocol includes the Microcom Networking Protocol (MNP) for reliability. Remote connections and internetworking are also supported.

Figure 4-2
Comparing 3Com 3+ Architecture with OSI

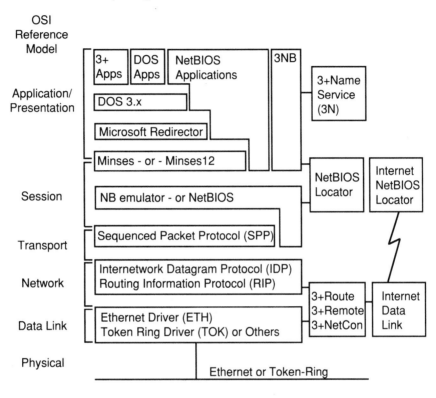

The Network layer is modeled after the XNS Internet Datagram Protocol (IDP) and provides datagram service. (Recall that datagrams are considered unreliable services since they offer no guarantee of packet delivery or packet sequencing.) The datagrams contain a three-part address (making up a total of 14 octets) that specifies a network, host, and socket. We'll look at IDP in detail in Section 4.3.

The 3+ Transport layer provides the reliability that its Network layer (IDP) lacks, and can be implemented with four different protocols. For virtual circuit connections, the XNS Sequenced Packet Protocol (SPP) provides reliable delivery of data in its proper sequence, with no incorrect, missing, or duplicate packets. Applications without packet sequencing requirements can use the XNS Packet

Exchange Protocol (PEP) which has lower packet overhead (not shown in Figure 4-2). Another user of the IDP datagram service is for the Routing Information Protocol (RIP) which keeps router tables updated. The Echo protocol (also not shown) is used to verify proper host operation. We'll study these Transport layer protocols in detail in Section 4.4.

The Session and Presentation layer functions of the XNS are described by the XNS Courier protocols. 3+ emulates these layers with either NetBIOS or a NetBIOS emulator for Session functions; and DOS and the Redirector for Presentation functions. The Redirector is part of the Microsoft Server/Redirector File Sharing Protocol. In between these two layers is an interface, known as MINSES (minimum session) or MINSES12 (minimum session for version 1.2). The purpose of the Redirector is to intercept all calls to DOS interrupt 21H and decide if local hardware (via the PC's BIOS) or network hardware (via a NetBIOS emulation and the MINDS protocols) is appropriate. It therefore redirects the INT 21H calls across the network, when necessary. The NetBIOS Locator provides the mechanism to identify users (names) on both local and remote networks.

The 3+ Application layer includes modules for name service (3N), a file utility (3F), a print service (3P), an administration tool (3M), internet NetBIOS support (3NB), dial-in remote access (3R), and electronic mail (MAIL.EXE). DOS and NetBIOS Applications are also supported. As before, let's begin our detailed tour of the 3+ protocols with the Data Link layer.

4.2 | 3+ Data Link Layer Protocols

In both 3+ and 3+Open, 3Com supports Ethernet/IEEE 802.3 and IEEE 802.5 at the Data Link layer. We'll look at these frame formats separately.

4.2.1 | 3Com Ethernet/IEEE 802.3 frames

As we saw in Chapter 1, there is one significant difference between the Ethernet standard (developed by DEC, Intel, and Xerox; see reference [1-8]) and IEEE 802.3 (see reference [1-2]): the use of the two-octet field immediately following the Destination and Source Addresses. Ethernet uses this field for a "Type" designation, identifying the higher layer protocol used within the Data field. IEEE 802.3 makes this the "Length" field, which contains the length (in octets) of the Data field. Fortunately, the allowable "Types" (formerly administered by Xerox, and now monitored by the IEEE) are outside the range of a valid "Length" (0001 - 05EEH) so that no confusion occurs. (See Appendix 1 for a listing of known Ethernet "types.")

3+ supports the Ethernet version and inserts the value of 0600H within the Type field to indicate that an IDP packet (direct from XNS) is contained within the Data field (see Figure 4-3). Headers for the IDP packet and the higher layer protocols also are encapsulated within the Data field. Ethernet frames range from 64 - 1518 octets in length, excluding the Preamble. Values outside that range are considered invalid and rejected by the Data Link layer, and so are not passed to the higher layer processes.

Figure 4-3
3Com 3+ and 3+Open Frame Format for Ethernet

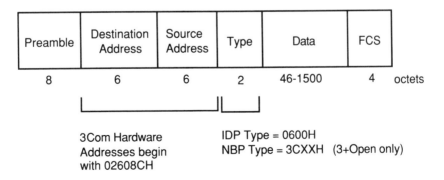

4.2.2 | 3Com IEEE 802.5 Frames

Support for 802.5 (token ring) networks includes both Logical Link Control (LLC) transmissions of user data and Medium Access Control (MAC) transmissions for ring management (see Figure 4-4). These two types of transmissions are delineated by the two least significant bits of the Frame Control Field: 00 designates a MAC frame and 01 designates an LLC frame. Further details on the specific MAC frame being transmitted are contained within the MAC header in the Information field. The MAC frame formats and the various token-ring processes will be discussed in detail in Section 5.3.

Another header within the 3+ Data field is a variation of the Subnetwork Access Protocol (SNAP), which was originally devised to allow IEEE 802 networks to communicate in a Transmission Control Protocol/Internetwork Protocol (TCP/IP) environment (see reference [4-7]). The SNAP header immediately follows the Source Address field. It consists of the DSAP and SSAP (both set to AAH), the 802.2 Control field (one octet), the Protocol ID or Organization Code (three octets, each set to 00H by 3+), and finally an Ethertype (set to 0600H) which indicates IDP.

Figure 4-4
3Com 3+ Frame Format for IEEE 802.5

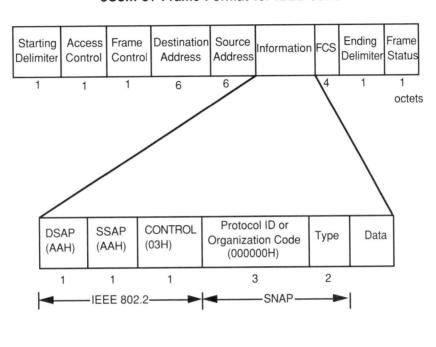

3Com Hardware Addresses
begin with 02608CH

IDP Type = 0600H
NBP Type = 3CXXH (3+Open only)

4.3   3+ Network Layer Protocols

3+ takes its Network layer structure from XNS IDP which routes packets (known as datagrams) through the internetwork. Note that the datagram implementation implies independence -- each packet contains sufficient addressing information to allow data to be transferred from source to destination via multiple routers.

The IDP header (see Figure 4-5) begins with a checksum which is usually set to FFFFH, since the Data Link layer frame has its own 32-bit Frame Check Sequence (FCS). The length field (two octets) defines the length of the packet in octets, beginning with the checksum. The

137

Transport Control is used by internetwork routers and includes a hop count (in the lower four bits) that determines the number of routers (or hops) that this packet has passed through. The initiator of the packet sets the hop count to zero, and the count is increased in increments as the packet passes through each router. The Packet Type defines the Transport layer protocol in use, and as defined by Xerox has five possible values. Of these five, 3+ supports four:

01 = Routing Information protocol (RIP)
02 = Echo Protocol (Echo)
03 = Error Protocol (Error) - not supported by 3+
04 = Packet Exchange Protocol (PEP)
05 = Sequenced Packet Protocol (SPP)

Addressing fields comes next, identifying first the Destination and then the Source. The Network (four octets), Host (six octets), and Socket (two octets) uniquely identify the network, hardware address, and service or virtual circuit, respectively, associated with each packet transmitted. Note that the Host addresses within the IDP packet may be different from the addresses contained in the Data Link layer frame. The frame contains the address of the immediate node, i.e. the next station to receive the frame, whereas the packet address contains the ultimate station to receive the packet. The immediate (Data Link layer) address is equivalent to the Network layer address when that Host is the final destination for the packet in question. Otherwise, a routing table supplies the immediate address.

The Data field at the end of the IDP packet would contain the higher layer information.

Figure 4-5
3Com 3+ IDP Packet

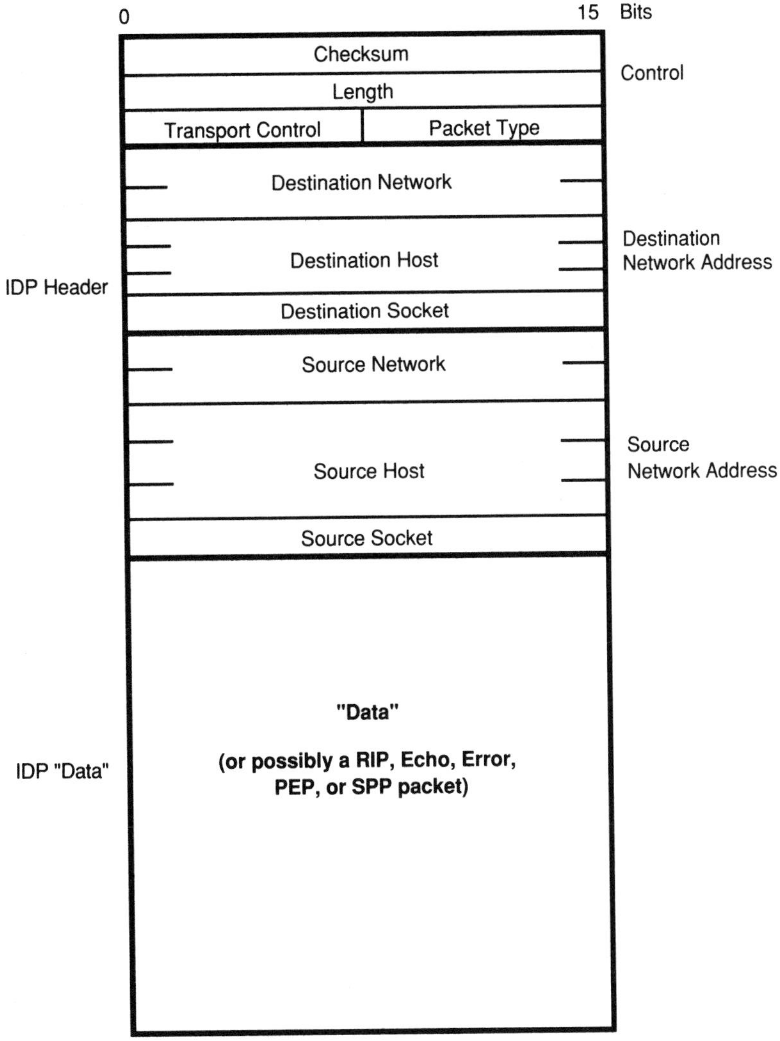

4.4 | 3+ Transport Layer Protocols

Four different Transport Layer Options (corresponding to the four packet types discussed above) are defined for 3+. We'll look at these separately.

4.4.1 | Routing Information Protocol (RIP)

In order to keep the router's routing tables current with network topology information about the internetwork, routers periodically broadcast RIP packets. There are two types of RIP packets, both defined by the Operation field (see Figure 4-6). Operation=1 is a request for routing information, where Operation=2 is a response containing routing information. The Object Network number field (four octets) contains the address of the distant network for which the information is requested. This number field would be set to FFFFFFFFH if the packet pertains to all networks. The Internetwork Delay (hop count) indicates how many router transitions or hops are necessary to reach the Object network. The minimum count is one hop, which indicates that the packet is destined for the local network.

Figure 4-6
3Com 3+ RIP Packet

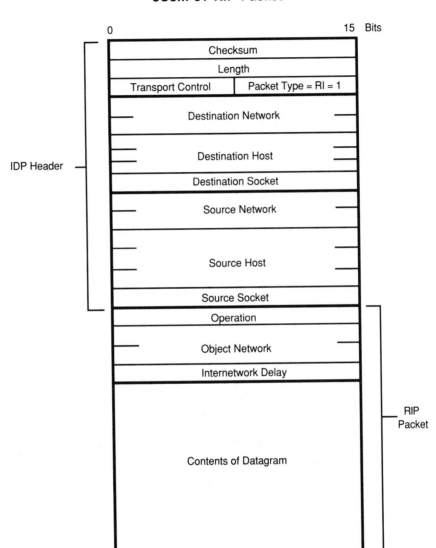

4.4.2 | Echo Protocol (Echo)

The Echo Protocol is used for diagnostic purposes (see Figure 4-7). It verifies the existence and proper operation of a Host, and determines the path to get to that Host. The Echo packet specifies that the data contained within that packet should be returned to the source. As with the RIP packets, an Operation=1 indicates an Echo Request and Operation=2 indicates an Echo Reply.

Figure 4-7
3Com 3+ Echo Packet

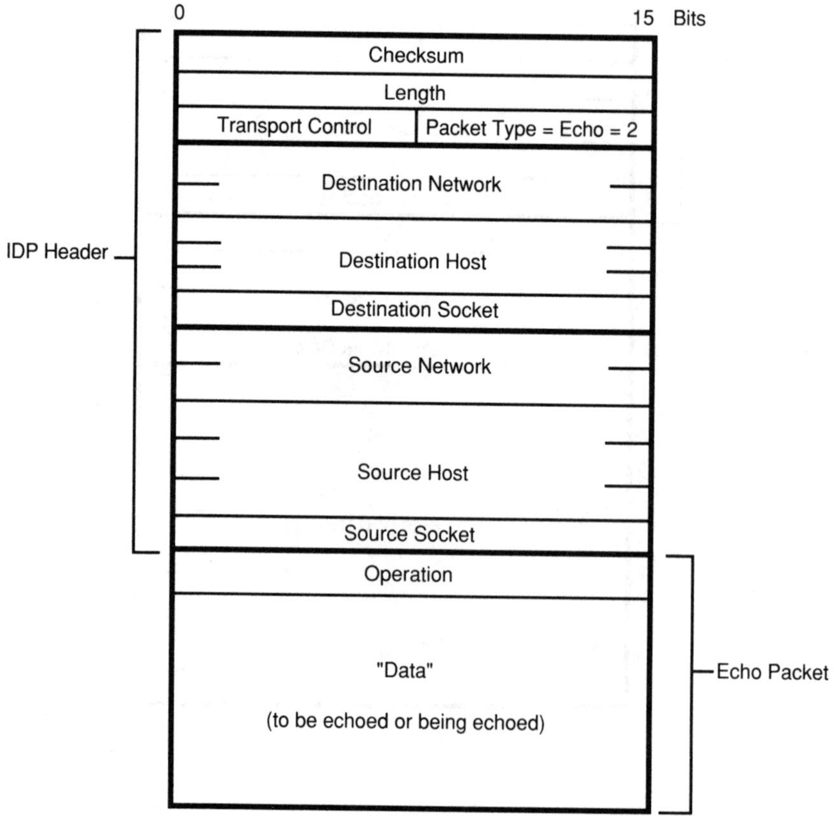

4.4.3 | Packet Exchange Protocol (PEP)

The Packet Exchange Protocol is used for transmissions that require greater reliability than that offered by an IDP packet, but which don't require the sequentiality available with SPP. In other words, PEP provides datagram service with retries.

For example, consider the need to identify a particular resource within the domain of the internetwork. The Identification field contains a transaction identifier that allows the request and response to be associated. The Client Type field (two octets, and similar to the Ethertype at the Data Link layer) identifies how the higher layers should interpret the data field (See Figure 4-8).

Some typical uses for PEP within 3+ include most transactions to name services, such as lookups, updates, etc., and the associated responses to these transactions.

Figure 4-8
3Com 3+ PEP Packet

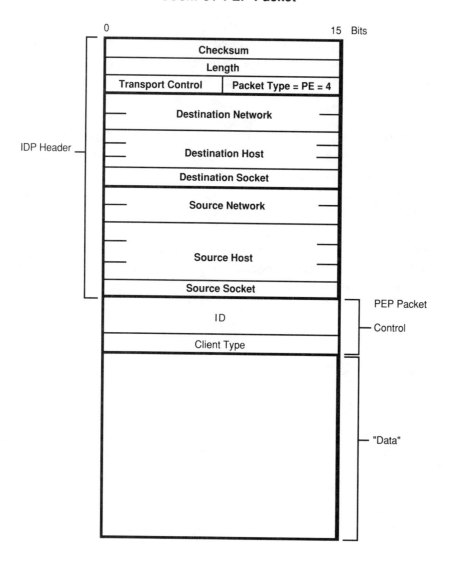

| 4.4.4 | ## Sequenced Packet Protocol (SPP)

The Sequenced Packet Protocol provides the virtual circuit service that the other Transport layer protocols lack and is most frequently used for LAN interaction between workstation and server. The additional information contained in the SPP header provides data integrity by guaranteeing sequence and delivery. It also allows the messages of differing lengths from the higher layers to be divided into multiple IDP packets, each of which can contain up to a full Ethernet frame of information (1514 octets), including the IDP header.

The SPP header immediately follows the IDP header (see Figure 4-9). The Connection Control field (one octet) controls the actions of SPP. The first part of this field is the System Packet bit, which is set when the data field is empty and therefore communicates control information only. Send Acknowledgement requires the receiver to acknowledge previously received packets. Attention indicates that the destination process should be informed immediately that this packet has arrived. End-of-Message terminates this message, and indicates that the next packet begins a subsequent message. The Datastream Type field (one octet) follows the Connection Control field and can be used by higher layer protocols to send control information outside of their normal flow of data.

Figure 4-9
3Com 3+ SPP Packet

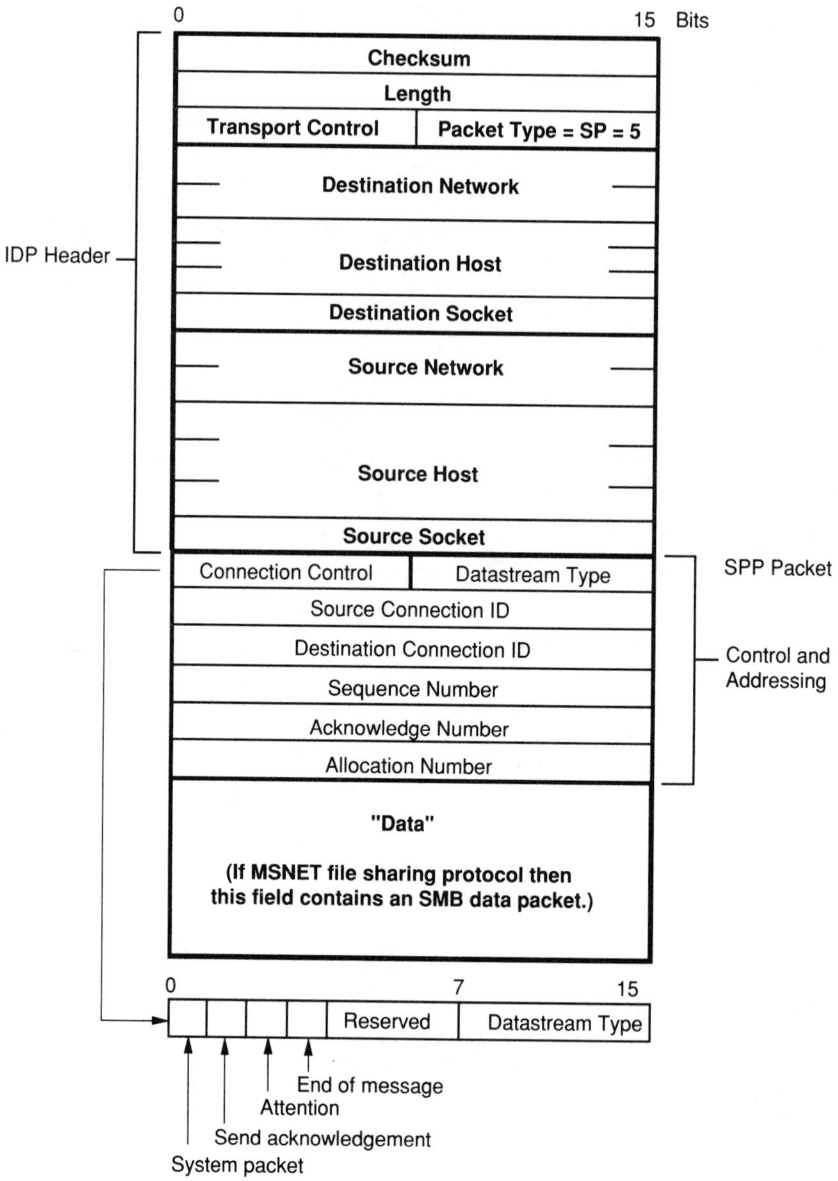

0	15 Bits
Checksum	
Length	
Transport Control	**Packet Type = SP = 5**
Destination Network	
Destination Host	
Destination Socket	
Source Network	
Source Host	
Source Socket	

IDP Header

Connection Control	Datastream Type
Source Connection ID	
Destination Connection ID	
Sequence Number	
Acknowledge Number	
Allocation Number	

SPP Packet

Control and Addressing

"Data"

(If MSNET file sharing protocol then this field contains an SMB data packet.)

0	7	15
		Reserved	Datastream Type

End of message
Attention
Send acknowledgement
System packet

Source and Destination Connection IDs (two octets each) assure that the sockets at each end of the transmission path are used correctly, and that they can be correctly identified should a failure occur and the connection needs to be restarted. The Sequence Number is the transmitting entity's sequence counter (starting with 0) which counts the packets sent over the connection. The Destination Connection ID uses this number to put all the packets back in the proper order without duplication. The Acknowledge Number is a piggy-backed acknowledgement from the receiver to the sender indicating the sequence number of the next packet expected from the distant process. The Allocation Number is used for flow control, indicating the maximum packet sequence number that can be accepted at the far end.

To provide an example of SPP, let's consider the interaction between a token-ring workstation (3Com 187065) and server (3Com 187062) shown in Figure 4-10. Frame 1 is an SMB command to create a file (MCGEE), which is completed in frame 2 (file handle=0002). Frame 4 is an SMB command to write 4096 octets of the file beginning at 0, and includes the first 1394 octets of data. Subsequent SPP packets (Frames 5 and 6) contain the balance of the data (1442 and 1260 octets, respectively). Frame 7 contains the SPP acknowledgement (acknowledge number=67). Frame 8 is the SMB confirmation that 4096 octets were written.

The details of the sequence (Figure 4-11) reveal some interesting points. Hop count=0 is verified by the identical Destination and Source network addresses, plus noting that the DLC address (from Figure 4-10) and XNS (IDP) Host address (from Figure 4-11) are identical. The SPP Sequence Number is 64 in frame 4, 65 in frame 5, and increments until the end of the data transmission (frame 6) while the Acknowledge Number remains at 63. When the file is completely received, Acknowledge then jumps from 63 to 67 (frame 7). Also interesting is the SPP Connection Control field in Frame 6 -- an Acknowledgement is requested, plus the End of Message is indicated. Frame 7 provides the requested acknowledgement, with a System Packet indicated in the Connection Control field.

Figure 4-10
3Com 3+ Protocols transmitted over a token ring network

Sniffer Network Analyzer data from 10-Sep-86 at 15:28:30,
file C:\CAPTURE\SAMPLES\3COM.TRC, Page 1

SUMMARY	Delta T	Destination	Source	Summary
M 1		3Com 187062 3Com 187065	SMB C Create \MCGEE
2	0.143	3Com 187065 3Com 187062	SMB R F=0002 Created
3	0.014	3Com 187062 3Com 187065	XNS SPP A D=0E3B S=01FF NR=63
4	0.027	3Com 187062 3Com 187065	SMB C F=0002 Write 4096 at 0
5	0.010	3Com 187062 3Com 187065	XNS SPP D=0E3B S=01FF NR=63 NS=65
6	0.010	3Com 187062 3Com 187065	XNS SPP D=0E3B S=01FF NR=63 NS=66
7	0.024	3Com 187065 3Com 187062	XNS SPP A D=01FF S=0E3B NR=67
8	0.050	3Com 187065 3Com 187062	SMB R OK
9	0.012	3Com 187062 3Com 187065	XNS SPP A D=0E3B S=01FF NR=64
10	0.016	3Com 187062 3Com 187065	SMB C F=0002 Write 579 at 4096
11	0.029	3Com 187065 3Com 187062	SMB R OK
12	0.014	3Com 187062 3Com 187065	XNS SPP A D=0E3B S=01FF NR=65
13	0.019	3Com 187062 3Com 187065	SMB C F=0002 Close
14	0.169	3Com 187062 3Com 187065	SMB C F=0002 Close
15	0.164	3Com 187062 3Com 187065	SMB C F=0002 Close
16	0.149	3Com 187065 3Com 187062	SMB R Closed
17	0.015	3Com 187062 3Com 187065	XNS SPP A D=0E3B S=01FF NR=66

Figure 4-11
3Com 3+ Protocol details

- - - - - - - - - - - - - - - - Frame 4 - - - - - - - - - - - - - - - - -

```
SMB:   ----- SMB Write Byte Range Command -----
SMB:
SMB:   Function = 0B (Write Byte Range)
SMB:   Tree id     (TID) = 6000
SMB:   Process id  (PID) = 167A
SMB:   File handle = 0002
SMB:   Number of bytes to write = 4096
SMB:   Offset in file = 0
SMB:   Total remaining write count = 4675
SMB:   [1394 byte(s) of write data]
SMB:   [2702 byte(s) are missing; may be in subsequent frames]
```

Figure 4-11 (continued)

```
- - - - - - - - - - - - - - - - Frame 5 - - - - - - - - - - - - - - - - -



XNS:    ----- XNS Header -----
XNS:
XNS:    Checksum = FFFF
XNS:    Length = 1484
XNS:    Transport control = 00
XNS:          0000 .... = Reserved
XNS:          .... 0000 = Hop count
XNS:    Packet type = 5 (SPP)
XNS:
XNS:    Dest   net = 00041C5E, host = 02608C187062, socket = 3004 (0BBC)
XNS:    Source net = 00041C5E, host = 02608C187065, socket = 3004 (0BBC)
XNS:
XNS:    ----- Sequence Packet Protocol (SPP) -----
XNS:
XNS:    Connection control = 00
XNS:            0... .... = Non-system packet
XNS:            .0.. .... = No acknowledgement requested
XNS:            ..0. .... = No attention
XNS:            ...0 .... = Not end of message
XNS:            .... 0000 = Reserved
XNS:
XNS:    Datastream type = 00
XNS:
XNS:    Source connection ID = 01FF
XNS:    Dest   connection ID = 0E3B
XNS:    Sequence    number = 65
XNS:    Acknowledge number = 63
XNS:    Allocation  number = 65
XNS:
XNS:    [1442 bytes of SPP data]


- - - - - - - - - - - - - - - - Frame 6 - - - - - - - - - - - - - - - - -



XNS:    ----- XNS Header -----
XNS:
XNS:    Checksum = FFFF
XNS:    Length = 1302
XNS:    Transport control = 00
XNS:          0000 .... = Reserved
XNS:          .... 0000 = Hop count
XNS:    Packet type = 5 (SPP)
XNS:
XNS:    Dest   net = 00041C5E, host = 02608C187062, socket = 3004 (0BBC)
```

149

Figure 4-11 (continued)

```
XNS:  Source net = 00041C5E, host = 02608C187065, socket = 3004 (0BBC)
XNS:
XNS:  ----- Sequence Packet Protocol (SPP) -----
XNS:
XNS:  Connection control = 50
XNS:          0... .... = Non-system packet
XNS:          .1.. .... = Acknowledgement requested
XNS:          ..0. .... = No attention
XNS:          ...1 .... = End of message
XNS:          .... 0000 = Reserved
XNS:
XNS:  Datastream type = 00
XNS:
XNS:  Source connection ID = 01FF
XNS:  Dest   connection ID = 0E3B
XNS:  Sequence   number = 66
XNS:  Acknowledge number = 63
XNS:  Allocation  number = 65
XNS:
XNS:  [1260 bytes of SPP data]


- - - - - - - - - - - - - - - - - Frame 7 - - - - - - - - - - - - - - - - - -


XNS:  ----- XNS Header -----
XNS:
XNS:  Checksum = FFFF
XNS:  Length = 42
XNS:  Transport control = 00
XNS:          0000 .... = Reserved
XNS:          .... 0000 = Hop count
XNS:  Packet type = 5 (SPP)
XNS:
XNS:  Dest   net = 00041C5E, host = 02608C187065, socket = 3004 (0BBC)
XNS:  Source net = 00041C5E, host = 02608C187062, socket = 3004 (0BBC)
XNS:
XNS:  ----- Sequence Packet Protocol (SPP) -----
XNS:
XNS:  Connection control = 80
XNS:          1... .... = System packet
XNS:          .0.. .... = No acknowledgement requested
XNS:          ..0. .... = No attention
XNS:          ...0 .... = Not end of message
XNS:          .... 0000 = Reserved
XNS:
XNS:  Datastream type = 00
XNS:
```

150

Figure 4-11 (continued)

```
XNS:   Source connection ID = OE3B
XNS:   Dest   connection ID = 01FF
XNS:   Sequence     number = 63
XNS:   Acknowledge number = 67
XNS:   Allocation  number = 68



- - - - - - - - - - - - - - - - Frame 8 - - - - - - - - - - - - - - - -



SMB:   ----- SMB Write Byte Range Response -----
SMB:
SMB:   Function = 0B (Write Byte Range)
SMB:   Tree id     (TID) = 6000
SMB:   Process id  (PID) = 167A
SMB:   Return code = 0,0 (OK)
SMB:   Number of bytes written = 4096
```

4.5 | 3+ Higher Layer Protocols

The third part of the 3+ "blend" (Ethernet, XNS, and DOS/Redirector) is evident in the higher layer protocols used with 3+. At the Session layer, an XNS-based implementation of NetBIOS is available for those applications that require NetBIOS (see reference [4-8]).

Both 3+ and 3+Open implement the SMB Protocol that was developed by Microsoft (see reference [4-9]). SMB is an Application layer protocol that allows a workstation to access a remote server in order to manipulate files and share printer access. The SMB commands are carried within a NBP data transmission.

Of particular interest to network analysts are the SMB error codes listed in Appendix A of reference [4-3]. There are six classes of SMB error messages listed, and class 04 (Table A-5) are unique to the 3Com extended server functions under 3+. The other error messages (class 00,01,02,03, and FF) are defined by the SMB protocol.

Both NetBIOS and SMB protocols will also be discussed in detail in Chapter 5 (interested readers should see sections 5.4 and 5.5). Applications supported by the 3+ utilities include Name service, File and Print service, and electronic mail.

4.6 | 3+Open Architecture

As we discussed in the beginning of this chapter, there are significant differences in both the architecture and the underlying protocols of the XNS-based 3+ and the NetBIOS-based 3+Open operating systems. You would expect this since 3+ runs under DOS and 3+Open runs under OS/2 LAN Manager. In order to maintain compatibility with the XNS-based 3+, the designers of 3+Open developed Demand Protocol Architecture, which allows a user at a DOS workstation to access multiple protocol stacks (see Figure 4-12). Let's begin at the lower layers, comparing Demand Protocol Architecture with the OSI model.

Figure 4-12
Comparing 3Com 3+Open LAN Manager Demand Protocol Architecture with OSI

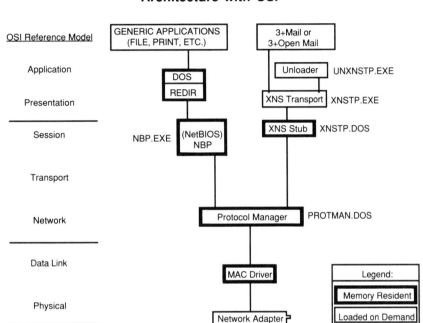

4.6.1   Network Driver Interface Specification

The link between the Network Operating System (NOS) and the Network Interface Card (NIC) or network adapter is a software driver. This driver downloads the information from the higher layers and fills the various fields (e.g. Address, Control, Data, etc.) of the Data Link layer frame. As a result of the close tie between the NOS and driver, a change of NOS (or protocols supported in the NOS) also necessitates a change in the NIC driver.

In an attempt to alleviate this dependency, 3+Com and Microsoft Corp. developed the Network Driver Interface Specification (NDIS), which was released in May 1988 as part of OS/2 LAN Manager. Since 3+Open is based upon OS/2 LAN Manager, NDIS is also part of 3+Open.

NDIS is divided into two major components: a MAC driver that controls access to the NIC; and a protocol driver that links to the higher layers. More specifically, the protocol driver links to the MAC driver (which in 3+Open is talking to the Ethernet or token ring hardware) and also to the Session layer (which for 3+Open is either NBP or XNS). Individual protocol stacks, such as NBP, XNS, TCP/IP, or DLC/NetBEUI , can thus be implemented independently. We'll discuss these in section 4.6.3. With NDIS, users are assured that the interfaces to any protocol stack will be consistent.

4.6.2 | The Protocol Manager

The Protocol Manager controls the binding between the MAC driver and the protocol driver. Specific information is stored in a file named PROTOCOL.INI, including the name of the protocol driver, the type of NIC, and other parameters. Up to four protocol drivers are allowed to share, or multiplex, a single NIC. A filter, known as Vector, manages this multiplexing process.

With 3+Open's Demand Protocol Architecture (DPA), the different protocols can thus be swapped dynamically, without having to reboot the workstation. For example, if a user needs to implement an XNS function, such as 3+Mail, a batch file runs the XNS Transport program (XNSTP.EXE) which starts the XNS protocol. The Protocol Manager driver (PROTMAN.DOS) determines which incoming frame of information is for the XNS stack, and which is for another stack, such as NBP. After the XNS application is finished, another program, UNXNSTP.EXE, checks to the XNS Stub (XNSTP.DOC) to determine if any other XNS protocols are running. If there are no other XNS protocols running, it unloads the XNS protocols. Changing to another protocol stack would be as easy as loading its protocol driver as above. References [4-10] and [4-11] provide further details on the DPA functions and parameters.

4.6.3   3+Open Supported Protocols

Under the Demand Protocol Architecture, a variety of protocol stacks are supported:

- XNS can be used as the primary protocol under NetBIOS (without using NBP), or as a secondary protocol stack for applications such as 3+Open/Mail. XNS provides both internetworking and support for mixed 3+ and 3+Open networks.

- NBP (NetBIOS Protocol) is an optimized execution of NetBIOS that has no underlying protocols. As a result, no internetworking capabilities, such as source routing, exist in NBP. (We'll study NBP in detail in Section 4.7).

- TCP/IP is used for either DOS or OS/2 workstations that need access to these popular internetworking protocols.

- DLC/NetBEUI provides IBM mainframe connectivity support, utilizing Microsoft's NetBIOS Extended User Interface (NetBEUI).

- AppleTalk is provided for Macintosh connectivity. AppleTalk Phase 1 (LocalTalk and EtherTalk) is currently available; Phase 2 support (TokenTalk) is planned for late 1990. (Chapter 7 is devoted to AppleTalk).

- Drivers are also being developed for OSI and IPX/SPX, which is used for connecting to Novell's NetWare.

To summarize the 3+Open Architecture, its true benefits are in its interoperability and flexibility. 3+Open provides both with elegance. We'll discuss 3+Open's premier protocol, NBP, in the next two sections.

| 4.7 | ## NetBIOS Protocol

The 3Com NetBIOS Protocol is an implementation of NetBIOS, and supports the 5CH interface. Fourteen different NBP packets have been defined, and each is identified by the Ethertype field in either the Ethernet (see Figure 4-3) or IEEE 802.5 (see Figure 4-4) frames. The NBP Ethertypes are shown below:

Ethertype	NBP Packet
3C00	Virtual Circuit Data
3C01	System
3C02	Connect Request
3C03	Connect Response
3C04	Connect Complete
3C05	Close Request
3C06	Close Response
3C07	Datagram Data
3C08	Broadcast Datagram Data
3C09	Claim Name
3C0A	Delete Name
3C0B	Remote Adapter Status Request
3C0C	Remote Adapter Status Response
3C0D	Reset

The above packets break into two categories: Virtual Circuits and Datagrams. the Virtual Circuit Data packet is used to provide reliable data transmission between network workstations. System packets are used to control those packets. All other NBP packets are datagrams, and are used when data reliability is not an overriding issue. The Connect datagrams are used to establish a virtual circuit, and the Close datagrams are used to break the connection. Claim Name and Delete Name packets are used to resolve NetBIOS-name-to-MAC-address mappings. The Remote Adapter datagrams are used to query other workstations. The Reset datagram indicates that a client process has submitted to the NetBIOS reset function, or that NBP has been booted.

The NBP Virtual Circuit packet header and data are contained within the Data Link layer frame (for either Ethernet or IEEE 802.5) and do not use the IDP header or other XNS-related protocols. For Virtual Circuits (see Figure 4-13), the NBP header includes both Destination and Source Socket numbers (which are one octet each and established by NetBIOS), followed by Destination and Source Connection IDs (two octets each), which are assigned to assure the uniqueness of this connection.

Figure 4-13
3Com NBP Virtual Circuit Packets

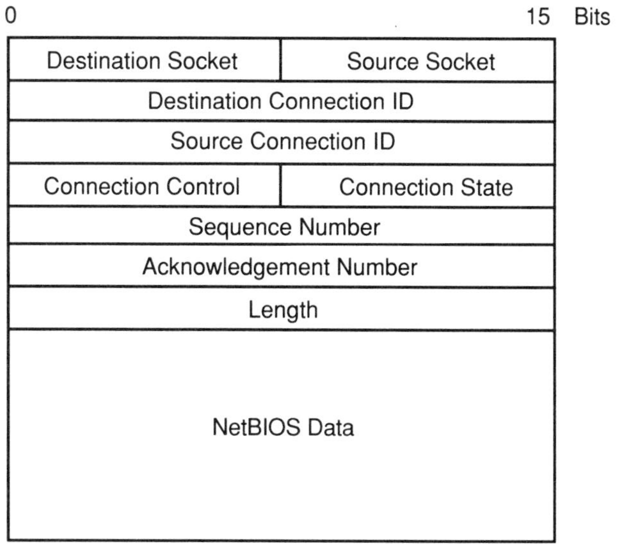

0	15 Bits
Destination Socket	Source Socket
Destination Connection ID	
Source Connection ID	
Connection Control	Connection State
Sequence Number	
Acknowledgement Number	
Length	
NetBIOS Data	

The Connection Control field (one octet) is next, defining four masks: End of Message, Resend, Send ACK, and Retransmission. The Connection State (one octet) indicates status of both transmitter and receiver. The Sequence and Acknowledgement fields (two octets each) indicate the transmit and receive (next expected) sequence numbers. Finally, the Length field (two octets) specifies the amount of user data (in octets) that will follow and is set to 000H if no more data is required. This number is limited by the Data Link layer frame in use, e.g., Ethernet frames with 1500 maximum data octets can have 1486 octets of user data. System packets are similar to the Virtual Circuit packets, except that they contain no user data and the packet Length field is set to 0000H.

Figure 4-14
3Com NBP Datagram Packet

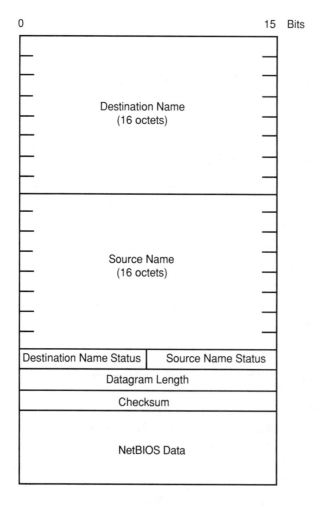

The NBP Datagram header (see Figure 4-14) begins with the Destination and Source NetBIOS names (16 octets each), and the Destination and Status indicators (one octet each) which provide status information for those names. The Datagram Length field (two octets) provides the number of octets of data that follows the Checksum field (also two octets). The Checksum is calculated from the bits starting with the Destination address in the MAC frame header and ending with the Datagram length field. We'll look at examples of NBP packets in section 4.8. Reference [4-12] discusses NBP in detail.

4.8 Protocol Analysis with 3+Open

To conclude our analysis of the 3+Open protocols, let's study two applications: a workstation login (Figure 4-15) and a print job (Figure 4-17).

The login of Vern's workstation to the server begins with the server sending NBP AckReq frames until it sees some activity (see Figure 4-15). The activity begins in frame 18, and the SMB protocol frames that follow (20 - 43) negotiate the protocol, connect Vern's workstation to various subdirectories on the server, and then send a connect confirmation (frame 45). Details of several SMB commands and responses are shown in Figure 4-16.

Figure 4-15
3Com 3+Open Login Analysis Summary

SUMMARY		Delta T	Destination	Source	Summary		
M	1		Vern	Server	NBP AckReq	D=AF27	S=7906
	2	1.5001	Vern	Server	NBP AckReq	D=AF27	S=7906
	3	1.5001	Vern	Server	NBP AckReq	D=AF27	S=7906
	4	1.5001	Vern	Server	NBP AckReq	D=AF27	S=7906
	5	1.5001	Vern	Server	NBP AckReq	D=AF27	S=7906
	6	1.5001	Vern	Server	NBP AckReq	D=AF27	S=7906
	7	1.5001	Vern	Server	NBP AckReq	D=AF27	S=7906
	8	1.5001	Vern	Server	NBP AckReq	D=AF27	S=7906
	9	1.5001	Vern	Server	NBP AckReq	D=AF27	S=7906
	10	1.5001	Vern	Server	NBP AckReq	D=AF27	S=7906
	11	1.5020	Vern	Server	NBP AckReq	D=AF27	S=7906
	12	1.4982	Vern	Server	NBP AckReq	D=AF27	S=7906
	13	1.5030	Vern	Server	NBP AckReq	D=AF27	S=7906

159

Figure 4-15 (continued)

```
14   1.4973   Vern     Server    NBP AckReq     D=AF27 S=7906
15   1.5001   Vern     Server    NBP AckReq     D=AF27 S=7906
16   1.5002   Vern     Server    NBP AckReq     D=AF27 S=7906
17   1.5034   Vern     Server    NBP AckReq     D=AF27 S=7906
18  33.2725   Vern     Server    NBP ConnRsp    D=VERN. S=SERVER
19   0.0013   Server   Vern      NBP ConnCmplt  D=SERVER S=VERN.
20   0.0012   Server   Vern      SMB C PC NETWORK PROGRAM 1.0
21   0.0144   Vern     Server    SMB R Negotiated Protocol 2
22   0.0024   Server   Vern      SMB C Setup account VERN
23   0.0438   Vern     Server    SMB R Setup
24   0.1329   Vern     Server    NBP AckReq     D=AF01 S=C4EE
25   0.0007   Server   Vern      NBP Ack        D=C4EE S=AF01
26   1.0178   Server   Vern      SMB C Connect A:\\SERVER\D$
27   0.0026   Vern     Server    SMB R A: Connected
28   0.1039   Vern     Server    NBP AckReq     D=AF01 S=C4EE
29   0.0007   Server   Vern      NBP Ack        D=C4EE S=AF01
30   0.9775   Server   Vern      SMB C Connect A:\\SERVER\C$
31   0.0025   Vern     Server    SMB R A: Connected
32   0.1464   Vern     Server    NBP AckReq     D=AF01 S=C4EE
33   0.0007   Server   Vern      NBP Ack        D=C4EE S=AF01
34   0.9365   Server   Vern      SMB C Connect
35   0.0025   Vern     Server    SMB R A: Connected
36   0.0893   Vern     Server    NBP AckReq     D=AF01 S=C4EE
37   0.0007   Server   Vern      NBP Ack        D=C4EE S=AF01
38   0.9921   Server   Vern      SMB C Connect A:\\SERVER\LOTUS
39   0.0024   Vern     Server    SMB R A: Connected
40   0.1332   Vern     Server    NBP AckReq     D=AF01 S=C4EE
41   0.0005   Server   Vern      NBP Ack        D=C4EE S=AF01
42   0.9648   Server   Vern      SMB C Connect A:\\SERVER\
43   0.0046   Vern     Server    SMB R A: Connected
44   0.1514   Vern     Server    NBP AckReq     D=AF01 S=C4EE
45   0.0007   Server   Vern      NBP Ack        D=C4EE S=AF01
```

Figure 4-16
3Com 3+Open Login Analysis Details

```
- - - - - - - - - - - - - - - - Frame 20 - - - - - - - - - - - - - - - - -

SMB:   ----- SMB Negotiate Protocol Command -----
SMB:
SMB:   Function = 72 (Negotiate Protocol)
SMB:   Tree id      (TID) = 0000
SMB:   Process id   (PID) = 0000
SMB:   Dialect = "PC NETWORK PROGRAM 1.0"
```

Figure 4-16 (continued)

```
SMB:  Dialect = "MICROSOFT NETWORKS 1.03"
SMB:  Dialect = "MICROSOFT NETWORKS 3.0"
SMB:

- - - - - - - - - - - - - - - - Frame 21 - - - - - - - - - - - - - - - - -

SMB:  ----- SMB Negotiate Protocol Response -----
SMB:
SMB:  Function = 72 (Negotiate Protocol)
SMB:  Tree id     (TID) = 0000
SMB:  Process id  (PID) = 0000
SMB:  Return code = 0,0 (OK)
SMB:  Flags = X1
SMB:  .... 0... = Pathnames are case sensitive
SMB:  .... ...1 = Supports subdialect (Lock&Read, Write&Unlock)
SMB:  Index of supported dialect = 2
SMB:  Security mode = 0003
SMB:   .... ....  .... ..1. = Encrypt passwords
SMB:   .... ....  .... ...1 = User level security
SMB:  Maximum size of server transmit-buffer = 4356 bytes
SMB:  Maximum number of multiplexed pending requests = 50
SMB:  Maximum number of virtual circuits per session = 1
SMB:  Block mode support = 0003
SMB:   .... ....  .... ..1. = Write Block Raw supported
SMB:   .... ....  .... ...1 = Read Block Raw supported
SMB:  Session Key = 000072AE
SMB:  Current date = 16-Feb-90 08:32:28
SMB:  Current time zone: FFFF
SMB:  Encryption key = "[Invalid data type]"
SMB:

- - - - - - - - - - - - - - - - Frame 22 - - - - - - - - - - - - - - - - -

SMB:  ----- SMB Session Setup & more Command -----
SMB:
SMB:  Function = 73 (Session Setup & more)
SMB:  Tree id     (TID) = 0000
SMB:  Process id  (PID) = 40D8
SMB:  Flags = 0X
SMB:  ...0 .... = Pathnames are not in canonicalized format
SMB:  Maximum size of consumer buffer = 1024 bytes
SMB:  Maximum number of multiplexed pending requests = 0
SMB:  Type = 0: First (only) virtual circuit
SMB:  Session key = 00000000
SMB:  Password = "VERN"
SMB:  Account name = "VERN"
SMB:
```

Figure 4-16 (continued)

```
SMB:  ----- SMB Tree Connect & more Command -----
SMB:
SMB:  Function = 75 (Tree Connect & more)
SMB:  Connect flags = 0000
SMB:   .... ....  .... ...0 = Do not disconnect TID
SMB:  Empty password
SMB:  Server = "\\SERVER\DOSAPPS"
SMB:  Service (device) = "A:"
SMB:
SMB:  ----- End of SMB chain -----
SMB:
```

- - - - - - - - - - - - - - - - Frame 23 - - - - - - - - - - - - - - - - - -

```
SMB:  ----- SMB Session Setup & more Response -----
SMB:
SMB:  Function = 73 (Session Setup & more)
SMB:  Tree id    (TID) = 100E
SMB:  Process id  (PID) = 40D8
SMB:  Request mode = 0000
SMB:   .... ....  .... ...0 = Not logged in as guest
SMB:
SMB:  ----- SMB Tree Connect & more Response -----
SMB:
SMB:  Function = 75 (Tree Connect & more)
SMB:  Return code = 0,0 (OK)
SMB:  Service (device) = "A:"
SMB:
SMB:  ----- End of SMB chain -----
SMB:
```

- - - - - - - - - - - - - - - - Frame 42 - - - - - - - - - - - - - - - - - -

```
SMB:  ----- SMB Tree Connect & more Command -----
SMB:
SMB:  Function = 75 (Tree Connect & more)
SMB:  Tree id    (TID) = 0000
SMB:  Process id  (PID) = 40D8
SMB:  Connect flags = 0000
SMB:   .... ....  .... ...0 = Do not disconnect TID
SMB:  Empty password
SMB:  Server = "\\SERVER\PARADOX3"
SMB:  Service (device) = "A:"
SMB:
SMB:  ----- End of SMB chain -----
SMB:
```

Figure 4-16 (continued)

```
- - - - - - - - - - - - - - - - - Frame 43 - - - - - - - - - - - - - - - - - - - -

SMB:   ----- SMB Tree Connect & more Response -----
SMB:
SMB:   Function = 75 (Tree Connect & more)
SMB:   Tree id     (TID) = 1009
SMB:   Process id  (PID) = 40D8
SMB:   Return code = 0,0 (OK)
SMB:   Service (device) = "A:"
SMB:
SMB:   ----- End of SMB chain -----
SMB:
```

The print job (Figure 4-17) begins with SMB packets that establish the connection to the laser printer (frames 1 - 8) and then begin to spool the file (beginning in frame 13). A three-way handshake built into NBP is shown clearly in frames 49 - 51 -- Connect Request, Connect Response, and Connect Complete. Details of those three NPB packets are shown in Figure 4-18. Note that these are NBP datagrams, and that within the Control field the Destination Connection ID changes. Frame 49 has B6F3H, (Server to Vern), Frame 50 has ADA2H (Vern to Server), concluding with B6F3H in Frame 51 (Server to Vern). The status of each flag within the Connection Control and Connection Status fields are also delineated. (For further details on the Sniffer protocol analysis, see reference [4-13].)

Figure 4-17
3Com 3+Open Printing Analysis Summary

SUMMARY		Delta T	Destination	Source	Summary
M	1		Server	Vern	SMB C Connect LPT1:\\SERVER
	2	0.0041	Vern	Server	SMB R LPT1: Connected
	3	0.0267	Server	Vern	SMB C Connect IPC\\SERVER\IPC$
	4	0.0047	Vern	Server	SMB R IPC Connected
	5	0.0037	Server	Vern	SMB C Transaction \PIPE\LANMAN
	6	0.0078	Vern	Server	SMB R Transaction
	7	0.0043	Server	Vern	SMB C T=4810 Disconnect
	8	0.0036	Vern	Server	SMB R OK
	9	0.0697	Vern	Server	NBP AckReq D=AF01 S=C4EE
	10	0.0007	Server	Vern	NBP Ack D=C4EE S=AF01
	11	29.8151	Vern	Server	NBP AckReq D=AF01 S=C4EE

Figure 4-17 (continued)

```
12   0.0007   Server   Vern     NBP  Ack         D=C4EE S=AF01
13   7.9978   Server   Vern     SMB  C Create Spool file VERN
14   0.1192   Server   Vern     NBP  AckReq      D=C4EE S=AF01
15   0.0005   Vern     Server   NBP  Ack         D=AF01 S=C4EE
16   0.2220   Vern     Server   SMB  R Created
17   0.0979   Vern     Server   NBP  AckReq      D=AF01 S=C4EE
18   0.0007   Server   Vern     NBP  Ack         D=C4EE S=AF01
19   0.0549   Server   Vern     SMB  C Spool Byte Range
20   0.0036   Vern     Server   SMB  R Spooled
21   0.1099   Server   Vern     SMB  C Spool Byte Range
22   0.0064   Vern     Server   SMB  R Spooled
23   0.1055   Vern     Server   NBP  AckReq      D=AF01 S=C4EE
24   0.0009   Server   Vern     NBP  Ack         D=C4EE S=AF01
25   0.0033   Server   Vern     SMB  C Spool Byte Range
26   0.0085   Vern     Server   SMB  R Spooled
27   0.0809   Vern     Server   NBP  AckReq      D=AF01 S=C4EE
28   0.0007   Server   Vern     NBP  Ack         D=C4EE S=AF01
29   0.0291   Server   Vern     SMB  C Spool Byte Range
30   0.0076   Vern     Server   SMB  R Spooled
31   0.1161   Server   Vern     SMB  C Spool Byte Range
32   0.0039   Vern     Server   SMB  R Spooled
33   0.1060   Server   Vern     SMB  C Spool Byte Range
34   0.0026   Vern     Server   SMB  R Spooled
35   0.1086   Vern     Server   NBP  AckReq      D=AF01 S=C4EE
36   0.0007   Server   Vern     NBP  Ack         D=C4EE S=AF01
37   0.0014   Server   Vern     SMB  C Spool Byte Range
38   0.0026   Vern     Server   SMB  R Spooled
39   0.0888   Vern     Server   NBP  AckReq      D=AF01 S=C4EE
40   0.0007   Server   Vern     NBP  Ack         D=C4EE S=AF01
41   0.0413   Server   Vern     SMB  C Spool Byte Range
42   0.0026   Vern     Server   SMB  R Spooled
43   0.0352   Server   Vern     SMB  C Spool Byte Range
44   0.0031   Vern     Server   SMB  R Spooled
45   0.0017   Server   Vern     SMB  C Close Spool File
46   0.0391   Vern     Server   SMB  R Closed
47   0.0667   Vern     Server   NBP  AckReq      D=AF01 S=C4EE
48   0.0005   Server   Vern     NBP  Ack         D=C4EE S=AF01
49   5.2200   Vern     Server   NBP  ConnReq     D=VERN. S=SERV
50   0.0014   Server   Vern     NBP  ConnRsp     D=SERVER. S=VERN
51   0.0009   Vern     Server   NBP  ConnCmplt   D=VERN. S=SERV
52   0.0024   Vern     Server   SMB  C Start Multi-Block Mess
53   0.0018   Server   Vern     SMB  C Start Multi-Block Mess
54   0.0014   Vern     Server   NBP  Ack         D=ADA2 S=B6F3
55   0.0037   Vern     Server   SMB  C Multi-Block Message Text
56   0.0027   Server   Vern     SMB  R Multi-Block Message Text
57   0.1060   Vern     Server   NBP  AckReq      D=ADA2 S=B6F3
58   0.0007   Server   Vern     NBP  Ack         D=B6F3 S=ADA2
59   0.0012   Server   Vern     NBP  AckReq      D=B6F3 S=ADA2
```

Figure 4-17 (continued)

```
60   0.0006   Vern     Server    NBP Ack        D=ADA2 S=B6F3
61   0.0082   Vern     Server    NBP Resend     D=ADA2 S=B6F3
62   0.0033   Vern     Server    SMB C Multi-Block Message Text
63   0.0007   Server   Vern      NBP Ack        D=B6F3 S=ADA2
64   0.0018   Server   Vern      SMB R Multi-Block Message Text
65   0.0014   Vern     Server    NBP Ack        D=ADA2 S=B6F3
66   0.0021   Vern     Server    SMB C End Multi-Block Message
67   0.0015   Server   Vern      SMB R End Multi-Block Message
68   0.0014   Server   Vern      NBP AckReq     D=B6F3 S=ADA2
69   0.0010   Vern     Server    NBP Ack        D=ADA2 S=B6F3
70   0.0160   Vern     Server    NBP CloseReq   D=VERN. S=SERV
71   0.0013   Server   Vern      NBP CloseRsp   D=SERVER. S=VERN
72   0.0009   Vern     Server    NBP CloseRsp   D=VERN. S=SERV
73   0.0009   Server   Vern      NBP Error      D=B6F3 S=ADA2 N
```

Figure 4-18
3Com 3+Open Printing Analysis Details

```
Frame 49 - - - - - - - - - - - - - - - - -

NBP:   ----- NBP Datagram Header -----
NBP:
NBP:   Dest    name  = 'VERN             .'
NBP:   Source name  = 'SERVER           .'
NBP:   Dest    state = 04 (Registered Unique Name)
NBP:   Source state = 04 (Registered Unique Name)
NBP:   Length = 24
NBP:   Checksum = 9522
NBP:
NBP:   ----- NBP Control Data -----
NBP:
NBP:   Dest    socket = 13
NBP:   Source socket = 00
NBP:   Dest    connection ID = B6F3
NBP:   Source connection ID = 0000
NBP:
NBP:   Connection control = 00
NBP:           ..0. .... = Non-system packet
NBP:           ...0 .... = Not a retransmission
NBP:           .... 0... = No error detected
NBP:           .... .0.. = No acknowledgement requested
NBP:           .... ..0. = No retransmit requested
NBP:           .... ...0 = Not end of message
NBP:
```

Figure 4-18 (continued)

```
NBP:   Connection state (idle) = 00
NBP:                   .0.. .... = No packets dropped
NBP:                   ..0. .... = No hangup in progress
NBP:                   ...0 .... = No packets on queue
NBP:                   .... 0... = No timeout since last clear
NBP:                   .... .0.. = Send packets
NBP:                   .... ..0. = Transmit window open
NBP:                   .... ...0 = Connection not distressed
NBP:
NBP:   Sequence    number = 0000
NBP:   Acknowledge number = A93B
NBP:   Packet length     = 1486
NBP:
NBP:   ----- NBP Connection Parameters -----
NBP:
NBP:   Maximum send and receive packet size = 1514 bytes
NBP:   Memory available for receive packets = 6656 bytes
NBP:   Smallest allocatable memory block    = 256 bytes
NBP:

- - - - - - - - - - - - - - - Frame 50 - - - - - - - - - - - - - - -

NBP:   ----- NBP Datagram Header -----
NBP:
NBP:   Dest   name  = 'SERVER         .'
NBP:   Source name  = 'VERN           .'
NBP:   Dest   state = 04 (Registered Unique Name)
NBP:   Source state = 04 (Registered Unique Name)
NBP:   Length = 24
NBP:   Checksum = 9422
NBP:
NBP:   ----- NBP Control Data -----
NBP:
NBP:   Dest   socket = 01
NBP:   Source socket = 13
NBP:   Dest   connection ID = ADA2
NBP:   Source connection ID = B6F3
NBP:
NBP:   Connection control = 00
NBP:              ..0. .... = Non-system packet
NBP:              ...0 .... = Not a retransmission
NBP:              .... 0... = No error detected
NBP:              .... .0.. = No acknowledgement requested
NBP:              .... ..0. = No retransmit requested
NBP:              .... ...0 = Not end of message
NBP:
```

Figure 4-18 (continued)

```
NBP:  Connection state (idle) = 00
NBP:                 .0.. .... = No packets dropped
NBP:                 ..0. .... = No hangup in progress
NBP:                 ...0 .... = No packets on queue
NBP:                 .... 0... = No timeout since last clear
NBP:                 .... .0.. = Send packets
NBP:                 .... ..0. = Transmit window open
NBP:                 .... ...0 = Connection not distressed
NBP:
NBP:  Sequence    number = A93B
NBP:  Acknowledge number = 00DD
NBP:  Packet length      = 1486
NBP:
NBP:  ----- NBP Connection Parameters -----
NBP:
NBP:  Maximum send and receive packet size = 1514 bytes
NBP:  Memory available for receive packets = 5120 bytes
NBP:  Smallest allocatable memory block    = 256 bytes
NBP:


- - - - - - - - - - - - - - - Frame 51 - - - - - - - - - - - - - - - - -

NBP:  ----- NBP Datagram Header -----
NBP:
NBP:  Dest   name  = 'VERN           .'
NBP:  Source name  = 'SERVER         .'
NBP:  Dest   state = 04 (Registered Unique Name)
NBP:  Source state = 04 (Registered Unique Name)
NBP:  Length = 24
NBP:  Checksum = 9322
NBP:
NBP:  ----- NBP Control Data -----
NBP:
NBP:  Dest   socket = 13
NBP:  Source socket = 01
NBP:  Dest   connection ID = B6F3
NBP:  Source connection ID = ADA2
NBP:
NBP:  Connection control = 00
NBP:            ..0. .... = Non-system packet
NBP:            ...0 .... = Not a retransmission
NBP:            .... 0... = No error detected
NBP:            .... .0.. = No acknowledgement requested
NBP:            .... ..0. = No retransmit requested
NBP:            .... ...0 = Not end of message
NBP:
```

Figure 4-18 (continued)

```
NBP:  Connection state (idle) = 00
NBP:                    .0.. .... = No packets dropped
NBP:                    ..0. .... = No hangup in progress
NBP:                    ...0 .... = No packets on queue
NBP:                    .... 0... = No timeout since last clear
NBP:                    .... .0.. = Send packets
NBP:                    .... ..0. = Transmit window open
NBP:                    .... ...0 = Connection not distressed
NBP:
NBP:  Sequence    number = 00DD
NBP:  Acknowledge number = A93B
NBP:  Packet length      = 1486
NBP:
NBP:  ----- NBP Connection Parameters -----
NBP:
NBP:  Maximum send and receive packet size = 1514 bytes
NBP:  Memory available for receive packets = 6656 bytes
NBP:  Smallest allocatable memory block    = 256 bytes
NBP:
```

3Com's advertisements state that their hardware and software "network more systems to more types of systems." Upon studying the protocols, validation of this claim is evident in two areas. The hardware platform supports DOS, OS/2, and Macintosh workstations. Protocol support includes XNS, TCP/IP, and SMB. Most importantly, 3Com's Demand Protocol Architecture allows for dynamic reconfigurations between the various alternatives -- truly a network that networks different networks.

4.9 | References

[4-1] 3Com, 3+ Theory of Operations, document 3C2504, February 1986.

[4-2] 3Com, 3+ Developer's Library, document 3CS670,

[4-3] 3Com, NetProbe Network Utility Guide, document 3914-00, September 1988.

[4-4] Dale Neibaur, "Understanding XNS: The prototypical internetwork protocol," Data Communications [ital], September 21, 1989, pp. 43–51.

[4-5] Xerox Corporation, Xerox Network Systems Architecture General Information Manual, document XNSG068504, 1985.

[4-6] Xerox Corporation, Internet Transport Protocols, document X515028112, 1981.

[4-7] "A Standard for the Transmission of IP Datagrams over IEEE 802 Networks," RFC-1042, DDN Information Center, February 1988.

[4-8] 3Com Corporation, NetBIOS Programmer's Reference, document 3C2512, 1987.

[4-9] Microsoft Corporation, Server/Redirector File Sharing Protocol, 1985.

[4-10] 3Com Corporation, 3+Open LAN Manager Technical Reference, document 3C2633, 1989.

[4-11] Microsoft LAN Manager Programmer's Reference, document 3C2634, 1988 (available from 3Com, document 3C2634).

[4-12] 3Com Corporation, "The 3+Open 1.1 NBP Protocol," February 5, 1990.

[4-13] Network General Corporation, Sniffer Portable Protocol Analyzer Operation Manual, 1986 – 1988.

CHAPTER FIVE

Analyzing IBM Token-Ring Related Protocols

As one of the principal developers of the token-ring network and a key contributor to the IEEE 802.5 standard, IBM has also incorporated a variety of protocols into its network software.

Originally developed for use with the broadband IBM PC Network, the PC LAN Program (PC LAN) software was later ported to run on token-ring local area networks. The OS/2 LAN Server is a network operating system for the next generation of OS/2-based network servers. The NetBIOS and Server Message Block (SMB) protocols are also key elements, as are the Data Link Layer Communications defined by the IEEE 802.5 standard. The purpose of this chapter is to provide an overview of the many protocols that are utilized on token ring networks, and to guide the reader to the wide range of references that are available.

We'll look at additional references from other sources as we go through this chapter. Many of the other IBM references in this chapter, such as reference [5-16], discuss the use of PC LAN with both broadband and token-ring hardware architectures. In view of the current technology, however, we will focus on the token-ring implementation.

IBM has produced a number of excellent references to assist with token-ring network design and troubleshooting. The Introduction and Planning Guide (reference [5-1]) discusses the hardware elements, cabling, network design, and documentation. The Architecture Reference (reference [5-2]) discusses the hardware and software intricacies in detail. The Problem Determination Guide (reference [5-3]) is a comprehensive troubleshooting reference.

5.1 | PC LAN Architecture and the OSI Model

The architecture of PC LAN can be described in several ways, depending upon your point of view.

From the perspective of DOS applications, PC LAN is considered to be an extension of DOS Version 3.3. It provides a transparent mechanism for an application running on one workstation to redirect its disk and printer I/O requests to another machine -- functions that we normally associate with DOS.

From a network perspective, PC LAN is considered to be a NetBIOS application in that it requires an interface to the NetBIOS protocol for communication via the network. Some mechanism must exist that will link the NetBIOS application interface with the token-ring (IEEE 802.5) hardware. These links are included in a family of device drivers, known collectively known as the PC LAN Support Program.

A third dimension comes from the perspective of the end user. That version initializes PC LAN by using the NET START command in the AUTOEXEC.BAT file, and then specifying the configuration to be used on that particular workstation. We'll begin dissecting PC LAN by looking at the user's configuration.

5.1.1 | PC LAN Services

PC LAN Version 1.3 has two different service offerings: Base Services, which include the functions defined in PC LAN Version 1.2; and Extended Services, which were added in Version 1.3.

The Base Services Requester resides at the workstation and can be configured in three different ways. The Redirector (RDR) intercepts the workstation I/O requests, redirects them to the appropriate network server, and receives the server's response. The DOS extension facility appears here because the workstation's requests appear as if they have been performed locally. The Receiver (RCV) performs the same function as the RDR, plus it logs the messages. The Messenger (MSG) performs both RDR and RCV functions, but adds more complex message handling functions. The Base Services Server (SVR) resides in a non-dedicated file and print server. It runs in the background, and responds to requests from the various workstations for disk and printer I/O.

The Extended Services option manages multiple servers as a single resource by defining a master server (domain controller) that further manages the network resources. Printer management is included to handle printer selection, print job queuing, etc. In addition, Extended Services provides greater system administration capabilities since the network administrator can define who has access to resources, what type of access is allowed, and the values of the various system performance parameters.

In most installations, workstations are configured as a Redirector (RDR), with at least one machine configured as a Server (SRV). The application program functions of printing and disk I/O utilize both the RDR (Redirector in Figure 5-1a) and SRV (PSPRINT and SHARE in Figure 5-1a). Printing applications that use DOS interrupts 21H or 17H are intercepted by the RDR. The RDR then determines if the intended target printer is attached to local PC hardware, such as a print job to the local printer, or to the network as with a print job to the network printer.

If the local hardware is required, the RDR sends the call to the local PC BIOS, and then to the local PC hardware. In this case, no network hardware is involved in the process. For network interactions, the RDR translates the request into an appropriate SMB message, then sends it to the server via Interrupt 5CH using the NetBIOS interface, and waits for the reply.

Figure 5-1a
IBM PC LAN architecture

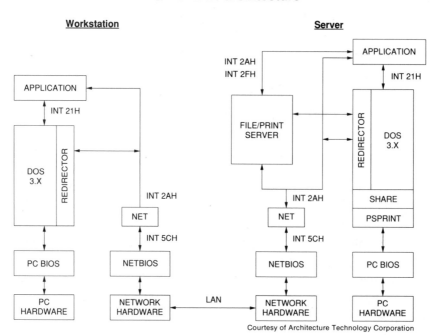

Courtesy of Architecture Technology Corporation

For disk I/O or a printer that is being accessed as if it is a file, DOS determines if the request is for a local or network device. If redirection is required, the request is passed to the RDR, which again translates it into an SMB message and transmits to the SVR via Interrupt 5CH using NetBIOS. Note that DOS is still the controlling factor for all these workstation interactions and that all DOS interrupts and file structures are maintained.

5.1.2 | PC LAN and OSI

To put PC LAN in the context of OSI (see Figure 5-1b), it could be said that PC LAN protocols encompass the Application and Presentation Layers of the OSI model, including the DOS, Redirector, SMB and executable Net program elements from Figure 5-1a. The NetBIOS driver provides a Session Layer interface. The PC LAN Support Program provides Transport and Network Layer functions, plus drivers for both the IEEE 802.2 and 802.5 interfaces at the Data Link Layer. The balance of the token-ring hardware, such as the NIC, cables, MSAU, etc., complete the Physical Layer.

Figure 5-1b
IBM PC LAN protocol interfaces

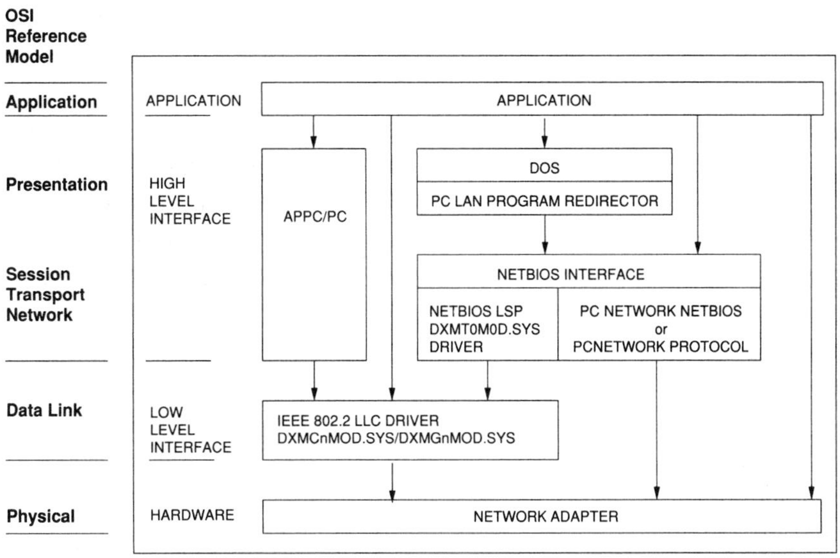

We'll look at the different interfaces of the PC LAN Support Program in the section 5.3, then investigate the NetBIOS interface and SMB protocol in detail in sections 5.5 and 5.6.

To put the entire picture of PC LAN and the related protocols together, several additional IBM documents might come in handy. The PC LAN Administration Guide (reference [5-4]), and the Support Program User's Guide (reference [5-5]) are invaluable resources during network installation. The PC LAN Installation Guide (reference [5-6]) and Parameter Guidelines Book (reference [5-7]) also are extremely useful for network optimization. An article in *LAN Magazine* (reference [5-8]) also provides insight into PC LAN optimization.

5.2 **OS/2 LAN Server Architecture and the OSI Model**

The OS/2 LAN Server Version 1.2 and IBM OS/2 Extended Edition version 1.2 products adhere to the guidelines established for IBM's System Application Architecture (SAA). Both products are required for the system operating as a server. For the client functions, a system will require either Extended Edition (which includes the LAN Requester) or DOS (version 3.3 or 4.0).

A variety of support interfaces are provided under the Communication Manager of Extended Edition, including SNA protocols, X.25, ASCII Terminal Emulation, and 3270 and 5250 Terminal Support. Most important to our discussion is the LAN support. The Communication Manager supports four different types of LAN hardware: IBM Token-Ring, IBM PC Network (both baseband and broadband), Ethernet Version 2.0 and IEEE 802.3. ETHERAND is the Communications Manager term for Ethernet and IEEE 802.3 protocol support. LAN applications may be written that interface with various Application Program Interfaces, or APIs (see Figure 5-2).

The Data Link Layer interface conforms to IEEE 802.2. It provides a communication platform for four higher-layer protocol stacks: NetBIOS, SNA LAN DLC, SQLLOO, and a direct 802.2 interface. The first higher layer interface is NetBIOS, and is used by the Remote Data Services (RDS) Requester for requests to and from DOS workstations; LAN Requester and LAN Server; and NetBIOS applications such as those using the Named Pipe category of program calls. The SNA LAN DLC refers to IBM's SNA interface for LAN communication, which supports both IEEE 802.2 and 802.5. SNA LAN DLC supports the Advanced Program to Program Communications (APPC) applications, such as Remote Data Services or RDS (for OS/2 users) and the 5250 emulation functions of Extended Edition. Both Logical Unit (LU) 2 (3270 display emulation) and LUA (a combination of LU 0, 1, 2, and 3) are supported as well. The host support APIs include SRPI (Server-Requester Programming Interface) that allow a workstation to request services from a host; and EHLLAPI (Emulator High-Level

Language Application Program Interface) for terminal emulation. The Structured Query Language LAN Only Option (SQLLOO) is a communication platform used by the OS/2 Database Manager.

Figure 5-2
IBM OS/2 Extended Edition Version 1.2
communications architecture

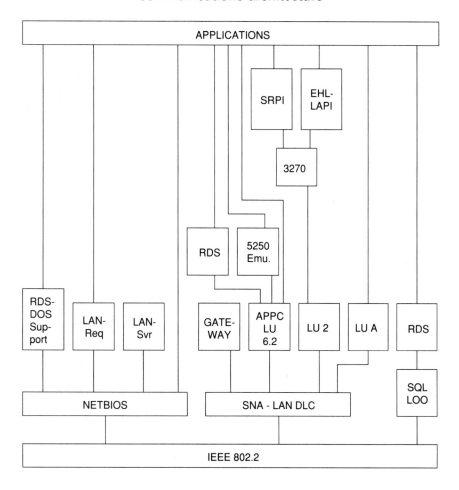

The OS/2 Extended Edition Version 1.2 contains the Communications Manager component with the APIs discussed above. In addition, Extended Edition includes the OS/2 LAN Requester component. The LAN Requester provides access to shared network resources by redirecting an application program or user request to the network. The OS/2 LAN Server, which is available as a separate product, provides the shared resource and responds to the LAN Requester. The OS/2 LAN Server also provides two other components: a DOS LAN Requester, which provides DOS user support; and the IBM LAN Support Program Version 1.1, which provides various DOS hardware drivers (to be discussed in section 5.3). Thus the OS/2 LAN Server provides both DOS and OS/2 support and a migration path for those users moving from DOS to OS/2.

Interested readers should consult references [5-9] and [5-10] for further details on the Communication Manager. Reference [5-11] provides details on the OS/2 LAN Server program.

5.3 | PC LAN Support Program

The IBM PC LAN Support Program (see reference [5-5]) provides the interface drivers that allow the individual workstation to communicate with the token-ring hardware. The Support Program replaced three other support interfaces that were previously used in PC LAN Version 1.1: TOKREUI.COM the token-ring NIC interface; TOKR3270.COM, the interface for the IBM 3270-PC; and NETBEUI.COM, the NetBIOS interface version. The device drivers can be used with both baseband and broadband PC network hardware, as well as the token-ring hardware, so they are much more flexible. As shown in Figure 5-1b, these drivers provide the links between the Application programs, NetBIOS, and the token-ring or PC Network hardware.

With the PC LAN Support Program, the drivers are initialized using the CONFIG.SYS file of the individual workstation The format is as follows:

DEVICE = DXM??MOD.SYS

Three different types of drivers exist. The first, DXMA0MOD.SYS is an interrupt arbitrator used by DOS and is required for all installations. The second type is used to drive the token ring or PC Network network hardware used at that workstation. There are five versions:

DXMC0MOD.SYS: token-ring support for IEEE 802.2;

DXMC1MOD.SYS: token-ring support for IEEE 802.2 and 3270;

DXMG0MOD.SYS: PC Network support for IEEE 802.2;

DXMG1MOD.SYS: PC Network support for IEEE 802.2 and 3270; and

DXMG2MOD.SYS: early vintage PC Network support for IEEE 802.2

The third driver, DXMT0MOD.SYS, supports NetBIOS functions.

An example of a CONFIG.SYS file for a token-ring network would be something like:

DEVICE = C:\DXMA0MOD.SYS (interrupt arbitrator driver)

DEVICE = C:\DXMC0MOD.SYS 400000000003 (Token-Ring driver)

DEVICE = C:\DXMT0MOD.SYS O=N S=9 (NetBIOS driver)

Once the proper options are designated in the CONFIG.SYS file, an entry containing the NET START command is added to the workstation's AUTOEXEC.BAT file to initializes PC LAN at that workstation. For example, to configure the workstation TRNMIS03 as a redirector and invoke the extended services, the command line would be:

NET START RDR TRNSMIS03 /XS

The parameters of the NET START command, the DXMT0MOD.SYS (NetBIOS) device driver, and other parameters set within the workstation's CONFIG.SYS and AUTOEXEC.BAT files can influence the proper operation and performance of the network. These are described in reference [5-4], chapter 7, and references [5-7] and [5-8]. We'll discuss the various PC LAN Program parameters in section 5.7, after looking at the Data Link Layer, NetBIOS interface, and SMB protocol.

5.4 Token Ring Data Link Layer Protocols

Two different types of Data Link Layer frames are defined by the IEEE 802.5 standard for token ring. The first is the Logical Link Control (LLC) frame used to transmit user data, such as files, electronic messages, etc. The second type is the Media Access Control (MAC) frame which performs ring management functions. These two frame types are distinguished by the first two bits of the Frame Control field within the 802.5 frame header (see Figure 1-9b). Setting the first two bits equal to 00 indicates a MAC frame, and setting them equal to 01 indicates a LLC frame. We'll summarize each of these frames separately. For a more detailed discussion, see Chapter 6 of the companion book, *LAN Troubleshooting Handbook*, or the IEEE 802.5 standard (reference [5-12]).

5.4.1 Logical Link Control (LLC) Frames

To facilitate transmission of user data, Logical Link Control frames contain an IEEE 802.2 LLC Protocol Data Unit (PDU) within the Information field (see Figure 5-3a). From the standpoint of protocol analysis, the Ending Delimiter field includes two bits designated A and C which can facilitate troubleshooting. The Address Recognized bit (A) is set by the receiver when it recognizes an address in an incoming frame. The Frame Copied bit (C) indicates that the destination workstation has, in fact, received the transmitted frame and copied the information into its buffer. (Whether the workstation responded properly to the transmission is another matter, however.)

Figure 5-3a
The 802.2 LLC PDU within an 802.5 frame

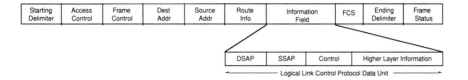

The Destination and Source Address fields, plus the Destination and Source Service Access Point Addresses (DSAP and SSAP, respectively) also should be noted as part of the analysis. Recall that a SAP acts as a port through which a higher layer application communicates with its lower layer. As such, the SAP allows multiple higher layer processes to share a common lower layer, in this case, the token-ring NIC. Consider these SAP addresses:

Example SAPs	Usage
00	Null
02	Individual LLC sublayer management
03	Group LLC sublayer management
04	SNA Path Control (individual)
05	SNA Path Control (group)
06	ARPANET's Internet Protocol
80	3Com XNS
AA	TCP/IP SNAP Protocol
E0	Novell NetWare
F0	IBM NetBIOS
F4	LAN Management (individual)
F5	LAN Management (group)
F8	IBM Remote Program Load
FE	ISO Network Layer
FF	Global

5.4.2 | Medium Access Control (MAC) Frames

Medium Access Control (MAC) frames are used for network management (see Figure 5-3b). The Information field within the MAC PDU consists of various fields (see Figure 5-4). A Length field indicates the length of the PDU in octets. A Class field indicates the Source and Destination Class. Commands, called Code Points, are the tasks the intended receiver is to perform. The Parameters, also called Subvectors, further elaborate on the Commands. The Major Vector ID (MVID) identifies the Destination and Source Class, including the functional addresses, such as Ring Station, Network Manager, Ring Parameter Server, Ring Error Monitor, etc. The Code Point identifies the exact MAC frame in use, such as Beacon, Duplicate Address Test, Active Monitor Present, etc.). The Subvector ID (SVID) further elaborates on the MVID and contains various parameters. The MAC details are extensively described in chapter 5 of reference [5-2].

Figure 5-3b
The MAC PDU within an 802.5 frame

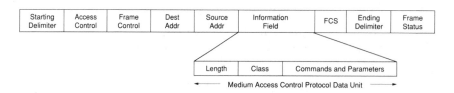

Starting Delimiter	Access Control	Frame Control	Dest Addr	Source Addr	Information Field	FCS	Ending Delimiter	Frame Status

Length	Class	Commands and Parameters

Medium Access Control Protocol Data Unit

There are 25 different types of MAC frames, and these are divided into four categories: Medium Control, which is concerned with the reliable operation of the network; Station Initialization, which is used when a station wishes to join the ring; Error Monitoring, which indicates soft errors that have occurred; and Network Management, which controls the network configuration and station parameters.

The MAC frames are transmitted from the Network Management Agent on the NIC, or Ring Station (RS), to one of several functional addresses: Active Monitor (AM), Ring Parameter Server (RPS), Ring Error Monitor (REM), or the Configuration Report Server (CRS). Note that these are functional rather than physical network addresses, and they would reside in a token-ring management software product such as IBM's LAN Manager or Proteon's TokenView.

Figure 5-4
The 802.5 MAC frame format

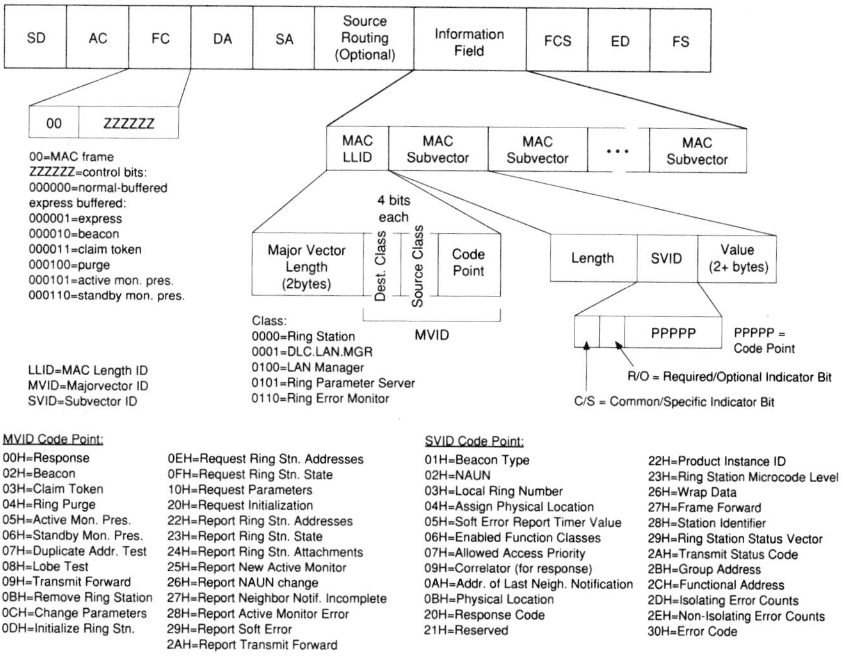

Courtesy of Architecture Technology Corporation

Once the MAC frame is transmitted to a particular functional address, other processes within the management software take over and perform functions such as setting parameters, e.g., workstation priority. For further information on the MAC frames, see section 5 of reference [5-2], section 3 of reference [5-13], or reference [5-14], from which Figure 5-4 was obtained. The 25 MAC frame formats are listed below:

1) Medium Control Frames

• Beacon (RS to all RS) -- transmitted when a Ring Station detects a hard failure, such as a wire fault, signal loss, or streaming station.

• Claim Token (RS to all RS) -- transmitted by any station that detects the absence of the Active Monitor and wishes to start the Claim Token process; or during the Contention process to determine the new AM.

• Ring Purge (AM to all RS) -- used by the Active Monitor to recover from a temporary error condition, release a new token, and reinitialize the token-passing process; or at the conclusion of the Claim Token process.

• Active Monitor Present (AM to all RS) -- transmitted every seven seconds or at the end of the Ring Purge process to indicate the presence of the Active Token Monitor.

• Standby Monitor Present (RS to all RS or AM) -- transmitted in response to an Active Monitor Present or another Standby Monitor Present frame during the Neighbor Notification process.

2) Station Initialization Frames

• Lobe Media Test (RS to itself) -- used during the initial phase of the ring insertion process to test the transmission media from the station to the wire center and back.

• Duplicate Address Test (RS to all RSs) -- used to verify the uniqueness of that station's address.

• Request Initialization (RS to RPS) -- asks the Ring Parameter Server for operational parameters, including local ring number, physical drop number, and error report timer value, during the Ring Initialization process.

• Initialize Ring Station (RPS to RS) -- transmits the parameters from the RPS to the station.

3) Error Monitoring Frames

• Report Error (RS to REM) -- indicates a count of soft errors that may be recovered by higher layer protocols.

• Report Monitor Error (RS to REM) -- informs the Ring Error Monitor of a problem in the Claim Token process, or a problem with the Active Monitor.

• Report Neighbor Notification Incomplete (RS to REM) -- indicates that the station has not received a transmission from its upstream neighbor during the Neighbor Notification process.

4) Network Management Frames

• Report New Monitor (AM to CRS) -- transmitted at the conclusion of the Claim Token process by the winning station.

• Report SUA Change (RS to CRS) -- reports a change in the stations stored upstream address as a result of information gathered during the Neighbor Notification process.

• Remove Ring Station (CRS to RS) -- sent from the Configuration Report Server to force a station to remove itself from the ring.

• Change Parameters (CRS to RS) -- allows the Configuration Report Server to change the local ring number, physical drop number, soft error report timer value, function class, and access priority number. It may also be used during the station initialization process.

The following frames are used by the Configuration Report Server to gather specific information about a particular station:

1) Request Station Address (CRS to RS)
2) Report Station Address (RS to CRS)
3) Request Station State (CRS to RS)
4) Report Station State (RS to CRS)
5) Request Station Attachment (CRS to RS)
6) Report Station Attachment (RS to CRS)

• Transmit Forward (CRS to RS) — used to test the path between various stations by retransmitting a given message.

• Report Transmit Forward (RS to CRS) — a confirmation from the station to the Configuration Report Server that a frame has been forwarded in the Transmit Forward process.

• Response (RS to CRS or RPS) — acknowledges a response to a Change Parameters (from CRS) or Initialize Ring Station (from RPS) frame.

An understanding of the various processes that generate the different MAC frames can assist in network troubleshooting. One example would be to use the Beacon frame transmitted by a workstation to detect a hard failure, such as broken cable or loss of signal.

For example, let's assume that Node A, which is upstream from Node B, has a defective transmitter. Node B would therefore detect a loss of signal and transmit a Beacon MAC frame, thus identifying its upstream neighbor) as Node A, as a possible failure point. When the MAC frame eventually reached Node A after traveling full circle around the ring), the failing node would begin the Beacon Transmit Auto Removal Test process to determine if it is faulty, and if the test shows it to be faulty, it will remove itself from the ring.

Capturing and decoding the MAC frames with a protocol analyzer can be a real timesaver when a network failure occurs. The TMS380 Chipset User's Guide (reference [5-13]) describes these processes in detail in section 3. We'll look at another MAC frame example in section 5.8.

5.5 The NetBIOS Interface

NetBIOS, the Network Basic Input/Output System, is a Session Layer interface developed by Sytek, Inc., for the broadband IBM PC Network. It is also supported by the IBM Token-Ring network, and emulated by a number of other vendors, including Novell. In the PC Network, NetBIOS was provided in a ROM chip resides on the NIC itself. For the Token-Ring, NetBIOS is part of the Local Area Network Support Program, and is found in a device driver labeled DXMT0MOD.SYS, as discussed in sections 5.3 and 5.7. Reference [5-14], Chapter 4 and Chapter 1 of reference [5-15] provide additional details on the history of NetBIOS.

A session is a logical connection between two NetBIOS names and must be established before any other communication between the workstations can occur. The NetBIOS protocol is used to establish that session, and also communicates between workstations during the session. NetBIOS defines four different type of commands, called Network Control Blocks or NCB commands, that are then used for the network communication purposes, thus controlling the NIC. The NCB commands are divided into four categories: General commands, Name Support commands, Session Support commands, and Datagram Support commands.

General commands allow the NIC to read status information or control other outstanding commands on the network. Name Support commands allow the workstation to be known by either a unique or group name on the network. Session Support commands allow the workstation to establish a logical connection, known as a session, with another workstation Session Support commands also send and receive messages during that session, obtain status information regarding the session, and terminate the session. These commands are used for reliable (acknowledged) transmissions, whereas Datagram Support commands are unacknowledged. With Datagram Support commands, messages can be sent to a name or a group name, broadcast to everyone on the network, or received from a name or group name. Datagram messages are also shorter in length (512 octets maximum) than Session commands, and require additional protocols to assure data reliability.

Since NetBIOS operates at the Session Layer, it is also helps maintain a database of workstation name and address relationships It then establishes and terminates the logical connections between the two names. The process for this information exchange occurs in four steps:

Step 1. The names are added to a local name table at each workstation using the various name management commands.

Step 2. A session is established using the LISTEN command at one workstation and the CALL command at the other.

Step 3. Data is then transferred (with guaranteed delivery) using the SEND and RECEIVE commands.

Step 4. The session is terminated with the HANG UP or RESET commands.

Before we can look further at the commands, however, we need to see how the NetBIOS command fits within a MAC frame.

5.5.1   Transmitting NetBIOS Commands

NetBIOS commands are encapsulated within the Data Link Layer information field corresponding to 802.3, 802.5, or whatever LAN architecture is in use. For IEEE 802.5 networks, the NetBIOS command is found between the frame header and the frame trailer. Recall that the frame header includes the Starting Delimiter, Access Control, Frame Control, Destination Address, Source Address, and the optional Routing Information fields, as shown in Figure 1-9b.

The frame trailer includes the Frame Check Sequence (FCS), Ending Delimiter, and Frame Status fields. Between the header and trailer is the Information field where the IEEE 802.2 LLC header and the NetBIOS header reside. (The 802.2 header was discussed in detail in section 1.4.1 and is shown in Figure 1-6a.)

Two formats exist for the NetBIOS header (Figure 5-5). The first is known as an Unnumbered Information (UI) frame in 802.2 terminology and is used for connectionless service. The connectionless header consists of the NetBIOS Header Length, a delimiter (which is always set to EFFFH), the NetBIOS command, two Optional Data fields, a Transmit/Response correlator to match received responses with transmitted queries, and finally the Destination and Source names.

The second type of header, which is used for connection-oriented service, is known as an Information (I) frame in 802.2 terminology. These frames contain sequence numbers (see Figure 1-6c) to guarantee reliable transmission of the data in sequence. For these connection-oriented frames, the NetBIOS header format is modified by inserting Destination and Source session numbers in place of Destination and Source names.

189

Figure 5-5
Encapsulating the NetBIOS command within an IEEE 802.5 frame

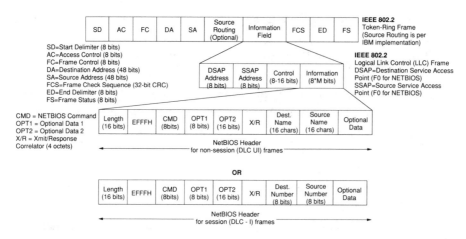

5.5.2 | NetBIOS Command Frames

The 22 different NetBIOS commands are grouped into the four categories previously discussed and fit inside the Information field of the 802.5 frame as shown in Figure 5-5. The third field of the NetBIOS header, the Command field, is a two-hex character designation for the particular command. Command codes are designated 00H - 13H are U frames, while commands designated 14H - 1FH are I frames. We'll look at the four categories of frames individually. Notice that each NetBIOS frame is given a name that suggests the NCB command in use. Reference [5-16], section 5 provides further details.

Name Management Frames provide name management functions:

Frame Name	Code	Function
ADD_GROUP_NAME_QUERY	00H	Check for duplicate group name on network
ADD_NAME_QUERY	01H	Check for duplicate name on network
ADD_NAME_RESPONSE	ODH	Negative response: add name is duplicate
NAME_IN_CONFLICT	02H	Duplicate names detected

Session Establishment and Termination Frames are used to establish, maintain, and terminate sessions:

Frame Name	Code	Function
NAME_QUERY	0AH	Request to locate a name on the network
NAME_RECOGNIZED	OEH	Name Recognized: NAME_QUERY response
SESSION_ALIVE	1FH	Verify session is still active
SESSION_CONFIRM	17H	SESSION_INITIALIZE acknowledgement
SESSION_END	18H	Session termination
SESSION_INITIALIZE	19H	A session has been set-up

Data Transfer Frames are used to transfer both session and non-session data:

Frame Name	Code	Function
DATA_ACK	14H	DATA_ONLY_LAST acknowledgement
DATA_FIRST_MIDDLE	15H	Session data message - first or middle frame
DATAGRAM	08H	Application-generated datagram
DATAGRAM_BROADCAST	09H	Application-generated broadcast datagram
DATA_ONLY_LAST	16H	Session data message - only or last frame
NO_RECEIVE	1AH	No receive command to hold received data
RECEIVE_CONTINUE	1CH	Indicates receive outstanding
RECEIVE_OUTSTANDING	1BH	Re-transmit last data - receive command up

Additional Frames:

Frame Name	Code	Function
STATUS_QUERY	03H	Request remote node status
STATUS_RESPONSE	OFH	Remote node status information
TERMINATE_TRACE	07H	Terminate traces at remote nodes
TERMINATE_TRACE	13H	Terminate traces at local and remote nodes

5.5.3 NetBIOS Examples

To illustrate the NetBIOS commands, we will examine the communication between two workstations (named Eagle One and IBM Portable) shown in Figure 5-6. In frame 59, IBM Portable issues a NAME_QUERY (command 0AH). The name is recognized (NetBIOS command 0EH in frame 60) and the session established and acknowledged (frames 61 and 63). A retransmission is requested (frame 67) and acknowledged (frames 71 and 75). Now that transmission is complete, the session is terminated with a SESSION_END (command 18H) in frame 77.

Figure 5-6
NetBIOS frames transmitted over an 802.5 network

Frame	Delta t	Destination	Source	Summary
59	1.651	NETBIOS	IBM Portable	NET Find name EAGLE<03>
60	0.011	IBM Portable	Eagle One	NET Name EAGLE<03> recognized
61	0.009	Eagle One	IBM Portable	NET D=02 S=04 Session initialize
62	0.002	IBM Portable	Eagle One	LLC R D=F0 S=F0 RR NR=113
63	0.007	IBM Portable	Eagle One	NET D=04 S=02 Session confirm
64	0.003	Eagle One	IBM Portable	LLC R D=F0 S=F0 RR NR=99
65	0.013	Eagle One	IBM Portable	SMB C Send Message
66	0.003	IBM Portable	Eagle One	LLC R D=F0 S=F0 RR NR=114
67	0.009	IBM Portable	Eagle One	NET D=04 S=02 Send more now
68	0.003	Eagle One	IBM Portable	LLC R D=F0 S=F0 RR NR=100
69	0.006	Eagle One	IBM Portable	SMB C Send Message
70	0.003	IBM Portable	Eagle One	LLC R D=F0 S=F0 RR NR=115
71	0.011	IBM Portable	Eagle One	Net D=04 S=02 Data ACK
72	0.003	Eagle One	IBM Portable	LLC R D=F0 S=F0 RR NR=101
73	0.041	IBM Portable	Eagle One	SMB R Send Message
74	0.004	Eagle One	IBM Portable	LLC R D=F0 S=F0 RR NR=102
75	0.005	Eagle One	IBM Portable	NET D=02 S=04 Data ACK
76	0.003	IBM Portable	Eagle One	LLC R D=F0 S=F0 RR NR=116
77	0.012	Eagle One	IBM Portable	NET D=02 S=04 Session end

Figure 5-7 shows the NetBIOS details of the sequence outlined above. References [5-16], [5-17], and [5-18] provide further information on the NetBIOS protocol. Programmers who want to write applications to the NetBIOS interface would find reference [5-19] useful.

Figure 5-7
NetBIOS frame details

```
- - - - - - - - - - - - - - - - - Frame 59 - - - - - - - - - - - - - - - -

NET:   ----- NETBIOS Name Query -----
NET:
NET:   Header length = 44, Data length = 0
NET:   Delimiter = EFFF (NETBIOS)
NET:   Command = 0A
NET:   Local session number = 4
NET:   Caller's name type = 00 (Unique name)
NET:   Receiver's name = EAGLE<03>
NET:   Sender's name = PORTABLE<00>
NET:
```

Figure 5-7 (continued)

```
- - - - - - - - - - - - - - - - Frame 60 - - - - - - - - - - - - - - - - -

NET:   ----- NETBIOS Name Recognized -----
NET:
NET:   Header length = 44, Data length = 0
NET:   Delimiter = EFFF (NETBIOS)
NET:   Command = 0E
NET:   Local session number = 2
NET:   Caller's name type = 00 (Unique name)
NET:   Transmit correlator = 001F
NET:   Response correlator = 003C
NET:   Receiver's name = PORTABLE<00>
NET:   Sender's name = EAGLE<03>
NET:

- - - - - - - - - - - - - - - Frame 61 - - - - - - - - - - - - - - - - - -

NET:   ----- NETBIOS Session Initialize -----
NET:
NET:   Header length = 14, Data length = 0
NET:   Delimiter = EFFF (NETBIOS)
NET:   Command = 19
NET:   Max data receive size = 2000
NET:   Transmit correlator = 003C
NET:   Response correlator = 0020
NET:   Remote session number = 2
NET:   Local session number = 4
NET:

- - - - - - - - - - - - - - - Frame 63 - - - - - - - - - - - - - - - - - -

NET:   ----- NETBIOS Session Confirm -----
NET:
NET:   Header length = 14, Data length = 0
NET:   Delimiter = EFFF (NETBIOS)
NET:   Command = 17
NET:   Max data receive size = 2000
NET:   Transmit correlator = 0020
NET:   Remote session number = 4
NET:   Local session number = 2
NET:
```

Figure 5-7 (continued)

```
- - - - - - - - - - - - - - - - - Frame 67 - - - - - - - - - - - - - - - - -

NET:   ----- NETBIOS Receive Outstanding -----
NET:
NET:   Header length = 14, Data length = 0
NET:   Delimiter = EFFF (NETBIOS)
NET:   Command = 1B
NET:   Remote session number = 4
NET:   Local session number = 2
NET:

- - - - - - - - - - - - - - - - - Frame 71 - - - - - - - - - - - - - - - - -

NET:   ----- NETBIOS Data Acknowledgement -----
NET:
NET:   Header length = 14, Data length = 0
NET:   Delimiter = EFFF (NETBIOS)
NET:   Command = 14
NET:   Transmit correlator = 0022
NET:   Remote session number = 4
NET:   Local session number = 2
NET:

- - - - - - - - - - - - - - - - - Frame 75 - - - - - - - - - - - - - - - - -

NET:   ----- NETBIOS Data Acknowledgement -----
NET:
NET:   Header length = 14, Data length = 0
NET:   Delimiter = EFFF (NETBIOS)
NET:   Command = 14
NET:   Transmit correlator = 003D
NET:   Remote session number = 2
NET:   Local session number = 4
NET:

- - - - - - - - - - - - - - - - - Frame 77 - - - - - - - - - - - - - - - - -

NET:   ----- NETBIOS Session End -----
NET:
NET:   Header length = 14, Data length = 0
NET:   Delimiter = EFFF (NETBIOS)
NET:   Command = 18
NET:   Termination indicator = 0 (HANGUP)
NET:   Remote session number = 2
NET:   Local session number = 4
NET:
```

5.6 | Server Message Block Protocol

The SMB protocol is the Application Layer protocol of the IBM PC LAN program and relies upon the NetBIOS protocol at the Session Layer for completeness. The function of the SMB protocol is to communicate with remote devices on the LAN, such as the server. As we saw in section 5.1, the workstation's redirector intercepts all the DOS function calls and provides a steering function. Calls requiring local hardware support, such as a local print job, are passed to DOS via the PC BIOS. Calls requiring network support, such as printing on the network printer, are translated into SMB commands for transmission to the remote device, and subsequent execution.

5.6.1 | SMB Protocol Commands

The SMB protocol commands are also divided into four different categories: Session Control, File, Print, and Message commands. Session Control commands start and end the connection between the redirector and the server, and verify the dialect between these two entities. File commands allow access to various files and directories on the server. Print commands support communication between the redirector and the server's printer. Message commands allow a program to transmit and receive either individual or broadcast messages. Each of these commands has a defined function code (one octet in length) at the beginning of the SMB transmission that specifies the desired interaction. Additional parameters, such as file attributes or retrieved data, are added as necessary. These commands are summarized below:

Session Control Commands start and stop the communication between the redirector at the workstation and the server. These include:

• Start connection (70H), which establishes the connection between the redirector and the shared resource at the server.

• End connection (71H), which terminates the connection between the redirector and the shared resource at the server.

• Verify dialect (72H), which is sent from the redirector to the server to verify the dialect in use.

File Access Commands allow the redirector to access remote files at the server once the session has been established. These include:

• Create directory (00H), which instructs the server to invoke the DOS MD (make directory) command.

• Delete directory (01H), which instructs the server to invoke the PC-DOS RD (remove directory) command

• Open file (02H), which instructs the server to open a file and return the file handle.

• Create file (03H), which instructs the server to create a new file and return the file handle.

• Close file (04H), which instructs the server to close a file specified by the file handle.

• Commit file (05H), which instructs the server to write all buffers for a file to its hard disk.

• Delete file (06H), which instructs the server to delete the file specified by the file name.

• Rename file (07H), which instructs the server to rename a file.

• Get file attributes (08H), which obtains the file's attributes from the server, the last access time, and the file size.

• Set file attributes (09H), which instructs the server to set file attributes.

• Check directory (10H), which instructs the server to determine the existence of a directory when the user invokes the PC-DOS CD · (change directory) command.

• Read byte block (0AH), which instructs the server to read a block of data from a file.

• Write byte block (0BH), which instructs the server to write a block of data to a file.

• Lock byte block (0CH), which instructs the server to lock a range of blocks within a file.

• Unlock byte block (0DH), which instructs the server to unlock a range of blocks within a file.

• Create Unique file (0EH), which instructs the server to generate a unique file name and return it to the redirector.

• Create new file (0FH), which instructs the server to generate a new file, assuming that the file name does not already exist.

• End of process (11H), which instructs the server to terminate the work associated with a connection.

• LSEEK (12H)-long seek, which instructs the server to move the file pointer.

• Get disk attributes (80H), which requests hard disk storage information from the server.

• Search multiple files (81H), which instructs the server to perform the PC-DOS FCB and ASCIIZ search functions.

197

Print Commands allow the redirector to send files to the server's printer and obtain status information about the print queue. These commands include:

• Create spool file (C0H), which instructs the server to initiate a file for spooling print data.

• Spool byte block (C1H), which instructs the server to write a block of data to a spool file.

• Close spool file (C2H), which indicates the end of the spool file to the server and tells the server that the file can be queued for printing.

• Return print queue (C3H), which instructs the server to return the contents of its print queue.

Message Commands enable an application program to send and receive messages. These include:

• Send single block message (D0H), which transmits a single block (128 characters, maximum) between two receivers.

• Send broadcast message (D1H), which sends a single block message to all receivers on the network.

• Forward user name (D2H), which requests a server to receive messages for an additional user name and add that name to its table.

• Cancel forward (D3H), which requests a server to delete a forwarded name from its table.

• Get machine name (D4H), which requests the machine name of a user name.

• Send start of multi-block message (D5H), which initiates a multi-block message.

• Send end of multi-block message (D6H), which indicates the end of a multi-block message.

• Send text of multi-block message (D7H), which sends up to 1,600 characters in 128-character blocks.

Now that the SMB commands have been outlined, in the following section we will show some of these commands in use.

5.6.2 | SMB Protocol Examples

To illustrate the SMB protocol in action, consider the interaction between a workstation, Eagle One, and a server, named IBM Portable, shown in Figure 5-8.

Figure 5-8
Server message block frames transmitted over a 802.5 network

Sniffer data collected on 9/20/86 at 18:04:02, file C:\SNIFFTOK\BDEMO.TRC.

	Frame	Delta t	Destination	Source	Summary
M	1		IBM Portable	Eagle One	LLC C D=F0 S=F0 RR NR=34 P
	2	0.000	Eagle One	IBM Portable	LLC R D=F0 S=F0 RR NR=53 F
	3	2.662	IBM Portable	Eagle One	SMB C Search \TEST.???
	4	0.001	Eagle One	IBM Portable	LLC R D=F0 S=F0 RR NR=54
	5	0.001	Eagle One	IBM Portable	NET D=02 S=01 Data ACK
	6	0.003	IBM Portable	Eagle One	LLC R D=F0 S=F0 RR NR=35
	7	0.010	Eagle One	IBM Portable	SMB R 1 entry found (done)
	8	0.003	IBM Portable	Eagle One	LLC R D=F0 S=F0 RR NR=36
	9	0.005	IBM Portable	Eagle One	NET D=01 S=02 Rcvd 40 bytes
	10	0.001	Eagle One	IBM Portable	LLC R D=F0 S=F0 RR NR=55
	11	0.009	IBM Portable	Eagle One	NET D=01 S=02 Send more now
	12	0.001	Eagle One	IBM Portable	LLC R D=F0 S=F0 RR NR=56
	13	0.001	Eagle One	IBM Portable	NET D=02 S=01 Data, 43 bytes
	14	0.003	IBM Portable	Eagle One	LLC R D=F0 S=F0 RR NR=37
	15	0.005	IBM Portable	Eagle One	NET D=01 S=02 Data ACK
	16	0.001	Eagle One	IBM Portable	LLC R D=F0 S=F0 RR NR=57
	17	0.021	IBM Portable	Eagle One	SMB C Continue search

199

Figure 5-8 (continued)

```
18   0.002   Eagle One     IBM Portable   LLC R D=F0 S=F0 RR NR=58
19   0.001   Eagle One     IBM Portable   NET D=02 S=01 Data ACK
20   0.003   IBM Portable  Eagle One      LLC R D=F0 S=F0 RR NR=38
21   0.007   Eagle One     IBM Portable   SMB R No more files
22   0.004   IBM Portable  Eagle One      LLC R D=F0 S=F0 RR NR=39
23   0.005   IBM Portable  Eagle One      NET D=01 S=02 Data ACK
24   0.001   Eagle One     IBM Portable   LLC R D=F0 S=F0 RR NR=59
25   0.140   IBM Portable  Eagle One      SMB C Open \TEST.BAT
26   0.002   Eagle One     IBM Portable   LLC R D=F0 S=F0 RR NR=60
27   0.001   Eagle One     IBM Portable   NET D=02 S=01 Data ACK
28   0.003   IBM Portable  Eagle One      LLC R D=F0 S=F0 RR NR=40
29   0.014   Eagle One     IBM Portable   SMB R F=0000 Opened
30   0.004   IBM Portable  Eagle One      LLC R D=F0 S=F0 RR NR=41
31   0.005   IBM Portable  Eagle One      NET D=01 S=02 Data ACK
32   0.001   Eagle One     IBM Portable   LLC R D=F0 S=F0 RR NR=61
33   0.016   IBM Portable  Eagle One      SMB C F=0000 Read 512 at 0
34   0.002   Eagle One     IBM Portable   LLC R D=F0 S=F0 RR NR=62
35   0.001   Eagle One     IBM Portable   NET D=02 S=01 Data ACK
36   0.003   IBM Portable  Eagle One      LLC R D=F0 S=F0 RR NR=42
37   0.006   Eagle One     IBM Portable   SMB R OK
38   0.003   IBM Portable  Eagle One      LLC R D=F0 S=F0 RR NR=43
39   0.005   IBM Portable  Eagle One      NET D=01 S=02 Rcvd 48 bytes
40   0.001   Eagle One     IBM Portable   LLC R D=F0 S=F0 RR NR=63
41   0.007   IBM Portable  Eagle One      NET D=01 S=02 Send more now
42   0.001   Eagle One     IBM Portable   LLC R D=F0 S=F0 RR NR=64
43   0.001   Eagle One     IBM Portable   NET D=02 S=01 Data, 52 bytes
44   0.003   IBM Portable  Eagle One      LLC R D=F0 S=F0 RR NR=44
45   0.005   IBM Portable  Eagle One      NET D=01 S=02 Data ACK
46   0.001   Eagle One     IBM Portable   LLC R D=F0 S=F0 RR NR=65
47   0.020   IBM Portable  Eagle One      SMB C F=0000 Close
48   0.002   Eagle One     IBM Portable   LLC R D=F0 S=F0 RR NR=66
49   0.001   Eagle One     IBM Portable   NET D=02 S=01 Data ACK
50   0.003   IBM Portable  Eagle One      LLC R D=F0 S=F0 RR NR=45
51   0.004   Eagle One     IBM Portable   SMB R Closed
```

The SMB commands from the workstation are followed by acknowledgements from the server at both the Logical Link Control (LLC) and NetBIOS (NET) Layers. In frame 3, the workstation requests a directory search (SMB function 81H) for the file TEST.???. The response comes in frame 7 and indicates C:TEST.BAT has been found. A subsequent search in frame 17 reveals no more files (frame 21).

The workstation requests a file open (SMB function 02H) in frame 25, which is confirmed with the file attributes (frame 29). Frame 33 initiates the process to read the file (SMB function 0AH), which produces 52 bytes of data in frame 37. The file is then closed (SMB function 04H) in frame 47 and confirmed (frame 51).

Figure 5-9 shows the details of the SMB commands and the associated parameters discussed above. For further information on the SMB protocol, see reference [5-20].

Figure 5-9
Server Message Block frame details

```
- - - - - - - - - - - - - - - - Frame 3 - - - - - - - - - - - - - - - -

SMB:  ----- SMB Search Directory Command -----
SMB:
SMB:  Function = 81 (Search Directory)
SMB:  Net path  (NPID) = A4E6
SMB:  Process id (PID) = 10C0
SMB:
SMB:  Return code = 0,0 (OK)
SMB:  File pathname = "\TEST.???"
SMB:  Maximum number of search entries to return = 11
SMB:  Attribute flags = 13
SMB:      00.. .... = Reserved
SMB:      ..0. .... = File(s) not changed since last archive
SMB:      ...1 .... = Directory file(s)
SMB:      .... 0... = No volume label info
SMB:      .... .0.. = No system file(s)
SMB:      .... ..1. = Hidden file(s)
SMB:      .... ...1 = Read only file(s)
SMB:  [Search parameter control block]
SMB:
SMB:  [End of "SMB Search Directory Command" packet.]
SMB:

- - - - - - - - - - - - - - - - Frame 7 - - - - - - - - - - - - - - - -

SMB:  ----- SMB Search Directory Response -----
SMB:
SMB:  Function = 81 (Search Directory)
SMB:  Net path  (NPID) = A4E6
SMB:  Process id (PID) = 10C0
SMB:
SMB:  Return code = 1,18 (No more files)
```

Figure 5-9 (continued)

```
SMB:   Entries returned = 1
SMB:       ..A. ....   C:TEST.BAT            52 bytes  20-Sep-86 17:57:36
SMB:
SMB:   [End of "SMB Search Directory Response" packet.]
SMB:


- - - - - - - - - - - - - - - - Frame 17 - - - - - - - - - - - - - - - - -

SMB:   ----- SMB Search Directory Command -----
SMB:
SMB:   Function = 81 (Search Directory)
SMB:   Net path  (NPID) = A4E6
SMB:   Process id (PID) = 10C0
SMB:
SMB:   Return code = 0,0 (OK)
SMB:   Continuation search
SMB:   [Search parameter control block]
SMB:
SMB:   [End of "SMB Search Directory Command" packet.]
SMB:


- - - - - - - - - - - - - - - - Frame 21 - - - - - - - - - - - - - - - - -

SMB:   ----- SMB Search Directory Response -----
SMB:
SMB:   Function = 81 (Search Directory)
SMB:   Net path  (NPID) = A4E6
SMB:   Process id (PID) = 10C0
SMB:
SMB:   Return code = 1,18 (No more files)
SMB:   Entries returned = 0
SMB:
SMB:   [End of "SMB Search Directory Response" packet.]
SMB:


- - - - - - - - - - - - - - - - Frame 25 - - - - - - - - - - - - - - - - -

SMB:   ----- SMB Open File Command -----
SMB:
SMB:   Function = 02 (Open File)
SMB:   Net path  (NPID) = A4E6
SMB:   Process id (PID) = 10C0
SMB:
SMB:   Return code = 0,0 (OK)
SMB:   File pathname = "\TEST.BAT"
```

Figure 5-9 (continued)

```
SMB:   Access flags = 00
SMB:       0... .... = Pass access to any sub-processes
SMB:       .000 .... = MS-DOS compatibility exclusive open
SMB:       .... 0000 = Open file for reading
SMB:   Attribute flags = 16
SMB:          00.. .... = Reserved
SMB:          ..0. .... = File(s) not changed since last archive
SMB:          ...1 .... = Directory file(s)
SMB:          .... 0... = No volume label info
SMB:          .... .1.. = System file(s)
SMB:          .... ..1. = Hidden file(s)
SMB:          .... ...0 = No read only file(s)
SMB:
SMB:   [End of "SMB Open File Command" packet.]
SMB:


- - - - - - - - - - - - - - - - Frame 29 - - - - - - - - - - - - - - - - -


SMB:   ----- SMB Open File Response -----
SMB:
SMB:   Function = 02 (Open File)
SMB:   Net path  (NPID) = A4E6
SMB:   Process id (PID) = 10C0
SMB:
SMB:   Return code = 0,0 (OK)
SMB:   File handle = 0000
SMB:   Attribute flags = 20
SMB:          00.. .... = Reserved
SMB:          ..1. .... = File(s) changed and not archived
SMB:          ...0 .... = No directory file(s)
SMB:          .... 0... = No volume label info
SMB:          .... .0.. = No system file(s)
SMB:          .... ..0. = No hidden file(s)
SMB:          .... ...0 = No read only file(s)
SMB:   Creation date = 19-Sep-86 17:57:36
SMB:   File size = 52
SMB:   Access flags = 02
SMB:       0... .... = Pass access to any sub-processes
SMB:       .000 .... = MS-DOS compatibility exclusive open
SMB:       .... 0010 = Open file for reading and writing
SMB:
SMB:   [End of "SMB Open File Response" packet.]
SMB:
```

Figure 5-9 (continued)

```
- - - - - - - - - - - - - - - - Frame 33 - - - - - - - - - - - - - - - - -

SMB:   ----- SMB Read Byte Range Command -----
SMB:
SMB:   Function = 0A (Read Byte Range)
SMB:   Net path  (NPID) = A4E6
SMB:   Process id (PID) = 10C0
SMB:
SMB:   Return code = 0,0 (OK)
SMB:   File handle = 0000
SMB:   Number of bytes to read = 512
SMB:   Offset in file = 0
SMB:   Total (estimated) read count = 512
SMB:
SMB:   [End of "SMB Read Byte Range Command" packet.]
SMB:


- - - - - - - - - - - - - - - Frame 37 - - - - - - - - - - - - - - - - -

SMB:   ----- SMB Read Byte Range Response -----
SMB:
SMB:   Function = 0A (Read Byte Range)
SMB:   Net path  (NPID) = A4E6
SMB:   Process id (PID) = 10C0
SMB:
SMB:   Return code = 0,0 (OK)
SMB:   Number of bytes read = 52
SMB:   [52 byte(s) of read data]
SMB:
SMB:   [End of "SMB Read Byte Range Response" packet.]
SMB:


- - - - - - - - - - - - - - - Frame 47 - - - - - - - - - - - - - - - - -

SMB:   ----- SMB Close File Command -----
SMB:
SMB:   Function = 04 (Close File)
SMB:   Net path  (NPID) = A4E6
SMB:   Process id (PID) = 10C0
SMB:
SMB:   Return code = 0,0 (OK)
SMB:   File handle = 0000
SMB:   Creation date = Unknown date/time
SMB:
SMB:   [End of "SMB Close File Command" packet.]
SMB:
```

Figure 5-9 (continued)

```
- - - - - - - - - - - - - - - - Frame 51 - - - - - - - - - - - - - - - - -

SMB:   ----- SMB Close File Response -----
SMB:
SMB:   Function = 04 (Close File)
SMB:   Net path  (NPID) = A4E6
SMB:   Process id (PID) = 10C0
SMB:
SMB:   Return code = 0,0 (OK)
SMB:
SMB:   [End of "SMB Close File Response" packet.]
SMB:
```

5.7 | PC LAN Program Parameters

A variety of the parameters introduced in section 5.3 are used to configure the PC LAN Program. The following sections discuss the details of NET START, NetBIOS, CONFIG.SYS, and AUTOEXEC.BAT.

For those of you who plan to implement the OS/2 LAN Server software, information about similar parameters is also available. Since this information is rather lengthy, interested readers are referred to section 11 of reference [5-10], and Appendices A and B of reference [5-11] for further details.

For PC LAN Program users, refer to Tables 5-1, 5-2, and 5-3 as you read.

5.7.1 | PC LAN NET START Parameters

The NET START command starts the Server, Messenger, Receiver, or Redirector services. The following command line is included in the workstation's AUTOEXEC.BAT file:

NET START configuration computername [/parameter]

Configuration: SRV, MSG, RCV, or RDR
Computername: name of the particular workstation
Parameters: 23 additional performance-affecting commands

The parameters that are used with all configurations are:

/XS	required for Extended Services.
/SRV:n	maximum number of servers with which the node can have concurrent sessions.
/ASG:n	maximum number of devices to be used simultaneously.
/SES:n	maximum number of NetBIOS sessions on the node.
/CMD:n	maximum number of NetBIOS commands on the node.
/NBC:n	maximum number of workstation buffers.
/NBS:n	maximum size (bytes) of the network buffer.
/PBx:n	maximum size (Kbytes) of the print buffer.

The parameters that are used for Server or Messenger configurations are:

/NSI	tells PC LAN not to keep the Base Services Full Screen Interface; a savings of about 32 Kbytes. This action is implied if the /XS parameter is specified.
/MBI:n	maximum size (bytes) of the message buffer.
/TSI:fb	sets the timeslice interval for foreground and background tasks.
/USN:n	maximum number of user names.

Of the above parameters, special attention should be paid to the buffer sizes (/NBC, /NBS, and /MBI) as well as the number of user names (/USN) since they are an important factor in determining the amount of RAM used by that node.

The parameters that are used only with Server configurations are:

/CAC:x   number of kilobytes of cache memory designated for disk buffering.

/REQ:n   number of concurrent workstation requests to be handled by the server.

/RQB:n   buffer size (bytes) for the request buffer.

/SHB:n   buffer size (bytes) for file sharing and block locking.

/SHL:n   defines the maximum number of active locked byte ranges in files on the server.

/PRB:n   defines size (bytes) of the server print buffer.

/PCx:n   maximum number of characters that the print server can send from the buffer to the printer in one operation.

/PRP:n   establishes the priority for printing the print buffer contents.

/SHR:n   maximum number of devices simultaneously shared by a server.

/RDR:n   maximum concurrent workstations connected to server.

Of the above parameters, the parameters that affect buffer sizes (REQ, RQB, and PRB) are especially important to server performance. See Table 5-1 for further information on the parameter limits.

Table 5-1
NET START Parameters

Parameter	Range	Mode	Extended Services Defaults	Base Services Defaults
XS		SRV, RCV, RDR	XS	na
ASG	1-32	SRV	10	5
		others	29	5
MBI	512-60K	SRV, MSG	512	1750
PRB	512-16K	SRV	512	2048
SHR	1-999	SRV	32	5
TSI	00-99	SRV, MSG	26	54
SES	1-254	SRV	Greater of 6 or (2*RDR) + USN + SRV + 2	Greater of 6 or RDR + USN + SRV + 2
		MSG	na	Greater of 6 or USN + SRV + 2
		RCV	(2*SRV) +2	6
		RDR	(2*SRV) +1	6
CMD	2-254	SRV	Greater of 8 or RDR + USN + REQ + 5	Greater of 8 or REQ + USN + 5
		MSG	na	Greater of 8 or USN + 4
		others	8	8
NBC	1-64	SRV	1	2
		<128K	2	2
		others	4	4
NBS	512-32K	SRV	512	1K
		<128K	512	512
		others	4K	4K
CAC	(K-bytes)	SRV only		
	128-3500	with EXM	88	112
	16-360	w/o EXM	88	112
NSI		SRV	na	
		MSG	na	
		others	na	na
SVR	1-31	SRV	2	3
na	Not applicable			

The following **NET START** parameter defaults are the same for Base and Extended Services:

Parameter	Range	Mode	Defaults
PCx	1-PRB	SRV	PRB
PRP	1-3	SRV	3
RDR	1-251	SRV	10
PBx	80-16K	x=1	
		<128K	512
		>128K	1024
		x=2 or 3	128
USN	0-12	SRV, MSG	1
EXM		SRV	
REQ	1-6	SRV	6
RQB	512-32K	SRV	8K
SHB	512-60K	SRV	2K
SHL	20-1000	SRV	20

5.7.2 | PC LAN NetBIOS Parameters

The DXT0MOD.SYS device driver enables NetBIOS operation and is entered into the workstation's CONFIG.SYS file. The coding format is:

```
DEVICE = d:\path\DXMTOMOD.SYS E p1=n1, p2=n2...
```

The various NetBIOS parameters (p1, p2, etc.) affect the communication capabilities of the workstation. These parameters are summarized as follows:

- E (ENABLE): enables interruption of the NetBIOS command and is only used with asynchronous communication.
- ST (STATIONS): sets maximum number of NetBIOS interface link stations.
- S (SESSIONS): sets maximum number of NetBIOS interface session.
- C (COMMANDS): sets maximum number of outstanding NetBIOS commands.
- N (NAMES): sets maximum number of NetBIOS interface names.
- O (OPEN.ON.LOAD): specifies whether the driver will open the NIC at load time.
- CR (CLOSE.ON.RESET): specifies whether the driver will close the NIC and then reopen it later should a RESET be issued.
- DG (DATAGRAM.MAX): determines if the maximum-length datagram will be determined by the NICs transmit buffer, DHB, yes or no.
- DN (DHB.NUMBER): establishes the number of transmit buffers at this NIC.
- DS (DHB.SIZE): defines the size of the NIC's transmit buffer.
- R (RECEIVE.BUFFER.SIZE): defines the size of the NIC's receive buffer.
- TT (TRANSMIT.TIMEOUT): sets the time period between query transmissions.

- TC (TRANSMIT.COUNT): sets the number of times queries are transmitted.
- MO (DLC.MAXOUT): determines the maximum outstanding transmissions without a receive acknowledgement.
- MI (DLC.MAXIN): sets the maximum outstanding receptions without a transmit acknowledgement.
- RA (RING.ACCESS): determines the NIC's ring access priority for NetBIOS messages.
- ES (EXTRA.SAPS): defines additional SAPs when the NIC is opened.
- EST (EXTRA.STATIONS): establishes the number of additional stations initialized by NetBIOS.
- RND (REMOTE.NAME.DIRECTORY): sets the number of remote names.
- RDC (REMOTE.DATAGRAM.CONTROL): used with RND to send datagrams to remote nodes.
- RV (RESET.VALUES): controls the values for ST and S when a reset is issued.
- ANR (ADAP.ADDR.NOT.REVERSED): determines if the NIC ROM address will be byte-reversed.
- RC (DLC.RETRY.COUNT): establishes the number of LLC retry attempts.
- T1 (DLC.T1): specifies the value of the LLC T1 timer.
- T2 (DLC.T2): specifies the value of the LLC T2 timer.
- TI (DLC.TI): specifies the value of the LLC TI timer.

Of these parameters, the ST, S, C, ES, EST, and DS parameters have the greatest impact on performance. See reference [5-6], section 4.2.2.6, for further information on the usage of the parameters; and references [5-7] and [5-8] for some practical examples of how to tune NetBIOS parameters for optimal performance. Table 5-2 summarizes the valid ranges for the NetBIOS parameters.

Table 5-2
NetBIOS device driver (DXMT0MOD.SYS) parameters

KEYWORD		ABBR	VALID VALUE	MIN	DEF
STATIONS	(1)	ST	0 - 254	1	6
SESSIONS		S	0 - 254	1	6
COMMANDS		C	0 - 254	1	12
NAMES		N	0 - 254	2	17
OPEN.ON.LOAD		O	Y/N	-	YES
DATAGRAM.MAX		DG	Y/N	-	NO
CLOSE.ON.RESET		CR	Y/N	-	NO
DHB.SIZE	(1)	DS	0, 200-9999	200	(3)
DHB.NUMBER	(1)	DN	0 - 9	-	(3)
RECEIVE.BUFFER.SIZE	(1)	R	0 - 9999	(2)	(3)
TRANSMIT.TIMEOUT		TT	0 - 20	0	1
TRANSMIT.COUNT		TC	0 - 10	0	6
DLC.MAXOUT		MO	0 - 9	0	2
DLC.MAXIN		MI	0 - 9	0	1
RING.ACCESS		RA	0 - 7	0	0
EXTRA.SAPS	(1)	ES	0 - 99	0	0
EXTRA.STATIONS	(1)	EST	0 - 99	0	0
REMOTE.NAME.DIRECTORY		RND	0 - 255	0	0
REMOTE.DATAGRAM.CONTROL		RDC	Y/N	-	NO
RESET.VALUES		RV	Y/N	-	NO
ADAP.ADDR.NOT.REVERSED		ANR	Y/N	-	NO
DLC.RETRY.COUNT		RC	0 - 255	0	8
DLC.T1		T1	0 - 10	0	5
DLC.T2		T2	0 - 11	0	2
DLC.TI		TI	0 - 10	0	3

NOTES:
(1) If this value is too large the adapter open will fail. Use Network Adapter resources. The maximum value allowed here typically exceeds current adapter maximum values.

(2) If a value is specified, its value is not checked by the NETBIOS Interface Device Driver. The value is checked by the adapter on open. Current adapters require a minimum value of 96.

(3) The default value set by the NETBIOS Interface Device is based upon the number of stations. Consult the following table:

Adapter	ST	DN	DS	R
TOKEN-RING	01-06	2	1048	280
PC ADAPTER	07-12	1	1048	192
with	13-18	1	600	144
8KB Shared	19-24	1	600	112
RAM	24+	1	600	96

Adapter	ST	DN	DS	R
ANY	01-32	2	2040	280
OTHER	33-48	2	1048	280
NETWORK	49-64	1	1048	280
ADAPTER	64+	1	600	144

5.7.3   PC LAN CONFIG.SYS and AUTOEXEC.BAT Parameters

Two other files, CONFIG.SYS and AUTOEXEC.BAT, can also affect PC LAN performance. How these files are configured sets the balance between RAM usage and system response time. The CONFIG.SYS options (Table 5-3) are:

- BUFFERS=20, which will improve the disk access of the server.
- FILES=100, which will allow the server to maintain multiple open files for each user.
- FCBS=m,n, which specifies the number of file control blocks that can be concurrently open. The parameters are m, which is the number of open files, and n, which is the number of files that cannot be automatically closed by DOS if the limit established by m is exceeded. Values of m, n = 16, 8 are usually good for server operations since the server treats remote FCB requests as file handle functions.
- LASTDRIVE=Z, which indicates the maximum number of real and virtual drives that can be used at one time.

The AUTOEXEC.BAT option is the FASTOPEN that improves performance by providing a file directory entry buffer. Table 5-3, taken from section 7 of reference [5-4] summarizes these above considerations.

Table 5-3
PC LAN parameters affecting performance

Paramter	Range	Explanation
NET START Command Paramters (1)		
XSS		Include to use Extended Services
SRV	1-31	Computers that can be used at one time
SES	1-254	Active NETBIOS sessions
CMD	2-254	Simultaneous NETBIOS commands on your computer
NBC	1-64	Number of network buffers (concurrent files)
NBS	512-32K	Size of network buffer
PBx	80-16K	Size of work station print buffer
PRB	512-16K	Print buffer holding data spooled to printer
PCx	1-PRB	Maximum characters sent from print buffer to printer at one time
PRP	1-3	Priority for printing contents of background print buffer
TSI	00-99	Foreground/background task time ratio
CAC (2)	128-3500	Size of disk cache (K bytes)
EXM		Use Extended Memory for cache
REQ	1-6	Concurrent work station requests to a server
RQB	512-32K	Server request buffer size
SHR (3)	1-999	Number of devices you can **NET SHARE** at one time
RDR	1-251	Concurrent network stations using server
CONFIG.SYS File Parameters		
BUFFERS	8--99	Total number of DOS buffers
	20	For Extended Services
FILES		Concurrently open files (speed impact)
	20	With a work station
	100 or more	With a server (minimal memory impact)
FCBS	1-255	Number of active files
LASTDRIVE	A-Z	Number of active real and virtual (4) drives
AUTOEXEC.BAT File Parameters		
FASTOPEN (5)	10-999	Files open concurrently for each drive

Notes on the Table of Parameters Affecting Performance:

(1) See table 5-1 for a complete list of the NET START parameters, including, the default values.
(2) Without Extended Memory, CAC is 0 or 16K -- 360K Cache can be used ineffectively, so that it degrades performance. If a file's records are not being read repetitively such as when a file is being printed, cache uses more time that it saves.
(3) Memory available may restrict this maximum value.
(4) Virtual drive refers to a fileset assigned as a drive.
(5) Number for FASTOPEN should be same number as FILES. See IBM Local Area Network Support Program User's Guide for information about other parameters in set in **AUTOEXEC.BAT** by the IBM PC LAN Support Program.

213

5.8 Protocol Analysis with Token Ring Protocols

As the previous sections attest, the IBM Token-Ring contains a number of protocols that perform specialized functions. In an attempt to put the entire package together into one comprehensive example, let us consider the process that occurs in Figure 5-10 when workstation mjl boots up and logs into network fileserver1.

Figure 5-10
Token-Ring Workstation Boot and Login Sequence Summary

Sniffer data collected on 2-Jan-90 at 16:33:04, file A:MJLBOOT.TRC, Page 1

SUMMARY		Delta T	Destination	Source	Summary
M	1		mjl	mjl	MAC Duplicate Address Test
	2	0.001	mjl	mjl	MAC Duplicate Address Test
	3	0.324	LAN Manager	mjl	MAC Report SUA Change
	4	0.013	Broadcast	mjl	MAC Standby Monitor Present
	5	0.001	Param Server	mjl	MAC Request Initialization
	6	0.001	Param Server	mjl	MAC Request Initialization
	7	0.000	Param Server	mjl	MAC Request Initialization
	8	0.000	Param Server	mjl	MAC Request Initialization
	9	0.006	NETBIOS	mjl	NET Check name TRNMIS03
	10	0.988	NETBIOS	mjl	NET Check name TRNMIS03
	11	0.499	NETBIOS	mjl	NET Check name TRNMIS03
	12	0.499	NETBIOS	mjl	NET Check name TRNMIS03
	13	0.499	NETBIOS	mjl	NET Check name TRNMIS03
	14	0.499	NETBIOS	mjl	NET Check name TRNMIS03
	15	0.500	NETBIOS	mjl	NET Check name TRNMIS03<03>
	16	0.999	NETBIOS	mjl	NET Check name TRNMIS03<03>
	17	0.499	NETBIOS	mjl	NET Check name TRNMIS03<03>
	18	0.499	NETBIOS	mjl	NET Check name TRNMIS03<03>
	19	0.499	NETBIOS	mjl	NET Check name TRNMIS03<03>
	20	0.499	NETBIOS	mjl	NET Check name TRNMIS03<03>
	21	0.430	Broadcast	mjl	MAC Standby Monitor Present
	22	0.069	NETBIOS	mjl	NET Check name TRNMIS03<00>
	23	0.999	NETBIOS	mjl	NET Check name TRNMIS03<00>
	24	0.499	NETBIOS	mjl	NET Check name TRNMIS03<00>
	25	0.499	NETBIOS	mjl	NET Check name TRNMIS03<00>
	26	0.499	NETBIOS	mjl	NET Check name TRNMIS03<00>
	27	0.499	NETBIOS	mjl	NET Check name TRNMIS03<00>
	28	0.500	NETBIOS	mjl	NET Check name TRNMIS03<05>
	29	0.999	NETBIOS	mjl	NET Check name TRNMIS03<05>
	30	0.499	NETBIOS	mjl	NET Check name TRNMIS03<05>
	31	0.500	NETBIOS	mjl	NET Check name TRNMIS03<05>

Figure 5-10 (continued)

```
32    0.499    NETBIOS       mjl           NET Check name TRNMIS03<05>
33    0.499    NETBIOS       mjl           NET Check name TRNMIS03<05>
34    0.445    Broadcast     mjl           MAC Standby Monitor Present
35    2.390    NETBIOS       mjl           NET Check name TRNMIS03<00>
36    0.678    NETBIOS       mjl           NET Check name TRNMIS03<00>
37    0.499    NETBIOS       mjl           NET Check name TRNMIS03<00>
38    0.499    NETBIOS       mjl           NET Check name TRNMIS03<00>
39    0.499    NETBIOS       mjl           NET Check name TRNMIS03<00>
40    0.499    NETBIOS       mjl           NET Check name TRNMIS03<00>
41    1.930    Broadcast     mjl           MAC Standby Monitor Present
42    6.989    Broadcast     mjl           MAC Standby Monitor Present
43    7.009    Broadcast     mjl           MAC Standby Monitor Present
44    6.989    Broadcast     mjl           MAC Standby Monitor Present
45    6.999    Broadcast     mjl           MAC Standby Monitor Present
46    0.156    NETBIOS       mjl           NET Find name MISDOM01
47    0.001    mjl           fileserver1   NET Name MISDOM01 recognized
48    0.001    fileserver1   mjl           LLC C D=F0 S=F0 SABME P
49    0.001    mjl           fileserver1   LLC R D=F0 S=F0 UA F
50    0.000    fileserver1   mjl           LLC C D=F0 S=F0 RR NR=0 P
51    0.000    mjl           fileserver1   LLC R D=F0 S=F0 RR NR=0 F
52    0.000    fileserver1   mjl           NET D=29 S=01 Session initialize
53    0.000    mjl           fileserver1   LLC R D=F0 S=F0 RR NR=1
54    0.001    mjl           fileserver1   NET D=01 S=29 Session confirm
55    0.001    fileserver1   mjl           LLC R D=F0 S=F0 RR NR=1
56    0.002    fileserver1   mjl           SMB C PC LAN PROGRAM 1.30
57    0.000    mjl           fileserver1   LLC R D=F0 S=F0 RR NR=2
58    0.002    mjl           fileserver1   SMB R Negotiated Protocol 0
59    0.001    fileserver1   mjl           LLC R D=F0 S=F0 RR NR=2
60    0.001    fileserver1   mjl           SMB C Connect A:\\MISDOM01\IBMXS
61    0.001    mjl           fileserver1   LLC R D=F0 S=F0 RR NR=3
62    0.003    mjl           fileserver1   SMB R T=3B65 Connected
63    0.001    fileserver1   mjl           LLC R D=F0 S=F0 RR NR=3
64    0.040    fileserver1   mjl           SMB C End of Process
65    0.001    mjl           fileserver1   LLC R D=F0 S=F0 RR NR=4
66    0.003    mjl           fileserver1   SMB R OK
67    0.001    fileserver1   mjl           LLC R D=F0 S=F0 RR NR=4
68    0.006    fileserver1   mjl           SMB C Get File Attributes
69    0.001    mjl           fileserver1   LLC R D=F0 S=F0 RR NR=5
70    0.005    mjl           fileserver1   SMB R OK
71    0.001    fileserver1   mjl           LLC R D=F0 S=F0 RR NR=5
72    0.005    fileserver1   mjl           SMB C Open \LISTS\LIST.U
73    0.001    mjl           fileserver1   LLC R D=F0 S=F0 RR NR=6
74    0.008    mjl           fileserver1   SMB R F=0000 Opened
75    0.001    fileserver1   mjl           LLC R D=F0 S=F0 RR NR=6
76    0.005    fileserver1   mjl           SMB C Get File Attributes
77    0.001    mjl           fileserver1   LLC R D=F0 S=F0 RR NR=7
78    0.005    mjl           fileserver1   SMB R OK
79    0.001    fileserver1   mjl           LLC R D=F0 S=F0 RR NR=7
```

Figure 5-10 (continued)

```
80   0.002   fileserver1   mjl           SMB C F=0000 Read 4096 at 0
81   0.001   mjl           fileserver1   LLC R D=F0 S=F0 RR NR=8
82   0.011   mjl           fileserver1   SMB R OK
83   0.001   fileserver1   mjl           LLC R D=F0 S=F0 RR NR=8
84   0.001   mjl           fileserver1   NET D=01 S=29 Data, 8 bytes
85   0.001   fileserver1   mjl           LLC R D=F0 S=F0 RR NR=9
86   0.018   fileserver1   mjl           SMB C F=0000 Close
87   0.001   mjl           fileserver1   LLC R D=F0 S=F0 RR NR=9
88   0.005   mjl           fileserver1   SMB R Closed
89   0.001   fileserver1   mjl           LLC R D=F0 S=F0 RR NR=10
90   3.213   NETBIOS       mjl           NET Find name MISDOM01<00>
91   0.001   mjl           fileserver1   NET Name MISDOM01<00> recognized
92   0.001   fileserver1   mjl           NET D=2A S=02 Session initialize
93   0.001   mjl           fileserver1   LLC R D=F0 S=F0 RR NR=10
94   0.001   mjl           fileserver1   NET D=02 S=2A Session confirm
95   0.001   fileserver1   mjl           LLC R D=F0 S=F0 RR NR=11
96   0.002   fileserver1   mjl           NET D=2A S=02 Data, 134 bytes
97   0.001   mjl           fileserver1   LLC R D=F0 S=F0 RR NR=11
98   0.001   mjl           fileserver1   NET D=02 S=2A Data ACK
99   0.001   fileserver1   mjl           LLC R D=F0 S=F0 RR NR=12
100  0.001   mjl           fileserver1   NET D=02 S=2A Data, 134 bytes
101  0.001   fileserver1   mjl           LLC R D=F0 S=F0 RR NR=13
102  0.000   fileserver1   mjl           NET D=2A S=02 Data ACK
103  0.001   fileserver1   mjl           NET D=2A S=02 Data, 134 bytes
104  0.000   mjl           fileserver1   LLC R D=F0 S=F0 RR NR=12
105  0.000   mjl           fileserver1   LLC R D=F0 S=F0 RR NR=13
106  0.000   mjl           fileserver1   NET D=02 S=2A Send more now
107  0.001   fileserver1   mjl           LLC R D=F0 S=F0 RR NR=14
108  0.001   fileserver1   mjl           NET D=2A S=02 Data, 134 bytes
109  0.001   mjl           fileserver1   LLC R D=F0 S=F0 RR NR=14
110  0.001   mjl           fileserver1   NET D=02 S=2A Data ACK
111  0.001   fileserver1   mjl           LLC R D=F0 S=F0 RR NR=15
112  0.052   mjl           fileserver1   NET D=02 S=2A Data, 134 bytes
113  0.001   fileserver1   mjl           LLC R D=F0 S=F0 RR NR=16
114  0.001   fileserver1   mjl           NET D=2A S=02 Data ACK
115  0.001   mjl           fileserver1   LLC R D=F0 S=F0 RR NR=15
116  0.053   fileserver1   mjl           NET D=2A S=02 Data, 134 bytes
117  0.001   mjl           fileserver1   LLC R D=F0 S=F0 RR NR=16
118  0.001   mjl           fileserver1   NET D=02 S=2A Data ACK
119  0.001   fileserver1   mjl           LLC R D=F0 S=F0 RR NR=17
120  0.106   mjl           fileserver1   NET D=02 S=2A Data, 134 bytes
121  0.001   fileserver1   mjl           LLC R D=F0 S=F0 RR NR=18
122  0.001   fileserver1   mjl           NET D=2A S=02 Data ACK
123  0.001   mjl           fileserver1   LLC R D=F0 S=F0 RR NR=17
124  0.194   fileserver1   mjl           SMB C Connect A:\\MISDOM01\IBMXS001
125  0.001   mjl           fileserver1   LLC R D=F0 S=F0 RR NR=18
126  0.005   mjl           fileserver1   SMB R T=E505 Connected
127  0.001   fileserver1   mjl           LLC R D=F0 S=F0 RR NR=19
```

Figure 5-10 (continued)

```
128   0.009   fileserver1   mjl           SMB C End of Process
129   0.001   mjl           fileserver1   LLC R D=F0 S=F0 RR NR=19
130   0.003   mjl           fileserver1   SMB R OK
131   0.001   fileserver1   mjl           LLC R D=F0 S=F0 RR NR=20
132   0.001   fileserver1   mjl           SMB C End of Process
133   0.001   mjl           fileserver1   LLC R D=F0 S=F0 RR NR=20
134   0.002   mjl           fileserver1   SMB R OK
135   0.001   fileserver1   mjl           LLC R D=F0 S=F0 RR NR=21
136   0.005   NETBIOS       mjl           NET Check name LANSMJ<03>
137   0.569   NETBIOS       mjl           NET Check name LANSMJ<03>
138   0.499   NETBIOS       mjl           NET Check name LANSMJ<03>
139   0.499   NETBIOS       mjl           NET Check name LANSMJ<03>
140   0.499   NETBIOS       mjl           NET Check name LANSMJ<03>
141   0.499   NETBIOS       mjl           NET Check name LANSMJ<03>
142   0.420   Broadcast     mjl           MAC Standby Monitor Present
143   0.008   fileserver1   mjl           LLC C D=F0 S=F0 RR NR=21 P
144   0.000   mjl           fileserver1   LLC R D=F0 S=F0 RR NR=20 F
145   0.075   fileserver1   mjl           SMB C Get File Attributes
146   0.001   mjl           fileserver1   LLC R D=F0 S=F0 RR NR=21
147   0.008   mjl           fileserver1   SMB R OK
148   0.001   fileserver1   mjl           LLC R D=F0 S=F0 RR NR=22
149   0.006   fileserver1   mjl           SMB C Open \PCLP13XS\LIST.U
150   0.001   mjl           fileserver1   LLC R D=F0 S=F0 RR NR=22
151   0.012   mjl           fileserver1   SMB R F=0000 Opened
152   0.001   fileserver1   mjl           LLC R D=F0 S=F0 RR NR=23
153   0.005   fileserver1   mjl           SMB C Get File Attributes
154   0.001   mjl           fileserver1   LLC R D=F0 S=F0 RR NR=23
155   0.005   mjl           fileserver1   SMB R OK
156   0.001   fileserver1   mjl           LLC R D=F0 S=F0 RR NR=24
157   0.003   fileserver1   mjl           SMB C F=0000 Read 4096 at 0
158   0.000   mjl           fileserver1   LLC R D=F0 S=F0 RR NR=24
159   0.005   mjl           fileserver1   SMB R OK
160   0.001   fileserver1   mjl           LLC R D=F0 S=F0 RR NR=25
161   0.005   fileserver1   mjl           SMB C F=0000 Close
162   0.001   mjl           fileserver1   LLC R D=F0 S=F0 RR NR=25
163   0.004   mjl           fileserver1   SMB R Closed
164   0.000   fileserver1   mjl           LLC R D=F0 S=F0 RR NR=26
165   0.002   fileserver1   mjl           NET D=2A S=02 Data, 134 bytes
166   0.001   mjl           fileserver1   LLC R D=F0 S=F0 RR NR=26
167   0.001   mjl           fileserver1   NET D=02 S=2A Data ACK
168   0.001   fileserver1   mjl           LLC R D=F0 S=F0 RR NR=27
169   0.079   mjl           fileserver1   NET D=02 S=2A Data, 134 bytes
170   0.001   fileserver1   mjl           LLC R D=F0 S=F0 RR NR=28
171   0.000   fileserver1   mjl           NET D=2A S=02 Data ACK
172   0.001   mjl           fileserver1   LLC R D=F0 S=F0 RR NR=27
173   0.166   fileserver1   mjl           SMB C Connect A:\\MISDOM01\IBMXS002
174   0.001   mjl           fileserver1   LLC R D=F0 S=F0 RR NR=28
175   0.005   mjl           fileserver1   SMB R T=4D Connected
```

Figure 5-10 (continued)

```
176   0.001   fileserver1   mjl           LLC R D=F0 S=F0 RR NR=29
177   0.009   fileserver1   mjl           SMB C End of Process
178   0.001   mjl           fileserver1   LLC R D=F0 S=F0 RR NR=29
179   0.003   mjl           fileserver1   SMB R OK
180   0.001   fileserver1   mjl           LLC R D=F0 S=F0 RR NR=30
181   0.001   fileserver1   mjl           SMB C End of Process
182   0.001   mjl           fileserver1   LLC R D=F0 S=F0 RR NR=30
183   0.002   mjl           fileserver1   SMB R OK
184   0.001   fileserver1   mjl           LLC R D=F0 S=F0 RR NR=31
185   0.001   fileserver1   mjl           SMB C End of Process
186   0.001   mjl           fileserver1   LLC R D=F0 S=F0 RR NR=31
187   0.002   mjl           fileserver1   SMB R OK
188   0.001   fileserver1   mjl           LLC R D=F0 S=F0 RR NR=32
189   0.003   fileserver1   mjl           NET D=2A S=02 Data, 134 bytes
190   0.001   mjl           fileserver1   LLC R D=F0 S=F0 RR NR=32
191   0.001   mjl           fileserver1   NET D=02 S=2A Data ACK
192   0.001   fileserver1   mjl           LLC R D=F0 S=F0 RR NR=33
193   0.090   mjl           fileserver1   NET D=02 S=2A Data, 134 bytes
194   0.001   fileserver1   mjl           LLC R D=F0 S=F0 RR NR=34
195   0.000   fileserver1   mjl           NET D=2A S=02 Data ACK
196   0.000   mjl           fileserver1   LLC R D=F0 S=F0 RR NR=33
```

The workstation must first perform the Ring Insertion Process in order to be both physically and logically connected to the ring. This process is embedding within the 802.5 controller chip (e.g. the Texas Instruments TMS380) and is therefore transparent to the end user. Five steps are involved: 1) the lobe media test checks the cable from the NIC to the MSAU and back; 2) the physical insertion activates the relay in the MSAU thus providing electrical continuity; 3) the uniqueness of the workstation address is verified; 4) participation in a ring poll is established to determine that workstation's upstream neighbor; and 5) the Ring Parameter Server is requested to initialize that workstation. (See reference [5-13], section 3.8.7 for further details). The steps undertaken by the Ring Insertion Process are shown in frames 1 through 5 of Figure 5-10.

Next, the workstation establishes a NetBIOS session with the server, which confirms that session (frames 46 through 54). The protocol (in this case for IBM PC LAN Version 1.30) is negotiated using SMB protocols (frames 56 and 58). Frame 60 begins the process by validating the user and setting the maximum transmit size (8240 shown in frame 62). The Domain Database (LIST.U) is then opened in frame 72. This process continues until the password is validated (frame 124), a check of the name (LANSMJ) is made (frame 136), and the process is finally completed (frame 173). Note the intermingling of DLC (layer 2), NET (layer 5), and SMB (layers 6-7) transmissions on the network. Many of these transactions are acknowledgements.

Figure 5-11 provides additional details of selected frames. See reference [5-21] for further information on token-ring network analysis with the Network General Sniffer protocol analyzer.

Figure 5-11
Token-Ring Workstation Boot Sequence Frame Details

```
Sniffer data collected on 2-Jan-90 at 16:33:04, file A:MJLBOOT.TRC, Page 1

- - - - - - - - - - - - - - - - - Frame 2 - - - - - - - - - - - - - - - - - -

DLC:  ----- DLC Header -----
DLC:
DLC:  Frame 2 arrived at  16:33:45.793  ; frame size is 18 (0012 hex) bytes.
DLC:  AC: Frame priority 0,  Reservation priority 0,  Monitor count 0
DLC:  FC: MAC frame,  PCF attention code: Express buffer
DLC:  FS: Addr recognized indicators: 00, Frame copied indicators: 00
DLC:  Destination: Station 400000000003, mjl
DLC:  Source     : Station 400000000003, mjl
DLC:
MAC:  ----- MAC data -----
MAC:
MAC:  MAC Command: Duplicate Address Test
MAC:  Source: Ring station, Destination: Ring station
MAC:


- - - - - - - - - - - - - - - - - Frame 3 - - - - - - - - - - - - - - - - - -

DLC:  ----- DLC Header -----
DLC:
DLC:  Frame 3 arrived at  16:33:46.117  ; frame size is 32 (0020 hex) bytes.
DLC:  AC: Frame priority 0,  Reservation priority 0,  Monitor count 0
DLC:  FC: MAC frame,  PCF attention code: None
DLC:  FS: Addr recognized indicators: 00, Frame copied indicators: 00
DLC:  Destination: Functional address C00000000010, LAN Manager
DLC:  Source     : Station 400000000003, mjl
DLC:
```

219

Figure 5-11 (continued)

```
MAC:  ----- MAC data -----
MAC:
MAC:  MAC Command: Report SUA Change
MAC:  Source: Ring station, Destination: LAN Manager
MAC:  Subvector type: Physical Drop Number 00000000
MAC:  Subvector type: Upstream Neighbor Address 400000000026
MAC:
```

- - - - - - - - - - - - - - - - Frame 4 - - - - - - - - - - - - - - - - -

```
DLC:  ----- DLC Header -----
DLC:
DLC:  Frame 4 arrived at  16:33:46.130  ; frame size is 32 (0020 hex) bytes.
DLC:  AC: Frame priority 0,  Reservation priority 0,  Monitor count 0
DLC:  FC: MAC frame,  PCF attention code: Standby monitor present
DLC:  FS: Addr recognized indicators: 11, Frame copied indicators: 11
DLC:  Destination: BROADCAST C000FFFFFFFF, Broadcast
DLC:  Source     : Station 400000000003, mjl
DLC:
MAC:  ----- MAC data -----
MAC:
MAC:  MAC Command: Standby Monitor Present
MAC:  Source: Ring station, Destination: Ring station
MAC:  Subvector type: Physical Drop Number 00000000
MAC:  Subvector type: Upstream Neighbor Address 400000000026
MAC:
```

- - - - - - - - - - - - - - - - Frame 5 - - - - - - - - - - - - - - - - -

```
DLC:  ----- DLC Header -----
DLC:
DLC:  Frame 5 arrived at  16:33:46.131  ; frame size is 62 (003E hex) bytes.
DLC:  AC: Frame priority 0,  Reservation priority 3,  Monitor count 0
DLC:  FC: MAC frame,  PCF attention code: None
DLC:  FS: Addr recognized indicators: 00, Frame copied indicators: 00
DLC:  Destination: Functional address C00000000002, Param Server
DLC:  Source     : Station 400000000003, mjl
DLC:
MAC:  ----- MAC data -----
MAC:
MAC:  MAC Command: Request Initialization
MAC:  Source: Ring station, Destination: Ring Parameter Server
MAC:  Subvector type: Adapter Software Level ...342279A
MAC:  Subvector type: Upstream Neighbor Address 400000000026
MAC:  Subvector type: Product Instance ID
MAC:      Machine type: 0000, Model: 000, Plant: 00, Sequence: 0000000
MAC:  Subvector type: Address Modifier 0000
MAC:
```

Figure 5-11 (continued)

```
- - - - - - - - - - - - - - - Frame 46 - - - - - - - - - - - - - - - - - -

NET:   ----- NETBIOS Name Query -----
NET:
NET:   Header length = 44, Data length = 0
NET:   Delimiter = EFFF (NETBIOS)
NET:   Command = 0A
NET:   Local session number = 1
NET:   Caller's name type = 00 (Unique name)
NET:   Receiver's name = MISDOM01
NET:   Sender's name = TRNMIS03<00>
NET:

- - - - - - - - - - - - - - - Frame 47 - - - - - - - - - - - - - - - - - -

NET:   ----- NETBIOS Name Recognized -----
NET:
NET:   Header length = 44, Data length = 0
NET:   Delimiter = EFFF (NETBIOS)
NET:   Command = 0E
NET:   Local session number = 41
NET:   Caller's name type = 00 (Unique name)
NET:   Transmit correlator = 0006
NET:   Response correlator = 4F43
NET:   Receiver's name = TRNMIS03<00>
NET:   Sender's name = MISDOM01
NET:

- - - - - - - - - - - - - - - Frame 52 - - - - - - - - - - - - - - - - - -

NET:   ----- NETBIOS Session Initialize -----
NET:
NET:   Header length = 14, Data length = 0
NET:   Delimiter = EFFF (NETBIOS)
NET:   Command = 19
NET:   Flags = 8F
NET:   1... .... = NO.ACK ability
NET:   .... 111. = Largest frame value = 7
NET:   .... ...1 = Version 2.0 or higher
NET:   Max data receive size = 2000
NET:   Transmit correlator = 4F43
NET:   Response correlator = 0007
NET:   Remote session number = 41
NET:   Local session number = 1
```

Figure 5-11 (continued)

- - - - - - - - - - - - - - - Frame 54 - - - - - - - - - - - - - - - - - - -

```
NET:   ----- NETBIOS Session Confirm -----
NET:
NET:   Header length = 14, Data length = 0
NET:   Delimiter = EFFF (NETBIOS)
NET:   Command = 17
NET:   Flags = 81
NET:   1... .... = NO.ACK ability
NET:   .... ...1 = Version 2.0 or higher
NET:   Max data receive size = 2000
NET:   Transmit correlator = 0007
NET:   Session correlator = 4F43
NET:   Remote session number = 1
NET:   Local session number = 41
NET:
```

- - - - - - - - - - - - - - - Frame 56 - - - - - - - - - - - - - - - - - - -

```
SMB:   ----- SMB Negotiate Protocol Command -----
SMB:
SMB:   Function = 72 (Negotiate Protocol)
SMB:   Tree id      (TID) = 0000
SMB:   Process id   (PID) = 0000
SMB:   Dialect = "PC LAN PROGRAM 1.30"
SMB:
```

- - - - - - - - - - - - - - - Frame 58 - - - - - - - - - - - - - - - - - - -

```
SMB:   ----- SMB Negotiate Protocol Response -----
SMB:
SMB:   Function = 72 (Negotiate Protocol)
SMB:   Tree id      (TID) = 0000
SMB:   Process id   (PID) = 0000
SMB:   Return code = 0,0 (OK)
SMB:   Flags = X1
SMB:   .... 0... = Pathnames are case sensitive
SMB:   .... ...1 = Supports subdialect (Lock&Read, Write&Unlock)
SMB:   Index of supported dialect = 0
SMB:
```

Figure 5-11 (continued)

```
- - - - - - - - - - - - - - - - Frame 60 - - - - - - - - - - - - - - - - - - - -

SMB:    ----- SMB Tree Connect Command -----
SMB:
SMB:    Function = 70 (Tree Connect)
SMB:    Tree id     (TID) = 0000
SMB:    Process id  (PID) = 0000
SMB:    File pathname = "\\MISDOM01\IBMXS"
SMB:    Password = ""
SMB:    Device name = "A:"
SMB:

- - - - - - - - - - - - - - - - Frame 62 - - - - - - - - - - - - - - - - - - - -

SMB:    ----- SMB Tree Connect Response -----
SMB:
SMB:    Function = 70 (Tree Connect)
SMB:    Tree id     (TID) = 0000
SMB:    Process id  (PID) = 0000
SMB:    Return code = 0,0 (OK)
SMB:    Maximum transmit size = 8240
SMB:    TID = 3B65
SMB:

- - - - - - - - - - - - - - - - Frame 64 - - - - - - - - - - - - - - - - - - - -

SMB:    ----- SMB End of Process Command -----
SMB:
SMB:    Function = 11 (End of Process)
SMB:    Tree id     (TID) = 3B65
SMB:    Process id  (PID) = 6049
SMB:

- - - - - - - - - - - - - - - - Frame 66 - - - - - - - - - - - - - - - - - - - -

SMB:    ----- SMB End of Process Response -----
SMB:
SMB:    Function = 11 (End of Process)
SMB:    Tree id     (TID) = 3B65
SMB:    Process id  (PID) = 6049
SMB:    Return code = 0,0 (OK)
SMB:

- - - - - - - - - - - - - - - - Frame 68 - - - - - - - - - - - - - - - - - - - -

SMB:    ----- SMB Get File Attributes Command -----
SMB:
SMB:    Function = 08 (Get File Attributes)
```

```
SMB:  Tree id      (TID) = 3B65
SMB:  Process id   (PID) = 505F
SMB:  File pathname = "\LISTS\LIST.U"
SMB:

- - - - - - - - - - - - - - - - - Frame 70 - - - - - - - - - - - - - - - - - -

SMB:  ----- SMB Get File Attributes Response -----
SMB:
SMB:  Function = 08 (Get File Attributes)
SMB:  Tree id      (TID) = 3B65
SMB:  Process id   (PID) = 505F
SMB:  Return code = 0,0 (OK)
SMB:  Attribute flags = 0020
SMB:      .... ....  ..1. .... = File(s) changed and not archived
SMB:      .... ....  ...0 .... = No directory file(s)
SMB:      .... ....  .... 0... = No volume label info
SMB:      .... ....  .... .0.. = No system file(s)
SMB:      .... ....  .... ..0. = No hidden file(s)
SMB:      .... ....  .... ...0 = No read only file(s)
SMB:  Creation date = 15-Mar-172 20:12:16
SMB:  File size = 1960 bytes
SMB:
SMB:  *** The SMB byte count records 2 extra data bytes
SMB:  Extra string parameter = ""
SMB:
```

As this chapter has described, IBM's Token-Ring and its related protocols make for a very rigorous operating system. With support for both DOS and OS/2-based network servers, the PC LAN and OS/2 LAN Server programs provide a rich networking software solution. The ties into IBM's SNA and SAA architectures are especially strong, and provide viable solutions for users who need connectivity to an IBM mid-range or mainframe processor.

5.9 | References

[5-1] IBM Token-Ring Network Introduction and Planning Guide, document GA27-3677.

[5-2] IBM Token-Ring Network Architecture Reference, document SC30-3374-02.

[5-3] IBM Token-Ring Network Problem Determination Guide, document SX27-3710.

[5-4] IBM PC Local Area Network Program Version 1.30, document number 84X0201, 1988.

[5-5] IBM Local Area Network Support Program User's Guide, document number 8575230, 1987.

[5-6] IBM PC LAN Program 1.3: A Guide to Installation and Use in a Working Environment, document number GG24-3267-00, 1988.

[5-7] Mark B. Arslan, "Guidelines for setting IBM LAN Support Program Parameters for Use With Selected IBM Products," document number GG22-9430-01, April 1989.

[5-8] Robert Panza, "Precision Tuning: Tinkering With IBM PC LAN Program Can Make it Much Faster," *LAN Magazine*, July 1989, pp. 78-97.

[5-9] IBM Operating System/2 Version 1.2 Information and Planning Guide, document G360-2650-03, second edition, 1990.

[5-10] IBM Operating System/2 Version 1.2 Server Installation and Configuration Guidelines, document number N/A, 1990.

[5-11] IBM Operating System/2 Local Area Network Server Version 1.2 Network Administrator's Guide, document G33F-9648-00, 1990.

[5-12] Institute of Electrical and Electronics Engineers, Token Ring Access Method and Physical Layer Specification, IEEE std 802.5 – 1989.

[5-13] TMS380 Adapter Chipset User's Guide, Texas Instruments, Inc., publication SPWU001, 1987.

[5-14]   J. Scott Haugdahl, *Inside the Token-Ring, Second Edition*, Architecture Technology Corporation, 1988.

[5-15]   J. Scott Haugdahl, *Inside NetBIOS*, Second Edition, Architecture Technology Corporation, 1988.

[5-16]   IBM Local Area Network Technical Reference, document SC30-3383-2, Third Edition, 1988.

[5-17]   IBM NetBIOS Application Development Guide, document S68X-2270-00, 1987.

[5-18]   IBM Token-Ring NetBIOS Program User's Guide, document 6467037.

[5-19]   W. David Schwaderer, *C Programmer's Guide to NetBIOS*, Howard W. Sams & Company, 1988.

[5-20]   IBM Personal Computer Seminar Proceedings, Volume 2, Number 8-1, May 1985, SMB Protocol.

[5-21]   Token-Ring Network Portable Protocol Analyzer Operation and Reference Manual, Network General Corporation, 1986-1988.

CHAPTER SIX

Analyzing Banyan VINES

Banyan Systems Inc.'s VINES, (Virtual Networking System) is unique among the LAN software offerings. Unlike other LAN operating systems, VINES is based upon UNIX System 5.3 rather than upon DOS or a vendor-proprietary operating system as is Novell's NetWare, IBM's PC LAN Program, and others. And like the banyan tree from which the company takes its name, VINES's strength as an operating system is in the way it creates branches for communication.

The branches of the banyan tree eventually grow to touch the ground where they re-root and start another tree. As you look at a banyan tree from a distance, it appears to have a number of "vines" (actually branches) that are touching the ground. In terms of computer networking, this re-rooting epitomizes the many communication paths available on a VINES network, and their accompanying protocols. As we will see, it is these multiple communication branches, and their associated internetworking options, that gives the VINES Operating System a unique strength in LAN and WAN connectivity, and therefore an important position in the network marketplace.

6.1 VINES Architecture and the OSI Model

The VINES architecture aligns itself very closely with the OSI Model, which is not surprising considering the large number of well-established protocols incorporated into VINES. For comparison, let's consider the various VINES elements and their relationship to the OSI model as shown in Figure 6-1a (VINES's relationship to the workstation) and Figure 6-1b (VINES's relationship to the server).

Also note the relationship between DOS which resides on the work-station and UNIX running on the server. Two Banyan references provide excellent information on the VINES architecture (reference [6-1]) and protocols (reference [6-2]).

Figure 6-1a
Banyan VINES elements and the OSI Model (workstation side)

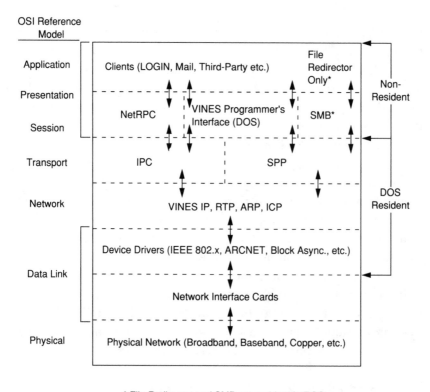

* File Redirector and SMB are resident in DOS

⇕ Flow of Data

(Courtesy of Banyan Systems Inc.)

Figure 6-1b
Banyan VINES elements and the OSI Model (server side)

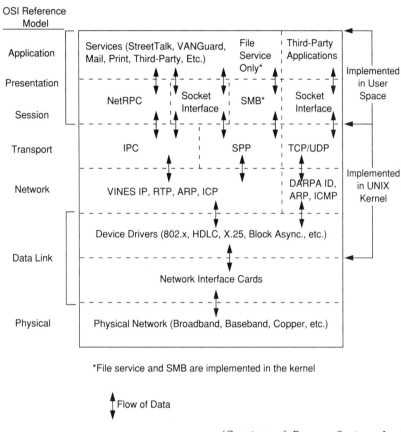

*File service and SMB are implemented in the kernel

↕ Flow of Data

(Courtesy of Banyan Systems Inc.)

The lower protocol layers encompass almost every conceivable LAN and WAN connection. The Physical Layer supports baseband and broadband LAN backbones, as well as synchronous and asynchronous connections for remote access. The Data Link Layer includes IEEE 802 standards such as 802.3 and 802.5, ARCNET, plus IBM host protocols such as SDLC (Synchronous Data Link Control) and BSC (Bisynchronous or Bisync).

At the top of the Data Link Layer (or bottom of the Network Layer, depending on your perspective) is the VINES Fragmentation Protocol (VFRP), which segments and reassembles the Network Layer packets into Data Link Layer frames. The VFRP is necessary because a transmission message may have a considerably longer frame length than the local area network or wide area link can handle. When transmission is too long, the VFRP breaks the message into smaller units, called fragments, and then hands the individual fragments to the Data Link Layer for transmission over the LAN cable.

The VINES Network Layer provides datagram service using both industry-standard protocols and Banyan's own proprietary protocols. A datagram is the VINES message that includes the Application Layer data and the appropriate headers at the Application through Network Layers. Datagram service transmits this message without acknowledgements. Banyan also provides reliable message delivery with acknowledgements and a guarantee that data is received in sequence. There is also a datastream service which acts as a data pipe between two processes rather than breaking the data up into atomic units such as messages. Both reliable message delivery and datastream service use virtual connections or "virtual circuits." These are called virtual circuits because they emulate a leased telephone line, providing first-in/first-out data delivery with no lost messages and a fixed delay. For these reasons, datagram services are called "unreliable" and reliable message delivery and datastream services are called "reliable," although the term "unreliable" has no correlation to reliability of the hardware or software itself.

The industry standard protocols implemented by VINES are the CCITT X.25 protocol, which is used for access to Public Data Networks (PDNs). VINES also uses the Internet Protocol (IP), Internet Control Message Protocol (ICMP), and Address Resolution Protocol (ARP), which are part of the U.S. Department of Defense (DoD) protocols. These DoD protocols were designed for the internetworking the dissimilar computer systems used by the various research facilities, universities, and defense contractors. Reference [6-4] describes the X.25

standard, and references [6-4] through [6-6] describe various DoD protocols.

Banyan's proprietary protocols (see reference [6-2]) include the VINES Internet Protocol (VIP), VINES Internet Control Protocol (VICP), VINES Address Resolution Protocol (VARP), and VINES Routing Update Protocol (VRTP). Both standard and proprietary protocols are used to route VINES datagrams between VINES servers, and between a VINES server and foreign networks such as PDNs. We'll look at these in greater detail in Section 6.3.

The Transport Layer supports two additional DoD protocols, the Transmission Control Protocol (TCP), and the User Datagram Protocol (UDP). It also supports two proprietary protocols. the VINES Interprocess Communications Protocol (VIPC) is used for both datagram (unreliable) and reliable message service. The VINES Sequenced Packet Protocol (VSPP) provides datastream service only. Both of these protocols are based upon XNS, the Xerox Network Services that also provides the basis for the Novell NetWare and 3Com 3+ operating systems.

The Session and Transport layers are implemented using the VINES NetRPC, the remote procedural call utility. Formerly called MatchMaker, NetRPC is a high-level programming language and compiler that provides independence between the Application Layer processes and the Transport Layer and communications subnetwork (Physical, Data Link, and Network Layer) implementations. NetRPC is a superset of the XNS Courier protocol.

The VINES Application Layer services completes the seven-layer model. These include file services, printing, and electronic mail functions; a NetBIOS emulation; and support for UNIX and DOS applications.

6.2 | The VINES Transmission Frame

Because such a large number of protocols can be embedded within a VINES transmission frame, a few definitions and illustrations are necessary at the outset (see Figure 6-2).

Figure 6-2
The Banyan VINES transmission frame

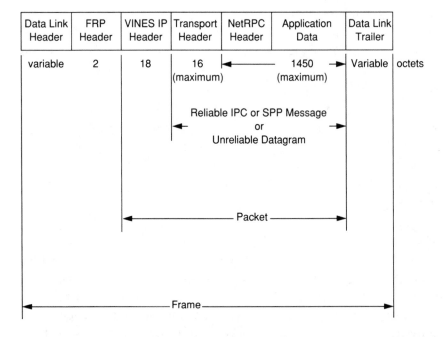

The frame begins and ends with a Data Link Layer header and trailer that is specific to the LAN in use, such as IEEE 802.3 or 802.5. Within the Data Link header would be the MAC and LLC headers, as discussed in Chapter 1.

Next comes a VINES Fragmentation Protocol (VFRP) header, which is used to break up and reassemble the Network Layer packets into multiple Data Link Layer frames. VFRP uses both sequencing and control mechanisms to recognize the beginning and end of a packet, and to properly order the fragments. We'll discuss each of the Data Link Layer headers in Section 6.3.

One frame, or possible multiple frames, contains a VINES internet packet. This begins with the VIP header, which includes node addressing information, an identifier for the higher layer protocol in use, and the length of the entire packet. We'll look at this header in detail in Section 6.4.

Next comes another Network Layer or Transport header. Depending upon the application, this could be an VRTP, VARP, or VICP Network Layer header; or an Interprocess Communications Protocol (IPC) or Sequenced Packet Protocol (SPP) Transport Layer header. An IPC virtual connection supports the transfer of reliable messages and may consist of one to four packets transmitted from a single source to a single destination. The SPP virtual connection acts as a datastream between two processes and has no theoretical data length limit. The IPC datagram is always one packet and is transmitted from a single source to one or more destinations. The Transport Layer protocols are discussed in Section 6.5.

The Session, Presentation, and Application Layer information completes the packet, beginning with the NetRPC header and application data, as required. Sections 6.6 and 6.7 are devoted to these protocols.

The Data Link trailer, which contains a Frame Check Sequence (FCS) and any other details such as the IEEE 802.5 Ending Delimiter, completes the transmission frame. We'll begin our tour of this transmission frame with the Data Link Layer.

6.3 | VINES Data Link Layer Protocols

As we already discussed, one of VINES's greatest advantages is in its communication capabilities. This strength becomes very evident when you consider the number of Data Link Layer protocols available. To

begin with, all major network architectures (ARCNET, Ethernet, token ring, and Starlan) are supported. Serial communication links between servers can use asynchronous or synchronous lines at speeds up to
64 Kbits/sec. Synchronous connections can utilize the LAPB (Link
Access Procedure-Balanced) option of the X.25 protocol to connect to
PDNs.

Remote host connections are also available, with emulations for
Digital Equipment Corporation's (DEC) VT52 and VT100 terminals as
well as the IBM 3101. To access remote IBM hosts, VINES uses a 3270
terminal emulator which allows a network workstations to emulate
the IBM 3279 color terminal. The VINES server appears as an IBM
3274 cluster controller with support for both SDLC and BSC (Bisync)
protocols. One connection between the server and the mainframe can
handle up to 96 concurrent sessions.

Now let's look in detail at the individual VINES Data Link Layer
headers for LANs.

6.3.1 | IEEE 802.2 LLC Header

For IEEE 802.x networks, the Data Link Layer header includes a
Logical Link Control (LLC) header. The LLC header, in turn, includes
the Destination Service Access Point (DSAP) and Source Service
Access Point (SSAP) addresses (review Section 1.4), plus control information.

Figure 6-3a shows these fields. It also provides the allowable values
for the DSAP and SSAP addresses used by various VINES applications.

Figure 6-3a
Banyan VINES IEEE 802.2 header

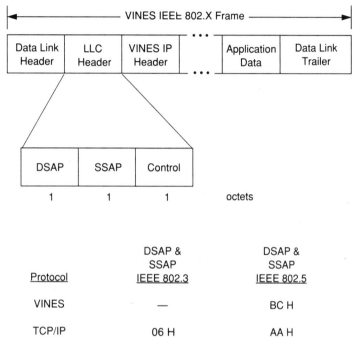

Protocol	DSAP & SSAP IEEE 802.3	DSAP & SSAP IEEE 802.5
VINES	—	BC H
TCP/IP	06 H	AA H
SNA	—	04 H

6.3.2 IEEE 802.3 Header

As we discussed in sections 1.4.2 and 1.4.3, one difference between IEEE 802.3 and Ethernet is that a Length field is used in IEEE 802.3 instead of the Type field used in Ethernet. Banyan is in the process of converting from the Ethernet frame to the IEEE 802.3 frame. As a result, the value given in the Length field indicates the type of VINES packet enclosed. These Type field values are shown in Figure 6.3b. This Length field is not interpreted at the Data Link Layer, but is passed to the higher layer (Network) process instead.

Figure 6-3b
Banyan VINES Ethernet or IEEE 802.3 header

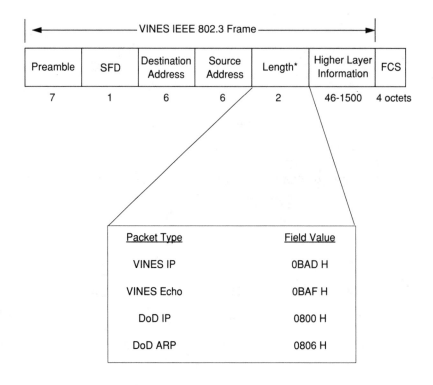

*VINES allows either an Ethernet frame (with a Type field) or an IEEE 802.3 frame (with a Length field). IEEE 802.3 frames also include an 802.2 Header, at the start of the Higher Layer Information field.

According to reference [6-2], section 2, future versions of VINES will include the SNAP header that we discussed in section 1.4.5. The LLC header (three octets) plus the SNAP header (five octets) are placed between the Length field and the Network Layer header within the 802.3 frame. The Length field will no longer indicate the VINES packet type, since the SNAP header will contain that information. Values for the 802.3 SNAP header will be:

08004A80C4H	VINES IP packets
08004A80C5H	VINES echo packets

6.3.3 | IEEE 802.5 Header

Token ring (IEEE 802.5) frames include both the LLC header and a VINES packet type immediately after the Routing Information field (see Figure 6-3c). Note that, although the 802.5 standard does not specify the length of the Information field, VINES limits it to 1,500 octets, which is similar to the maximum size of an 802.3 transmission frame.

Future versions of VINES will replace the packet type field with the SNAP header. Similar to the 802.3 implementation, the SNAP header for 802.5 frames will reside between the LLC header and the Network Layer header that is part of the higher layer information field. Values for the 802.5 SNAP header will be:

0000000800 H	DARPA IP packets
0000000806 H	DARPA ARP packets

DARPA is the Defense Advanced Research Project Agency. Two protocols used by that agency are the Internet Protocol (IP) and the Address Resolution Protocol (ARP). See section 2 of reference [6-2] for further details.

Figure 6-3c
Banyan VINES IEEE 802.5 header

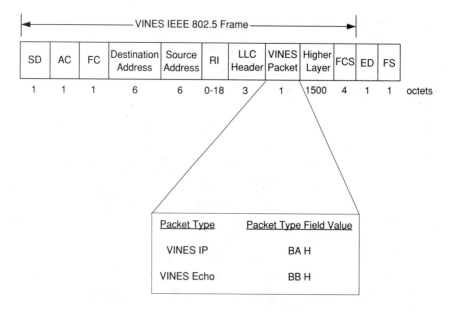

6.3.4 ARCNET Header

ARCNET, which is not an IEEE standard, has a different Data Link Layer header format (see Figure 6-3d). Included in the VINES ARCNET frame is a vendor ID, the VINES packet type, and a VINES fragmentation header. The maximum length of the higher layer information is 508 octets. The Fragmentation Protocol (VFRP) is a two-octet header which is used with Omninet, ARCNET, IBM PC Network, High-level Data Link Control (HDLC), and block asynchronous frames. The first octet of the VFRP header is a Control field that indicates if this particular frame begins or ends the VINES IP packet. The second field is a Sequence Number indicating where in the transmission sequence this frame belongs.

Figure 6-3d
Banyan VINES ARCNET header

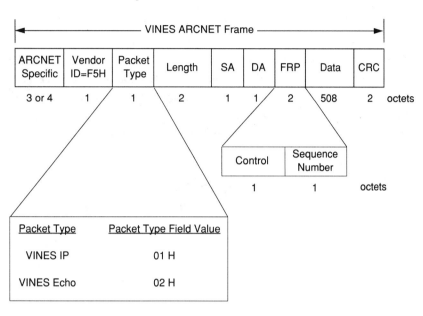

6.4   VINES Network Layer Protocols

Banyan defines the Internet Packet (shown within Figure 6-2) as a transmission entity that is routed between nodes within a VINES network. The packet consists of a maximum of 1,450 octets of information (not counting the Network and Transport Layer headers), and begins with the VINES Internet Protocol (VIP) header. Depending upon the type of transmission, either a Network Layer header or a Transport Layer header plus any data is added.

In this section we'll discuss the Network Layer protocols, Section 6.5 will be devoted to the VINES Transport Layer.

6.4.1	**The VINES IP Header**

The Internet Packet header is a derivative of XNS (see Figure 6-4) and is used to route packets through the VINES network. Taken in order, the field begin with a checksum, which is optional and is usually set to FFFFH as in NetWare, unless the Data Link Layer does not provide error control. This is followed by the packet length (which can be a maximum of 1,450 octets), Transport Control information, and a Protocol Type field. Then come the Destination and Source Network Addresses, which are six octets each.

Figure 6-4
Banyan VINES IP, IPC, and SPP headers

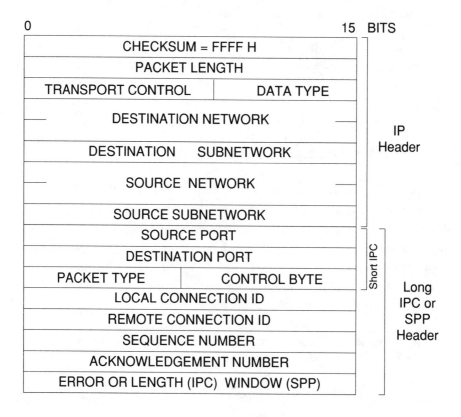

240

The Protocol Type field indicates the higher layer protocol being used within the packet. The following values are defined:

Protocol Type Field Value	Protocol Name
1	Interprocess Communications Protocol (IPC)
2	Sequenced Packet Protocol (SPP)
4	Address Resolution Protocol (ARP)
5	Routing Update Protocol (RTP)
6	Internet Control Protocol (ICP)

The addresses are presented in a NETWORK.SUBNETWORK format, with four octets allowed for the network address and two octets for the subnetwork. The VINES internetwork address (layer 3) is independent of the node address on the NIC (layer 2). The Network address (32 bits) defines the VINES logical network, which consists of both service nodes, which are usually servers, and client nodes, which are usually workstations. The service nodes are capable of routing packets and assign VINES internet addresses to client nodes. The network number is the serial number of that service node, and the subnetwork number uniquely identifies each client node. A service node uses the value of 1 for its subnetwork number.

6.4.2 | Other Network Layer Headers

VINES has three other Network Layer headers with specific purposes, as described in reference [6-2]:

1) VINES Routing Update Protocol (RTP) is used to distribute information about the network topology among the various servers.

2) Address Resolution Protocol (ARP) is used to assign internet addresses to nodes that do not already have them.

3) Internet Control Protocol (ICP) is used as a Network Layer support protocol and transmits exception information (e.g. address mismatches) and routing cost information.

These protocols are first identified in the Protocol Type Field of the IP header. The RTP, ARP, or ICP packet then follows the IP header. (The IPC or SPP headers would not exist for these cases.)

6.4.3 VINES Network Layer Protocol Examples

To exemplify the VINES Network Layer, let's consider a VINES client node (station john9) that is logging into a VINES service node (server merlinbb) over an 802.3 network (see Figure 6-5). Frame 2 (Figure 6-6) shows several clear illustrations of the Network Layer protocols discussed above as john9 attempts to login to server merlinbb. The Data Link Control (DLC) header begins with the Destination (3Com 755649) and Source (3Com 767628) addresses. Next comes the Ethertype (0BADH) assigned to VINES.

Figure 6-5
Banyan VINES Login Sequence

```
Sniffer Network Analyzer data from 30-Jan-90 at 13:07:40,
file A:JMULOGIN.ENC, Page 1

SUMMARY  Delta T    Destination   Source        Summary

M    1              Broadcast    merlinbb      VRTP  R Router update (1 nets,
     2   5.9811     merlinbb     john9         MATCH Call Port=0013 (Unknown)
     3   0.1551     john9        merlinbb      MATCH Return Port=0013
     4   0.0974     merlinbb     john9         MATCH Call Port=0013 (Unknown)
     5   0.2677     john9        merlinbb      VIPC  Ack   NS=9      NR=11
     6   0.0261     Broadcast    john9         VRTP  C Endnode Hello
     7   0.1525     john9        merlinbb      MATCH Return Port=0013
     8   0.0350     merlinbb     john9         SMB C T=14F Disconnect
     9   0.0049     john9        merlinbb      SMB C T=14F Disconnect
    10   0.0021     merlinbb     john9         VSPP  Disconnect D=0211 S=0202
    11   0.0060     merlinbb     john9         MATCH Call Port=0013 (Unknown)
    12   0.0165     john9        merlinbb      MATCH Return Port=0013
    13   0.0071     john9        merlinbb      VSPP  Data  NS=1      NR=0
    14   0.0011     merlinbb     john9         VSPP  Ack   NS=0      NR=1
    15   0.2152     merlinbb     john9         VIPC  Ack   NS=12     NR=11
```

Figure 6-5 (continued)

```
16   0.5109  john9     merlinbb  VSPP  Data  NS=2      NR=0
17   0.1342  john9     merlinbb  VSPP  Data  NS=3      NR=0
18   0.0089  merlinbb  john9     STRTK C *** UNDOCUMENTED
19   0.0025  john9     merlinbb  VSPP  Data  NS=4      NR=0
20   0.0064  john9     merlinbb  VSPP  Data  NS=5      NR=0
21   0.0010  merlinbb  john9     VSPP  Ack   NS=0      NR=5
22   0.0389  john9     merlinbb  STRTK R OK *** UNDOCUMENTED
23   0.0042  merlinbb  john9     VIPC  Data  NS=1      NR=0
24   0.0139  john9     merlinbb  VIPC  Data  NS=1      NR=1
25   0.0150  merlinbb  john9     STRTK C *** UNDOCUMENTED
26   0.0185  john9     merlinbb  STRTK R OK *** UNDOCUMENTED
27   0.0039  merlinbb  john9     VIPC  Data  NS=15     NR=13
28   0.2945  john9     merlinbb  VIPC  Ack   NS=13     NR=15
29   0.0427  merlinbb  john9     VIPC  Ack   NS=1      NR=1
30   0.0028  merlinbb  john9     VRTP  C Endnode update request
31   0.0081  john9     merlinbb  VRTP  R Router update (1 nets,
32   0.0067  john9     merlinbb  VRTP  ILLEGAL OPERATION
33   0.5952  john9     merlinbb  VIPC  Data  NS=14     NR=15
34   0.0131  merlinbb  john9     STRTK C *** UNDOCUMENTED
35   0.0200  john9     merlinbb  STRTK R OK *** UNDOCUMENTED
36   0.0038  merlinbb  john9     VIPC  Data  NS=17     NR=15
37   0.1746  john9     merlinbb  VIPC  Data  NS=16     NR=17
38   0.0094  merlinbb  john9     STRTK C *** UNDOCUMENTED
39   0.0199  john9     merlinbb  STRTK R OK *** UNDOCUMENTED
40   0.0038  merlinbb  john9     VIPC  Data  NS=19     NR=17
41   0.0432  john9     merlinbb  VIPC  Data  NS=18     NR=19
42   0.0098  merlinbb  john9     STRTK C *** UNDOCUMENTED
43   0.0188  john9     merlinbb  STRTK R OK *** UNDOCUMENTED
44   0.0040  merlinbb  john9     VIPC  Data  NS=21     NR=19
45   0.0466  john9     merlinbb  VIPC  Data  NS=20     NR=21
46   0.0089  merlinbb  john9     STRTK C *** UNDOCUMENTED
47   0.0195  john9     merlinbb  STRTK R OK *** UNDOCUMENTED
48   0.0037  merlinbb  john9     VFILE C Report Status
49   0.0097  john9     merlinbb  VFILE R OK
50   0.0173  merlinbb  john9     STRTK C Lookup  Class=Service
51   0.0196  john9     merlinbb  STRTK R OK Lookup Type=Service
52   0.0044  merlinbb  john9     VIPC  Data  NS=25     NR=23
53   0.0804  john9     merlinbb  VIPC  Data  NS=24     NR=25
54   0.0172  merlinbb  john9     STRTK C *** UNDOCUMENTED
55   0.0252  john9     merlinbb  STRTK R OK *** UNDOCUMENTED
56   0.0037  merlinbb  john9     VIPC  Data  NS=27     NR=25
57   0.2793  john9     merlinbb  VIPC  Ack   NS=25     NR=27
58   0.0834  john9     merlinbb  VIPC  Data  NS=26     NR=27
59   0.0076  merlinbb  john9     VSPP  Disconnect D=0D1B S=0356
60   0.0042  merlinbb  john9     MATCH Call Port=0013 (Unknown)
61   0.1884  john9     merlinbb  MATCH Return Port=0013
62   0.0046  merlinbb  john9     STRTK C *** UNDOCUMENTED
63   0.0183  john9     merlinbb  STRTK R OK *** UNDOCUMENTED
```

Figure 6-5 (continued)

```
64    0.0037   merlinbb     john9         MAIL  C Count New Messages
65    0.3393   john9        merlinbb      VIPC  Ack    NS=28      NR=30
66    0.3325   john9        merlinbb      MAIL  R OK
67    0.4024   merlinbb     john9         VIPC  Ack    NS=30      NR=29
```

The VINES IP header follows, indicating a packet length of 96 octets. The Transport Control fields are then filled, followed by the Protocol Type of that packet (1 for VIPC). The Destination and Source network addresses are the same (00201E23H). The Destination subnetwork is the server (address 0001H) and the source subnetwork is 8044H (john9). This packet is a NetRPC (MatchMaker) "Call" packet, so the IPC and NetRPC headers follow the IP header. The initial response from the server is received in frame 3 (also shown in Figure 6-6).

Figure 6-6
Banyan VINES Login Sequence Details

```
Sniffer Network Analyzer data from 30-Jan-90 at 13:07:40,
file A:JMULOGIN.ENC, Page 1


- - - - - - - - - - - - - - - - Frame 2 - - - - - - - - - - - - - - - -

DLC:  ----- DLC Header -----
DLC:
DLC:  Frame 2 arrived at  13:07:54.3026 ; frame size is 110 (006E hex) bytes.
DLC:  Destination: Station 3Com  755649, merlinbb
DLC:  Source     : Station 3Com  767628, john9
DLC:  Ethertype = 0BAD (Banyan VINES)
DLC:
VIP:  ----- VINES IP Header -----
VIP:
VIP: Checksum = FFFF (Null checksum)
VIP: Packet length = 96
VIP:
VIP: Transport control = 1F
VIP:         00.. .... = Unused
VIP:         ..0. .... = Do not return metric notification packet
VIP:         ...1 .... = Return exception notification packet
VIP:         .... 1111 = Hop count remaining (15)
VIP:
VIP: Protocol type = 1 (Interprocess Communications Protocol - VIPC)
VIP:
VIP: Destination network.subnetwork = 00201E23.0001
```

Figure 6-6 (continued)

```
VIP: Source network.subnetwork      = 00201E23.8044
VIP:
VIPC: ----- VINES IPC Header -----
VIPC:
VIPC: Source port     = 0355
VIPC: Destination port = 0013
VIPC:
VIPC: Packet type = 1 (Data)
VIPC:
VIPC: Control = 60
VIPC: 0... .... = Do not send immediate acknowledgment
VIPC: .1.. .... = End of message
VIPC: ..1. .... = Beginning of message
VIPC: ...0 .... = Do not abort current message
VIPC: .... 0000 = Unused
VIPC:
VIPC: Source connection ID      = 01AD
VIPC: Destination connection ID = 0044
VIPC:
VIPC: Sequence number       = 10
VIPC: Acknowledgment number = 8
VIPC:
VIPC: Length = 62
VIPC:
MATCH: ----- VINES MATCHMAKER Header -----
MATCH:
MATCH: Packet type = 0 (Call)
MATCH:
MATCH: Transaction ID    = 0
MATCH: Program number    = 0
MATCH: Version number    = 1
MATCH: Procedure value   = 24
MATCH: Procedure arguments = 00 02 00 15 6A 6D . . .


- - - - - - - - - - - - - - - Frame 3 - - - - - - - - - - - - - - - -


DLC: ----- DLC Header -----
DLC:
DLC:  Frame 3 arrived at  13:07:54.4578 ; frame size is 118 (0076 hex) bytes.
DLC:  Destination: Station 3Com  767628, john9
DLC:  Source     : Station 3Com  755649, merlinbb
DLC:  Ethertype = 0BAD (Banyan VINES)
VIP: ----- VINES IP Header -----
VIP: Checksum = FFFF (Null checksum)
VIP: Packet length = 104
VIP:
VIP: Transport control = 1F
VIP:         00.. .... = Unused
```

Figure 6-6 (continued)

```
VIP:            ..0. .... = Do not return metric notification packet
VIP:            ...1 .... = Return exception notification packet
VIP:            .... 1111 = Hop count remaining (15)
VIP:
VIP: Protocol type = 1 (Interprocess Communications Protocol - VIPC)
VIP:
VIP: Destination network.subnetwork = 00201E23.8044
VIP: Source network.subnetwork      = 00201E23.0001
VIPC: ----- VINES IPC Header -----
VIPC: Source port       = 0013
VIPC: Destination port = 0355
VIPC:
VIPC: Packet type = 1 (Data)
VIPC:
VIPC: Control = 60
VIPC: 0... .... = Do not send immediate acknowledgment
VIPC: .1.. .... = End of message
VIPC: ..1. .... = Beginning of message
VIPC: ...0 .... = Do not abort current message
VIPC: .... 0000 = Unused
VIPC:
VIPC: Source connection ID       = 0044
VIPC: Destination connection ID = 01AD
VIPC:
VIPC: Sequence number       = 9
VIPC: Acknowledgment number = 10
VIPC: Length = 70
MATCH: ----- VINES MATCHMAKER Header -----
MATCH: Packet type = 2 (Return)
MATCH:
MATCH: Transaction ID   = 0
MATCH: Procedure results = 00 20 1E 23 00 01 . . .
```

6.5 VINES Transport Layer Protocols

The VINES Transport Layer provides the end-to-end communication between two user processes. These users might be operating on different machines or in different cities. Two proprietary Transport Layer Protocols are implemented: IPC and SPP.

Three types of services are provided. An IPC datagram is a discrete, single transmission that is not acknowledged and may arrive out of sequence. A datagram contains one VINES IP packet and may have up to 1,450 octets of data. An IPC reliable message is an acknowledged transmission that arrives in sequence and may contain one to four VINES IP packets. It may carry up to 5,800 octets of data. These transmissions are also collectively known as an IPC Virtual Connection, which is a process-to-process communication path that allows for the exchange of an unlimited amount of data. These connections are acknowledged and flow controlled.

Flow control is an issue between data sender and data receiver. The problem that must be solved is how to keep a fast sender from overwhelming a slow receiver with more data than it can accept and process at a time. Printers demonstrate the flow control process with the XON/XOFF protocol.

From the user's point of view, SPP provides a means of sending and receiving an endless stream of data, whereas "reliable" IPC is viewed by the user as a method of sending discrete, reliable, ordered, messages of limited length (i.e., a multi-VIP packet reliable datagram).

For example, you could ask VINES to send 64K octets of data on an SPP connection. You assume that the data will be sent reliably, and in sequence, to the other end of the connection. The only indication of failure would be if the user receives a disconnect.

Reliable IPC, on the other hand, allows you to send 5,800 octets (4 * 1,450) at a time, maximum, and you are told of the successful reception of the data. If the data is not received you get a "timeout" error. Each message you send is done in order, but there is no flow control.

Common to both IPC and SPP is the VINES Transport Layer addressing scheme, which contains two levels. Higher layer protocols access the VINES Transport Layer at a socket. Associated with that socket is a message queue called a port. Each port has an eight-octet (64-bit) address. The high-order six octets are the internet address of that node. The low-order two octets specify the local port number. Ports can either be well-known, such as those reserved for VINES and third-party applications such as StreetTalk, or transient, which are assigned dynamically as necessary. Given this common foundation, let's discuss the IPC and SPP protocols in more detail.

6.5.1 | VINES IPC and SPP Protocol Headers

The VINES IPC protocol provides both unreliable datagram and reliable message services. VINES SPP is used for virtual connection (datastream) services. Both IPC and SPP use the same IP header format at layer 3, and then use different header formats at layer 4 (review Figure 6-4).

The IPC header also has two different formats. The short header (six octets in length) is used for unreliable datagram services and includes the Source and Destination Port addresses (two octets each), the Packet Type (one octet), plus a Control byte. Since datagram service is defined as being unsequenced, no sequence counters or acknowledgements are included. The IPC packet types are:

Packet Field Value	Packet Type	Usage
0	Datagram	IPC Only
1	Data	Reliable IPC and SPP
2	Error	Reliable IPC and SPP
3	Disconnect	Reliable IPC and SPP
4	Probe	Reliable IPC and SPP
5	Acknowledgement	Reliable IPC and SPP

The long header (16 octets in length) is used for reliable IPC messages and SPP virtual connections. In addition to the first six octets of the short IPC header, several fields have been added to support the reliable transmissions. The Local and Remote Connection fields (two octets each) identify both the sending and receiving entities. The Sequence number (two octets) indicates the sending sequence number for this packet. The Acknowledgement number (two octets) indicates the last packet accepted by the receiver. The Error field is used for error packets only. The Length and Control Byte fields are used in data packets only. Data from the higher layers would then follow the IPC header.

The Sequenced Packet Protocol (SPP) is used to provide virtual connection (or datastream) service. Its header is identical to the long IPC header (Figure 6-4), except that the field just prior to the data field (Length) in the IPC header is replaced with a Window field which handles flow control. Flow control at the Transport Layer (SPP for VINES) assures that a process on one workstation does not overwhelm a process at another workstation or server with too much data. The number in the Window field indicates the highest sequence number that can be accepted by the receiving SPP entity.

6.5.2 | VIPC Example

Returning to the login sequence (Figure 6-5), let's examine frames 2 and 3 in detail (Figure 6-6). The VINES IPC header defines the Source (0355H) and Destination (0013H) ports, along with a Packet Type (1) for a data packet. The Source Connection ID is 01ADH and the Destination Connection ID is 0044H. The Length field specifies a data packet length of 62 octets, which contains a NetRPC (MatchMaker) Call packet.

Frame 3 is the response from the server. Note that the Source and Destination port numbers are reversed from frame 2, as are the Source and Destination connection numbers. This data packet has a length of 70 octets and is a NetRPC (MatchMaker) Return packet.

6.5.3 | VSPP Example

An exchange of sequenced data is shown in frames 16 and 17 (Figure 6-7). Notice that all the Source and Destination fields at layers 2, 3, and 4 are the same for frames 16 and 17, since these are two sequential frames transmitted from the server (merlinbb) to the workstation (john9). The SPP header is similar to the IPC headers discussed above, except for the last three entries: Sequence, Acknowledgement, and Window.

Note that the Sequence changes in increments (2 in frame 16 and then 3 in frame 17) The Acknowledgement stays the same (0), since no packets have been received from the workstation between frames 16 and 17. The Window value (4) remains constant as well. The data concluding both frames was part of the user profile downloaded from the server to the workstation at login time.

Figure 6-7
Banyan VINES Login Sequence SPP Details

```
Sniffer Network Analyzer data from 30-Jan-90 at 13:07:40,
file A:JMULOGIN.ENC, Page 1


- - - - - - - - - - - - - - - Frame 16 - - - - - - - - - - - - - - - - -

DLC:  ----- DLC Header -----
DLC:
DLC:  Frame 16 arrived at  13:07:55.8008 ; frame size is 83 (0053 hex) bytes.
DLC:  Destination: Station 3Com  767628, john9
DLC:  Source     : Station 3Com  755649, merlinbb
DLC:  Ethertype = 0BAD (Banyan VINES)
DLC:
VIP: ----- VINES IP Header -----
VIP:
VIP: Checksum = FFFF (Null checksum)
VIP: Packet length = 69
VIP:
VIP: Transport control = 1F
VIP:        00.. .... = Unused
VIP:        ..0. .... = Do not return metric notification packet
VIP:        ...1 .... = Return exception notification packet
VIP:        .... 1111 = Hop count remaining (15)
VIP:
VIP: Protocol type = 2 (Sequenced Packet Protocol - VSPP)
VIP:
VIP: Destination network.subnetwork = 00201E23.8044
VIP: Source network.subnetwork      = 00201E23.0001
VSPP: ----- VINES SPP Header -----
VSPP:
VSPP: Source port      = 0D1B
VSPP: Destination port = 0356
```

Figure 6-7 (continued)

```
VSPP:
VSPP: Packet type = 1 (Data)
VSPP:
VSPP: Control = 60
VSPP: 0... .... = Do not send immediate acknowledgment
VSPP: .1.. .... = End of message
VSPP: ..1. .... = Beginning of message
VSPP: ...0 .... = Do not abort current message
VSPP: .... 0000 = Unused
VSPP:
VSPP: Source connection ID      = 002D
VSPP: Destination connection ID = 01B1
VSPP:
VSPP: Sequence number      = 2
VSPP: Acknowledgment number = 0
VSPP: Window               = 4
VSPP:
VSPP: Data = 02 2F 62 3A 22 6A . . .
- - - - - - - - - - - - - - - - Frame 17 - - - - - - - - - - - - - - - - - -

DLC: ----- DLC Header -----
DLC:
DLC: Frame 17 arrived at  13:07:55.9350 ; frame size is 604 (025C hex) bytes.
DLC: Destination: Station 3Com  767628, john9
DLC: Source     : Station 3Com  755649, merlinbb
DLC: Ethertype = 0BAD (Banyan VINES)
DLC:
VIP: ----- VINES IP Header -----
VIP:
VIP: Checksum = FFFF (Null checksum)
VIP: Packet length = 590
VIP:
VIP: Transport control = 1F
VIP:        00.. .... = Unused
VIP:        ..0. .... = Do not return metric notification packet
VIP:        ...1 .... = Return exception notification packet
VIP:        .... 1111 = Hop count remaining (15)
VIP:
VIP: Protocol type = 2 (Sequenced Packet Protocol - VSPP)
VIP:
VIP: Destination network.subnetwork = 00201E23.8044
VIP: Source network.subnetwork      = 00201E23.0001
VIP:
VSPP: ----- VINES SPP Header -----
VSPP:
VSPP: Source port      = 0D1B
VSPP: Destination port = 0356
VSPP:
```

Figure 6-7 (continued)

```
VSPP: Packet type = 1 (Data)
VSPP:
VSPP: Control = 60
VSPP: 0... .... = Do not send immediate acknowledgment
VSPP: .1.. .... = End of message
VSPP: ..1. .... = Beginning of message
VSPP: ...0 .... = Do not abort current message
VSPP: .... 0000 = Unused
VSPP: Source connection ID      = 002D
VSPP: Destination connection ID = 01B1
VSPP: Sequence number      = 3
VSPP: Acknowledgment number = 0
VSPP: Window              = 4
VSPP: Data = 01 6C 70 74 32 20 . . .
```

6.6 VINES Session and Presentation Layer Protocols

The VINES Session Layer coordinates communication between two different processes on the network. The Presentation Layer makes sure that these two processes can understand one another by making syntax (data format) conversions as necessary.

Both of these VINES layers are implemented with the NetRPC protocols. (NetRPC was formerly known as the MatchMaker Remote Procedural Calls for Session layer, and MatchMaker Data Type Representations for Presentation layer.) Within the RPC mechanism, a workstation that needs a service (known as a client) makes a request to a provider (known as a service). The client and service can exist on different nodes, or on different networks for that matter.

We looked at the RPC header (Figure 6-2) when we were discussing the overall VINES frame structure. The exact makeup of that header varies with the exact type of NetRPC message. There are seven types of NetRPC messages:

Call: which is from a client requesting a specific service.

Reject: which indicates to the client that the RPC could not be processed.

Abort: which indicates that the RPC was aborted.

Return: which provides the results of the RPC to the client.

Search: which enables the client to locate a particular distributed service within the network.

Search-all: which is used when the client wants to locate a set of services.

Return address: which is the response to a Search or Search-all.

Since each of these remote procedure calls vary in function, the RPC header varies in length and contents as well. See reference [6-2], chapter 5, for more details.

6.7 VINES Application Layer Protocols

The VINES Application Layer protocols support a variety of VINES and third-party applications. These protocols can be divided into three different categories.

The first category is the Basic Services, which support network administration, electronic mail, network security, and MS/PC-DOS file service. StreetTalk, which is VINES global naming service, and VANGuard, which provides security features, are two examples of these basic services. Next, Gateway Services support the connectivity options within VINES, such as 3270/SNA, 3270/BSC, and asynchronous terminal emulation capabilities. Finally, the Utility Services are concerned with network integrity, backup, and recovery functions.

Reference [6-7] is a directory of applications compatible with the VINES operating system. References [6-8] and [6-9] are useful for application developers.

6.8 | Protocol Analysis with VINES

As a final example of the VINES protocols in action, let's consider the interaction between two servers: merlinbb, (from our earlier example) and denver50 (the server on another network).

The protocol analyzer was placed on the LAN cable between these two servers and most of the interaction occurs between the NIC in merlinbb, which is connected to the internetwork (denoted as merdenlink), and the other server (denver50). In this example, a workstation on the merlin backbone network (john9) logs into the remote server (denver50) shown in Figure 6-8.

Figure 6-8
Banyan VINES Server to Server Communication

```
Sniffer Network Analyzer data from 30-Jan-90 at 13:41:12.
file A:SRVRLINK.ENC. Page 1

SUMMARY  Delta T      Destination    Source         Summary

M    1                Broadcast      denver50       VRTP  R Router update (1 nets.
     2    0.9986      Broadcast      merdenlink     VRTP  R Router update (1 nets.
     3    1.6187      Broadcast      3Com  915753   VRTP  C Endnode Hello
     4    1.5227      denver50       3Com  756067   VSPP  Ack   NS=8      NR=49
     5    4.0674      Broadcast      john10         VRTP  C Endnode Hello
     6    5.5961      Broadcast      3Com  756067   VRTP  C Endnode Hello
     7    0.0627      3Com  756067   denver50       VSPP  Ack   NS=49     NR=8
     8    0.1712      merdenlink     3Com  915753   VSPP  Ack   NS=8      NR=49
     9   10.5866      denver50       merdenlink     STRTK C Operation
    10    0.0254      merdenlink     denver50       STRTK R OK Operation
    11    0.0415      denver50       merdenlink     VSRV  C ** UNDOCUMENTED
    12    0.0055      merdenlink     denver50       VSRV  R OK
    13    0.0124      denver50       merdenlink     MATCH Call Port=0013 (Unknown)
    14    0.0075      merdenlink     denver50       MATCH Call Port=0013 (Unknown)
    15    0.0078      denver50       merdenlink     MATCH Return Port=0013
    16    0.0111      merdenlink     denver50       MATCH Return Port=0013
    17    0.0057      denver50       merdenlink     VICP  Metric=0.4
```

Figure 6-8 (continued)

```
18   0.0913   denver50     merdenlink   MATCH Call Port=0013 (Unknown)
19   0.3007   merdenlink   denver50     VIPC  Ack
20   0.0010   merdenlink   denver50     VIPC  Ack    NS=3      NR=3
21   0.0050   merdenlink   denver50     MATCH Return Port=0013
22   0.0549   denver50     merdenlink   MATCH Call Port=0013 (Unknown)
23   0.0078   merdenlink   denver50     MATCH Return Port=0013
24   0.0067   merdenlink   denver50     VSPP  Data   NS=1      NR=0
25   0.0065   denver50     merdenlink   VICP  Metric=0.4
26   0.0014   denver50     merdenlink   VSPP  Ack    NS=0      NR=1
27   0.3187   denver50     merdenlink   VIPC  Ack    NS=3      NR=3
28   0.1882   merdenlink   denver50     VSPP  Data   NS=2      NR=0
29   0.0024   merdenlink   denver50     VSPP  Data   NS=3      NR=0
30   0.0161   denver50     merdenlink   STRTK C *** UNDOCUMENTED
31   0.0095   merdenlink   denver50     STRTK C Operation
32   0.0183   denver50     merdenlink   STRTK R OK Operation
33   0.0069   merdenlink   denver50     STRTK R OK *** UNDOCUMENTED
34   0.0104   denver50     merdenlink   VIPC  Data   NS=5      NR=4
35   0.0061   merdenlink   denver50     VIPC  Data   NS=5      NR=5
36   0.0219   denver50     merdenlink   STRTK C *** UNDOCUMENTED
37   0.0156   merdenlink   denver50     STRTK R OK *** UNDOCUMENTED
38   0.0102   denver50     merdenlink   VIPC  Data   NS=7      NR=6
39   0.0060   merdenlink   denver50     VIPC  Data   NS=7      NR=7
40   0.0215   denver50     merdenlink   STRTK C *** UNDOCUMENTED
41   0.0112   merdenlink   denver50     STRTK C Operation
42   0.0158   denver50     merdenlink   STRTK R OK Operation
43   0.0075   merdenlink   denver50     STRTK R OK *** UNDOCUMENTED
44   0.0314   denver50     merdenlink   STRTK C *** UNDOCUMENTED
45   0.0099   merdenlink   denver50     STRTK C Operation
46   0.0166   denver50     merdenlink   STRTK R OK Operation
47   0.0068   merdenlink   denver50     STRTK R OK *** UNDOCUMENTED
48   0.0064   denver50     merdenlink   VSPP  Ack    NS=0      NR=3
49   0.0228   denver50     merdenlink   STRTK C *** UNDOCUMENTED
50   0.0123   merdenlink   denver50     STRTK C Operation
51   0.0151   denver50     merdenlink   STRTK R OK Operation
52   0.0079   merdenlink   denver50     STRTK R OK *** UNDOCUMENTED
53   0.0296   denver50     merdenlink   STRTK C *** UNDOCUMENTED
54   0.0109   merdenlink   denver50     STRTK C Operation
55   0.0175   denver50     merdenlink   STRTK R OK Operation
56   0.0067   merdenlink   denver50     STRTK R OK *** UNDOCUMENTED
57   0.0374   denver50     merdenlink   STRTK C Lookup   Class=Service
58   0.0110   merdenlink   denver50     STRTK C Operation
59   0.0155   denver50     merdenlink   STRTK R OK Operation
60   0.0083   merdenlink   denver50     STRTK R OK Lookup Type=Service
61   0.0352   denver50     merdenlink   VSPP  Disconnect D=03DB S=020D
62   0.0044   denver50     merdenlink   MATCH Call Port=0013 (Unknown)
63   0.0439   merdenlink   denver50     MATCH Return Port=0013
64   0.0102   denver50     merdenlink   STRTK C *** UNDOCUMENTED
65   0.0102   merdenlink   denver50     STRTK C Operation
```

Figure 6-8 (continued)

```
66   0.0164   denver50       merdenlink    STRTK R OK Operation
67   0.0064   merdenlink     denver50      STRTK R OK *** UNDOCUMENTED
68   0.3338   denver50       merdenlink    VIPC  Ack    NS=14     NR=14
69   0.0180   merdenlink     denver50      VIPC  Ack    NS=10     NR=10
70   3.1625   3Com  915753 merdenlink      VSPP  Ack    NS=49     NR=8
```

Details of the server-to-server communication begin in frame 9 (see Figure 6-9) with the calling server (merdenlink) using the StreetTalk protocols to locate the remote server. A response is provided in frame 10. Then the NetRPC (MatchMaker) protocols begin the process of connecting the workstation (john9) to the remote server (denver50). Frames 13 and 14 initiate and confirm the beginning of this procedure, and Frame 15 passes the various arguments from the first server (merlinbb) to the second (denver50). These arguments (not shown) include the StreetTalk name (ddemo@demogroup@denver50), plus the NIC address (3Com 767628) of the calling NIC (john9). This process continues until the remote login is complete after frame 61. For further details on VINES protocol analysis with the Network General Sniffer protocol analyzer, see reference [6-10].

The seamless manner in which this remote login was completed illustrates VINES's strength in both LAN and WAN communications. The local workstation (john9) could connect to a remote server (denver50), which then established a remote, asynchronous connection from Denver to Boston via a dial-up connection. The entire process took only a few seconds and was painless for the user — an excellent example of the VINES protocols in action.

Figure 6-9
Banyan VINES Server to Server Communication Details

```
Sniffer Network Analyzer data from 30-Jan-90 at 13:41:12,
file A:SRVRLINK.ENC, Page 1

- - - - - - - - - - - - - - - - Frame 9 - - - - - - - - - - - - - - - - -


STRTK: ----- VINES StreetTalk Header -----
STRTK:
STRTK: Matchmaker packet type = 0 (Call)
STRTK: Procedure value = 16 (Operation)
STRTK:
STRTK:

- - - - - - - - - - - - - - - - Frame 10 - - - - - - - - - - - - - - - -


STRTK: ----- VINES StreetTalk Header -----
STRTK:
STRTK: Matchmaker packet type = 2 (Return)
STRTK: Procedure value = 16 (Operation) [Found in frame 9]
STRTK:
STRTK:

- - - - - - - - - - - - - - - - Frame 11 - - - - - - - - - - - - - - - -


VSRV: ----- VINES SERVER SERVICE Header -----
VSRV:
VSRV: Matchmaker packet type = 0 (Call)
VSRV: Procedure value = 19 (** UNDOCUMENTED FUNCTION **)
VSRV:
VSRV:

- - - - - - - - - - - - - - - - Frame 12 - - - - - - - - - - - - - - - -


VSRV: ----- VINES SERVER SERVICE Header -----
VSRV:
VSRV: Matchmaker packet type = 2 (Return)
VSRV:
```

Figure 6-9 (continued)

```
- - - - - - - - - - - - - - - - - Frame 13 - - - - - - - - - - - - - - - - - -

MATCH: ----- VINES MATCHMAKER Header -----
MATCH:
MATCH: Packet type = 0 (Call)
MATCH:
MATCH: Transaction ID    = 0
MATCH: Program number    = 0
MATCH: Version number    = 1
MATCH: Procedure value   = 0
MATCH: Procedure arguments = 79 4C
MATCH:

- - - - - - - - - - - - - - - - Frame 14 - - - - - - - - - - - - - - - - - -

MATCH: ----- VINES MATCHMAKER Header -----
MATCH:
MATCH: Packet type = 0 (Call)
MATCH:
MATCH: Transaction ID    = 0
MATCH: Program number    = 0
MATCH: Version number    = 1
MATCH: Procedure value   = 16
MATCH: Procedure arguments = 00 03 00 20 1E 23 . . .
```

6.9 | References

[6-1] Banyan Systems Inc., VINES Architecture Definition, document 092015-001, 1988.

[6-2] Banyan Systems Inc., VINES Protocol Definition, document DA254-00, 1989.

[6-3] The International Telegraph and Telephone Consultation Committee, Recommendation X.25, Blue Book Volume VIII - Fascicle VIII.2, 1989.

[6-4] Most documentation on ARPANET, TCP/IP, and related protocols are contained in Request for Comment (RFC) papers circulated within the research community. These are available from the DDN Network Information Center, SRI International, (415) 859-3695 or (800) 235-3155.

Of special interest is *RFC-1000, the Request for Comments Reference Guide.*

[6-5]   Internet Protocol (IP), RFC-791, DDN Network Information Center, September 1981.

[6-6]   Transmission Control Protocol, RFC-793, DDN Network Information Center, September 1981.

[6-7]   Banyan Systems Inc., Application Directory, document 092012-003, April 1989.

[6-8]   Banyan Systems Inc., VINES Application Developer's Guide, document 092044-000, 1989.

[6-9]   Banyan Systems Inc., VINES Programmer's Interface (DOS), document 092014-002, 1986.

[6-10]   Ethernet Network Portable Protocol Analyzer Operation and Reference Manual, Network General Corporation, 1986-1988.

CHAPTER SEVEN

Analyzing Apple Computer's AppleTalk

Apple Computer's AppleTalk is an operating system with an architecture designed using the same philosophy behind developing the Apple Macintosh: to provide an easy-to-use user interface with "plug-and-play" networking capabilities. The concept of "plug-and-play" was designed into the Macintosh itself, since there is a LocalTalk network interface built into the computer. For example, a Mac connected to a LaserWriter printer could be easily configured with only a twisted-pair cable between them. This type of twisted-pair connection has come to be called LocalTalk, where the network architecture itself is referred to as AppleTalk.

There are many companies supporting AppleTalk networks. For example, Farallon Computing Inc., duPont Electronics, and Dayna Communications offer twisted-pair and fiber-optic cabling alternatives. Many firms, including Apple, Adaptec Inc., Everex, Racal-Interlan, Standard Microsystems Corporation, and Thomas-Conrad Corporation, supply network interface cards (NICs) for Ethernet/IEEE 802.3, token ring (IEEE 802.5), and ARCNET networks. Repeaters are available from such firms as TOPS Division, Sun Microsystems Inc., and Hayes Microcomputer Products Inc. Routers for internetworking are available from Apple and Kinetics Inc. Gateways for using TCP/IP within AppleTalk protocols can be obtained from Kinetics and Cayman Systems Inc. In addition, other operating systems vendors support the Macintosh and AppleTalk protocols within their networks, including TOPS, 3Com, and Novell. Apple provides AppleTalk protocol stacks for MS-DOS and DEC VMS environments as well. In summary, AppleTalk is a well-respected architecture with more than 2 million nodes installed on more than 250,000 networks.

What's more, Apple continues to enhance the AppleTalk architecture. AppleTalk Phase 1 (1985) can handle up to 254 node connections per network. Phase 2 (1989) adds extended addressing that can accommodate up to 16 million unique nodes. Support for token-ring networks (IEEE 802.5) also has been added with Phase 2. Phases 1 and 2 are also referred to as non-extended and non-extended networks, respectively. There are some differences between Phases 1 and 2 protocols, primarily at the Network Layer for routers. We'll point out those differences as they are encountered throughout this chapter.

Several references are invaluable for a more detailed study of the AppleTalk protocols. The Macintosh series (reference [7-1]) has good information about Macintosh communication issues as well as AppleTalk. The AppleTalk System Overview (reference [7-2]) provides a high-level tutorial on the network from Apple's perspective, while reference [7-3] discusses the TOPS network and other vendors' products. Bit-level detail on all the AppleTalk protocols is given in references [7-4] and [7-5], which cover AppleTalk Phase 1 and Phase 2, respectively.

To begin, we'll compare the AppleTalk architecture with the OSI Reference Model.

7.1 AppleTalk and the OSI Model

As in previous chapters, we'll begin our tour through the OSI model at the Physical and Data Link Layers (see Figure 7-1). AppleTalk defines Ethernet (the DEC, Intel, and Xerox versions) and LocalTalk in Phase 1; and CSMA/CD bus networks (IEEE 802.3) and token ring (IEEE 802.5) in Phase 2. In addition, Phase 2 packets use the IEEE 802.2 and Subnetwork Access Protocol (SNAP) headers (review section 1.4.5) within 802.3 or 802.5 frames.

Figure 7-1
Comparing AppleTalk with the OSI Model

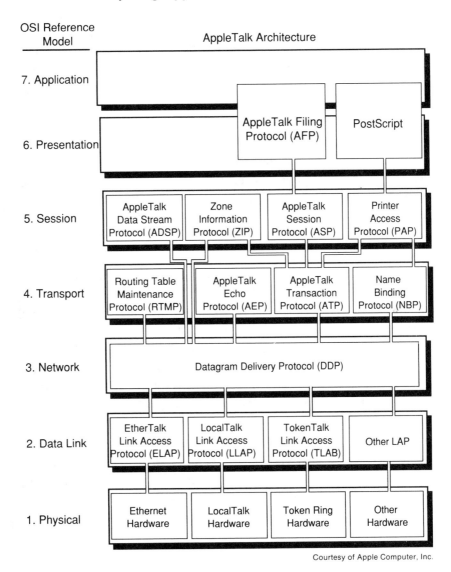

Courtesy of Apple Computer, Inc.

The Network Layer is implemented using the Datagram Delivery Protocol (DDP) which provides for communication between two sockets, which are the addressable entities within a node. Another protocol, the AppleTalk Address Resolution Protocol or AARP (not shown in Figure 7-1), provides the address translations between the hardware (Data Link Layer) address and the higher layer (DDP) address.

The Transport Layer includes four different protocols. The Routing Table Maintenance Protocol (RTMP) updates the internet routers with current information about the network. The AppleTalk Echo Protocol (AEP) is used for maintenance and delay measurements and allows one node to send a datagram to another and have that node echo back to the source. The Name Binding Protocol (NBP) provides translations between character names and the corresponding internet socket addresses on a distributed basis, and without a central database. Finally, the AppleTalk Transaction Protocol (ATP) provides reliable, sequential, socket-to-socket transmissions, plus "exactly-once" transmissions.

Four protocols also are available at the Session Layer. The AppleTalk Session Protocol (ASP) opens, maintains, and closes sessions between sockets. The AppleTalk Data Stream Protocol (ADSP) provides reliable, byte-streamed service between two sockets. The Zone Information Protocol (ZIP) maintains an internet-wide map of the zones within the network, and maps zone names to specific network numbers. Finally, the Printer Access Protocol (PAP) is used for transactions between network devices and Apple LaserWriter printers.

Two protocols are defined at the Presentation and Application Layers. The first is the AppleTalk Filing Protocol (AFP), which handles remote file access. The second is PostScript, a language understood by LaserWriter printers for desktop publishing. We'll look in detail at the individual layers next.

7.2 | AppleTalk Data Link Layer Protocols

As we have touched on, there are differences between AppleTalk Phases 1 and 2. One of the significant changes is the increase in the number of addressable nodes allowable per network, from 254 in Phase 1 to more than 16 million in Phase 2.

Phase 1 uses the Destination/Source node ID (one octet each) from the Link Access Protocol (LAP) header to uniquely identify each node. In an internet environment, an additional two-octet network number specifies the physical cable to which that node is attached. Phase 1 only allows one network number per cable.

In Phase 2, extended addressing always includes the network number (two octets) plus the node ID (one octet) of the DDP header. Phase 2 allows more than one network number, specified as a contiguous range, per cable. Extended addressing permits up to 16,515,334 nodes to exist on the physical network. We'll discuss the use of this addressing for both IEEE 802.3 and IEEE 802.5 networks.

7.2.1 | LocalTalk Link Access Protocol

The LocalTalk Link Access Protocol (LLAP) frame is an integral part of LocalTalk's communication capabilities, which are built into every Macintosh and LaserWriter (see Figure 7-2a). The LLAP header includes the Destination and Source Node IDs and the LLAP Type field that specifies the type of packet contained within the Data field. LLAP specifies packet types 01 - 7FH for data packets and types 80 - FFH for control packets.

Control packets do not contain a data field, but data packets can contain up to 600 octets of information. The low-order 10 bits of the first two octets within the data field contain the length (0 - 600) of the data field. Then comes the Frame Check Sequence (FCS), which is followed by a Flag (7EH), and an Abort Sequence (12 - 18 ONES) that indicates the end of the frame.

Figure 7-2a
AppleTalk LLAP Frame

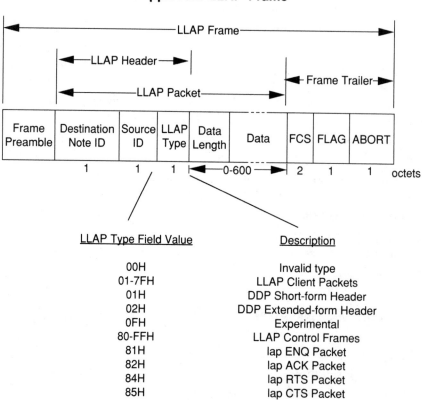

LLAP Type Field Value	Description
00H	Invalid type
01-7FH	LLAP Client Packets
01H	DDP Short-form Header
02H	DDP Extended-form Header
0FH	Experimental
80-FFH	LLAP Control Frames
81H	lap ENQ Packet
82H	lap ACK Packet
84H	lap RTS Packet
85H	lap CTS Packet

7.2.2 EtherTalk 1.0 (Phase 1) Link Access Protocol

The EtherTalk Link Access Protocol (ELAP) encapsulates the LAP information within an Ethernet frame (see Figure 7-2b). The first 14 octets are the Ethernet header, including the Ethernet Destination and Source Addresses (six octets each) and the Ethernet Type (two octets), which is set to 809BH for AppleTalk. Next are the AppleTalk Address and Type fields, as with LLAP, and then the

Data Length and Data fields. Note that a Pad may be required to satisfy the minimum length requirement for an Ethernet frame.

Figure 7-2b
AppleTalk Ethernet Frame

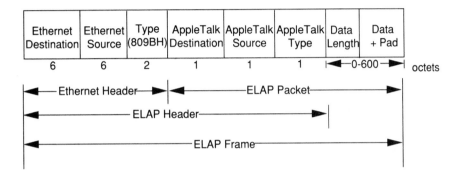

7.2.3 EtherTalk 2.0 (Phase 2) and TokenTalk Link Access Protocols

Apple has revised the Data Link Layer frame formats in AppleTalk Phase 2 so they conform to IEEE 802.2, 802.3, and 802.5 standards (see Figure 7-2c). In Phase 2, the Data Link header for either 802.3 or 802.5 is followed by the 802.2 and SNAP headers. The LLC header contains the DSAP and SSAP addresses (both set to AAH) and a Control field (set to 03H for unnumbered information). The next five octets are the SNAP header containing the Organization Code (080007H for Apple) and EtherType (809BH for AppleTalk Phase 2). Following the SNAP header is the DDP header (note that there is no LAP header) and DDP data that will be discussed in detail in Section 7.3.

Figure 7-2c
AppleTalk Phase 2 802.3/802.5 Frames

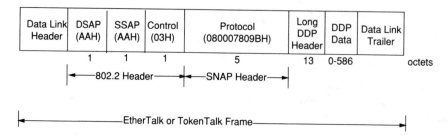

Data Link Header	DSAP (AAH)	SSAP (AAH)	Control (03H)	Protocol (080007809BH)	Long DDP Header	DDP Data	Data Link Trailer
	1	1	1	5	13	0-586	octets

|←——802.2 Header——→|←—SNAP Header—→|

|←————————EtherTalk or TokenTalk Frame————————→|

7.2.4 | Address Resolution Protocol

The AppleTalk Address Resolution Protocol (AARP) is the mechanism used to translate between the Data Link Layer (hardware) address and the higher layer protocol address. Each node maintains an Address Mapping Table (AMT) for each higher layer protocol suite in use, and AARP maps between any two sets of the hardware and higher layer addresses.

If a node receives an AARP Request for a protocol address that matches its own, it sends an AARP Response containing its hardware address. In this instance the AMT is not involved. If a node wishes to transmit a packet, the AMT is checked by AARP. If a match for the desired higher layer protocol stack is not found, an AARP Request is initiated in order to find a match, as above. AARP dynamically performs this function using one of three different packet types: Request, Response, and Probe.

When a node is initialized, AARP assigns a tentative address for each protocol set on that node, which in most cases is just AppleTalk). AARP then broadcasts Probe packets to determine if any other node is using that address. A Response packet from another node would indicate that the address is already in use and the process must be repeated with a new tentative address. If the address is unique, the tentative address is considered permanent, and the node will now reply to any AARP Request or Probe packets that contain its protocol address.

The AARP packet follows the Data Link Layer header. For Phase 1 networks, AARP is designated with Ethernet protocol type = 80F3H (see Figure 7-3a). For Phase 2 networks, AARP is designated with the SNAP type = 00000080F3H (see Figure 7-3b). The AARP packet contains a Hardware type field (two octets) specifying Ethernet or Token-Ring, and the Protocol type field (also two octets) which identifies the protocol family. Next is the Hardware and Protocol address lengths (one octet each), followed by the Function (Request, Response, or Probe). The addresses are then transmitted, and are defined by the function of that packet (see Figure 7-3a). Phase 2 AARP packets are preceded by the Phase 2 Data Link header, e.g. 802.3 + 802.2 + SNAP or 802.5 + 802.2 + SNAP (shown in Figure 7-3b), but these packets are otherwise identical. A value of 0 in the Destination Hardware Address field indicates that an unknown quantity is being requested in Request and Probe packets.

Figure 7-3a
AppleTalk AARP Packet (Phase 1 and Phase 2)

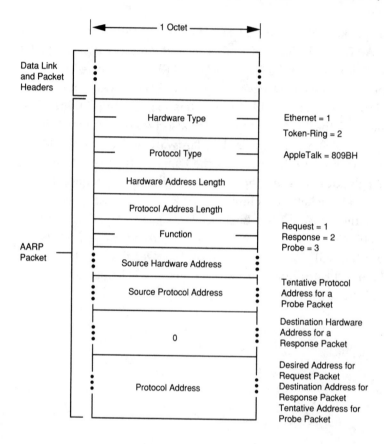

Figure 7-3b
AppleTalk AARP Packet Header (Phase 2)

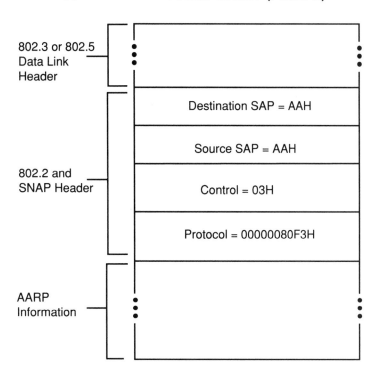

An example of several of the AppleTalk protocols at work is shown in Figure 7-4. Details of frame 109 (Figure 7-5) show that it is an AARP packet. Workstation DECnet006418 (maciicx) is broadcasting a Probe to determine if anyone is using destination address 2000.7 (network number 2000, node number 7, given in decimal).

Figure 7-4
AppleTalk Protocol Examples

```
SUMMARY   Delta T   Destination    Source        Summary

     99   3.8799   Broadcast      kahuna      RTMP R Node=29225.147 Routing entries=14
    100   3.1661   Broadcast      VAX1        RTMP R Node=29225.254 Routing entries=18
    101   0.9184   090007FFFFFF   macrouter   RTMP R Node=2000.10 Routing entries=18
    102   0.0051   Broadcast      macrouter   RTMP R Node=29225.141 Routing entries=5
    103   0.8560   DEC Routers    VAX1        DRP ROUTER  Hello  S=6.14   BLKSZ=1498
    104   1.0002   DEC Endnode    VAX1        DRP ROUTER  Hello  S=6.14   BLKSZ=1498
    105   2.9673   macrouter      VAX1        ADSP Probe            CID=D2C1  WIN=4096
    106   0.0009   maciicx        macrouter   ADSP Probe            CID=D2C1  WIN=4096
    107   1.0901   Broadcast      kahuna      RTMP R Node=29225.147 Routing entries=14
    108   3.1623   Broadcast      VAX1        RTMP R Node=29225.254 Routing entries=18
    109   0.0981   090007FFFFFF   maciicx     AARP Probe Node=2000.7
    110   0.1942   090007FFFFFF   maciicx     AARP Probe Node=2000.7
    111   0.1995   090007FFFFFF   maciicx     AARP Probe Node=2000.7
    112   0.1995   090007FFFFFF   maciicx     AARP Probe Node=2000.7
    113   0.1995   090007FFFFFF   maciicx     AARP Probe Node=2000.7
    114   0.0172   090007FFFFFF   macrouter   RTMP R Node=2000.10 Routing entries=18
    115   0.0051   Broadcast      macrouter   RTMP R Node=29225.141 Routing entries=5
    116   0.1772   090007FFFFFF   maciicx     AARP Probe Node=2000.7
    117   0.1993   090007FFFFFF   maciicx     AARP Probe Node=2000.7
    118   0.1995   090007FFFFFF   maciicx     AARP Probe Node=2000.7
    119   0.1995   090007FFFFFF   maciicx     AARP Probe Node=2000.7
    120   0.1995   090007FFFFFF   maciicx     AARP Probe Node=2000.7
    121   0.2052   090007FFFFFF   maciicx     ZIP C GetNetInfo ZONE=EBC EtherTlkPhase2
    122   0.0028   maciicx        macrouter   ZIP R NetInfoReply RANGE=2000-2000
    123   4.7539   Broadcast      kahuna      RTMP R Node=29225.147 Routing entries=14
    124   0.9293   DEC Routers    VAX1        DRP ROUTER  Hello  S=6.14   BLKSZ=1498
    125   1.0000   DEC Endnode    VAX1        DRP ROUTER  Hello  S=6.14   BLKSZ=1498
    126   0.2246   macrouter      maciicx     NBP C Request ID=1 (Mac //cx:Macintosh IIcx@EBC
    127   0.0051   090007000088   macrouter   NBP C Lookup ID=1 (Mac //cx:Macintosh IIcx@EBC
    128   0.5106   macrouter      maciicx     NBP C Request ID=1 (Mac //cx:Macintosh IIcx@EBC
    129   0.0052   090007000088   macrouter   NBP C Lookup ID=1 (Mac //cx:Macintosh IIcx@EBC
    130   0.4748   Broadcast      VAX1        RTMP R Node=29225.254 Routing entries=18
```

Figure 7-5
AppleTalk Address Resolution Protocol Example

```
Sniffer Network Analyzer data from 22-Feb-90 at 08:57:38,
file A:VLOGLOCK.ENC, Page 1

- - - - - - - - - - - - - - - - Frame 109 - - - - - - - - - - - - - - - - -

AARP:----- AARP -----
AARP:
AARP:  Hardware type                = 1 (10Mb Ethernet)
AARP:  Protocol type                = 809B (AppleTalk)
AARP:  Hardware length              = 6 bytes
AARP:  Protocol length              = 4 bytes
AARP:  Command                      = 3 (Probe)
AARP:  Source hardware address      = DECnet006418 (maciicx)
AARP:  Source protocol address      = 2000.7
AARP:  Destination hardware address = 000000000000
AARP:  Destination protocol address = 2000.7
AARP:
AARP:[Normal end of "AARP".]
AARP:
```

7.3   AppleTalk Network Layer Protocol

The Datagram Delivery Protocol (DDP) is the Network Layer protocol used by all the higher layers. While the Data Link Layer frames deliver information between nodes on a single network, DDP is responsible for delivering datagrams between sockets (higher layer process addresses) on the internet. The internet consists of individual AppleTalk networks connected by routers, and these routers, in turn, could be connected via telephone circuits, a public data network, or higher speed LAN backbones such as IEEE 802.3 or 802.5.

Node addresses within the internet consist of a network number (two octets) followed by a node ID (one octet). Sockets are addressed with a network number (two octets), node ID (one octet), and a socket number (one octet). Network number 0 is reserved for unknown networks. On AppleTalk Phase 2, however, only broadcast to net zero is supported, i.e. Net=0, Node=FFH means "all nodes on my network (cable)".

The DDP datagram consists of 0 - 586 octets of data, and is preceded by either a short (Phase 1 only) or long format header (see Figures 7-6a and 7-6b). The short header (LLAP type=1) is used when both source and destination sockets are on the same network; the extended-form header (LLAP type=2) is used for internet transmissions. Note that extended networks (Phase 2) always use long format headers.

Figure 7-6a
AppleTalk Short Format DDP Packet Header (Phase 1 only)

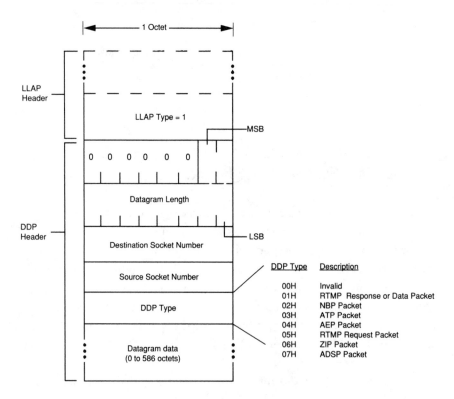

Figure 7-6b
AppleTalk Phase 2 DDP Packet Format (Extended Header)

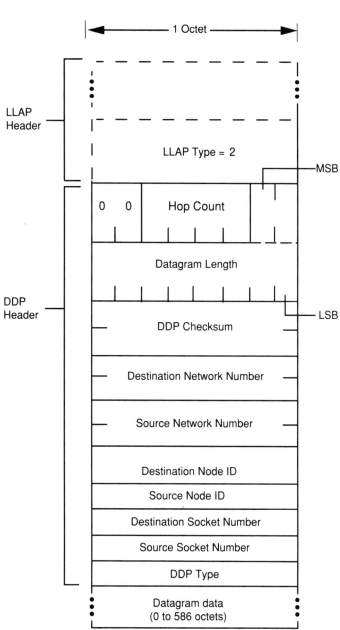

The short header contains the Datagram length (which is part of the first two octets), Destination and Source socket numbers, and the DDP type which describes the higher layer protocol within the DDP packet. The datagram Data completes the DDP packet.

The long header includes a hop count field that measures the number of internet router hops that the packet traverses. The source node sets this field to 0, and each router advances the field in increments of one. The maximum number of hops is 15. The Datagram Length field follows the hop count field, completing the first two octets.

The next field is a DDP checksum, which is computed beginning with the Destination network field through the Data field. The Destination/Source network fields (two octets each), Destination/Source node IDs (one octet each), and Destination/Source socket numbers (one octet each) contain the full network address for this datagram. Next comes the DDP Type field (see Figure 7-6a), followed by up to 586 octets of data. The maximum length of the DDP datagram (excluding the LAP header) is thus 599 octets.

An example of a DDP packet, including ATP data, is shown in Figure 7-7. This is a Phase 1 Ethernet packet (the Ethertype = 809BH), and the LAP protocol header specifies the LAP protocol type=2 for the long DDP header. The source of this packet is an AppleTalk node on the other side of the router (macrouter), therefore, the hop count has been set to equal 1. The Destination node (VAX1) is on this network. The Destination and Source network information then comes next, and the DDP header concludes with the protocol type of its data field (DDP type=3), indicating ATP data. We'll look at ATP more closely in section 7.4.1.

The addressing conventions and associated routing philosophies are one area that distinguishes AppleTalk Phase 1 from AppleTalk Phase 2. Those implementers considering migration to Phase 2 should consult reference [7-5] for further details on specific algorithms.

References [7-6] and [7-7] provide upgrade information for administrators.

Figure 7-7
AppleTalk Datagram Delivery Protocol Example

```
Sniffer Network Analyzer data from 22-Feb-90 at 08:16:14,
file A:PRINTDIR.ENC, Page 1

DLC:  ----- DLC Header -----
DLC:
DLC:  Frame 30 arrived at  08:16:27.6003 ; frame size is 60 (003C hex) bytes.
DLC:  Destination: Station DECnet000E18, VAX1
DLC:  Source      : Station 3Com  580975, macrouter
DLC:  Ethertype = 809B (AppleTalk)
DLC:
LAP:----- LAP header -----
LAP:
LAP:  Destination node  = 254
LAP:  Source node       = 141
LAP:  LAP protocol type = 2 (Long DDP)
LAP:
DDP:----- DDP header -----
DDP:
DDP:  Hop count        = 1
DDP:  Length           = 21
DDP:  Checksum         = 0000
DDP:  Destination Network Number = 12345
DDP:  Destination Node           = 172
DDP:  Destination Socket         = 129
DDP:  Source Network Number      = 2000
DDP:  Source Node                = 7
DDP:  Source Socket              = 250
DDP:  DDP protocol type = 3 (ATP)
DDP:
ATP:----- ATP header -----
ATP:
ATP:  Client         =
ATP:  Function       = 1 (Request)
ATP:  Control field  = 0X
ATP:          ..0. .... = At-least-once transaction
ATP:  Request bitmap = 00
ATP:          .... .... = Request bitmap
ATP:  Transaction id = 22225
ATP:  User data      = 05820000
ATP:
ATP:[Normal end of "ATP header".]
ATP:
```

| 7.4 | **AppleTalk Transport Layer Protocols**

The AppleTalk Transport Layer includes four different protocols. The AppleTalk Transaction Protocol assures reliable, end-to-end datagram delivery. The Name Binding Protocol provides name-to-address translation. The AppleTalk Echo Protocol provides a means to verify data transmissions. And the Routing Table Maintenance Protocol assists the datagram routing process.

We'll look at each of these protocols separately.

| 7.4.1 | **AppleTalk Transaction Protocol**

A transaction is a request on behalf of one socket, such as a client, for another socket, such as a server, to perform a higher layer function and then report the status of the operation. This is the function of ATP. ATP is the backbone of the AppleTalk protocols since it provides reliable transport services between Source and Destination sockets. Three different packets can be sent: Transaction Request (TReq), which is a transaction initiated by the requester; Transaction Response (TResp), which is returned by the responder reporting the outcome of the transaction; and Transaction Release (TRel), which releases the request from the responding ATP's transaction list. A Transaction identifier (TID) is used at each end to distinguish that particular transaction. A successful transaction is thus conducted as a three-way handshake — TReq (request), TResp (response), and then TRel (acknowledgement from requesting end releasing the transaction).

The ATP packet (see Figure 7-8) includes a Control field that defines the function (TReq, TResp, or TRel), plus three other flags to define Exactly Once (XO), End of Message (EOM), or Send Transaction Status (STS).

Figure 7-8
AppleTalk ATP Packet

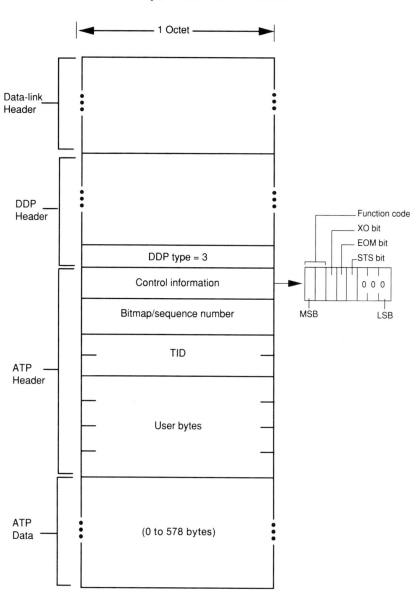

The next field is a bitmap/sequence number that is used to guarantee the packet sequence. The TID field is next, followed by four octets of user data, and then 0 - 578 octets of ATP data. Phases 1 and 2 ATP packets that are identical with the exception of additional TRel timer values in the Command field. We saw one example of ATP in Figure 7-7, and will look at another in Section 7.6.

7.4.2 | Name Binding Protocol

The Name Binding Protocol (NBP) provides a distribution mechanism to provide address translation between entity names (of the form object: type @ zone) and the four-octet internet address (of the form network number, node ID, socket number). Name binding is the process applied by a distributed database to look up addresses between nodes. It is distributed in that there is no centrally-located database of address names, and so NBP is used to find these entities using broadcast messages.

Four services are involved in this process: name registration, name deletion, name look up, and name confirmation. NBP packets (DDP type=2) come in four types: BrRq (Broadcast Request), LkUp (Look Up), LkUp-Reply (Look Up Reply), and FwdReq (Forward Request), each of which is defined by a function code within the NBP packet (see Figure 7-9). Within the packet is an NBP tuple, which contains the NAME - ADDRESS pairs of interest. The FwdReq packet was added for Phase 2.

An example of NBP is shown in Figure 7-10 (which shows a detail of frames 126 - 129 from Figure 7-4). Maciicx (frame 126 and 128) is asking its router (macrouter) to check all networks in its zone to see if anyone else is using its name ("maciicx").

Figure 7-9
AppleTalk NBP Packet

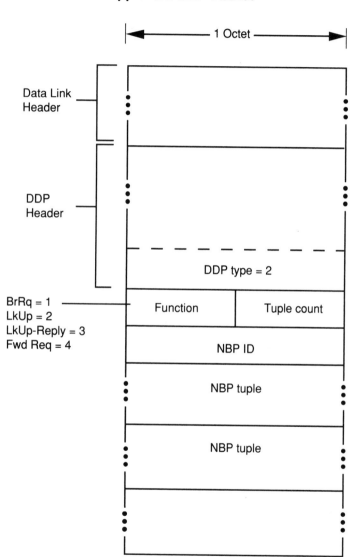

Figure 7-10
AppleTalk Name Binding Protocol Example

```
Sniffer Network Analyzer data from 22-Feb-90 at 08:57:38,
file A:VLOGLOCK.ENC, Page 1

- - - - - - - - - - - - - - - Frame 126 - - - - - - - - - - - - - - - -


NBP:----- NBP header -----
NBP:
NBP:  Control       = 1 (Broadcast Request)
NBP:  Tuple count   = 1
NBP:  Transaction id = 1
NBP:
NBP:  ---- Entity # 1 ----
NBP:
NBP:  Node          = 2000.7,  Socket = 254
NBP:  Enumerator = 0
NBP:  Object        = "Mac //cx"
NBP:  Type          = "Macintosh IIcx"
NBP:  Zone          = "EBC EtherTlkPhase2"
NBP:
NBP:[Normal end of "NBP header".]
NBP:

- - - - - - - - - - - - - - - Frame 127 - - - - - - - - - - - - - - - -


NBP:----- NBP header -----
NBP:
NBP:  Control       = 2 (Lookup)
NBP:  Tuple count   = 1
NBP:  Transaction id = 1
NBP:
NBP:  ---- Entity # 1 ----
NBP:
NBP:  Node          = 2000.7,  Socket = 254
NBP:  Enumerator = 0
NBP:  Object        = "Mac //cx"
NBP:  Type          = "Macintosh IIcx"
NBP:  Zone          = "EBC EtherTlkPhase2"
NBP:
NBP:[Normal end of "NBP header".]
NBP:
```

Figure 7-10 (continued)

```
- - - - - - - - - - - - - - - - Frame 128 - - - - - - - - - - - - - - - - -

NBP:----- NBP header -----
NBP:
NBP:  Control         = 1 (Broadcast Request)
NBP:  Tuple count     = 1
NBP:  Transaction id = 1
NBP:
NBP:  ---- Entity # 1 ----
NBP:
NBP:  Node           = 2000.7,  Socket = 254
NBP:  Enumerator = 0
NBP:  Object         = "Mac //cx"
NBP:  Type           = "Macintosh IIcx"
NBP:  Zone           = "EBC EtherTlkPhase2"
NBP:
NBP:[Normal end of "NBP header".]
NBP:


- - - - - - - - - - - - - - - - Frame 129 - - - - - - - - - - - - - - - - -

NBP:----- NBP header -----
NBP:
NBP:  Control         = 2 (Lookup)
NBP:  Tuple count     = 1
NBP:  Transaction id = 1
NBP:
NBP:  ---- Entity # 1 ----
NBP:
NBP:  Node           = 2000.7,  Socket = 254
NBP:  Enumerator = 0
NBP:  Object         = "Mac //cx"
NBP:  Type           = "Macintosh IIcx"
NBP:  Zone           = "EBC EtherTlkPhase2"
NBP:
NBP:[Normal end of "NBP header".]
NBP:
```

7.4.3 | AppleTalk Echo Protocol

Each AppleTalk node contains a socket, known as the Echoer socket, that is used to return (or echo) incoming data back to the sender. AEP uses DDP type=4, and has only two functions: Echo Request and Echo Reply (see Figure 7-11). Phase 1 and Phase 2 use the same packet format, and echoed data (0 - 586 octets) is sent to the destination node and returned to the sender. AEP is used for two applications: to determine if a particular node is accessible over an internet; or to obtain an estimate of the round-trip delay time for a data transmission to a particular node.

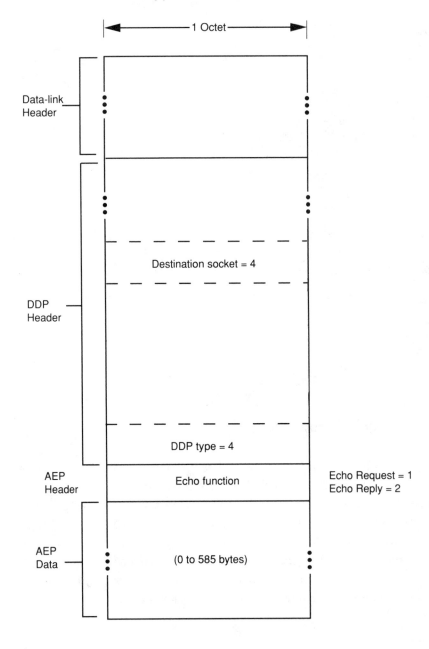

Figure 7-11
AppleTalk AEP Packet

| 7.4.4 | ## Routing Table Maintenance Protocol |

AppleTalk uses RTMP to maintain information about internetwork addresses and connections. It is one of the many protocols that interfaces with the internet router, which is the device used to connect two distinct AppleTalk networks. A local router can be used to connect two networks that are physically close together. A pair of half routers can be used for wide area network configurations, and usually employs dial-up or leased telephone lines.

The router itself must provide interfaces to several protocols and processes. The data link port provides the connection to the local network's DDP. The Routing Table contains the information necessary to forward the datagrams. The Routing Table Maintenance Protocol (RTMP), Zone Information Protocol (ZIP), and Name Binding Protocol (NBP) each play an important role in the routing process.

To route an incoming datagram, the Routing Table contains an entry for each possible destination network number (or network range). There are five elements contained in to each entry: the data link port number, the destination network number, the node ID of the next router, the number of hops needed to reach the destination network, and a cross-reference into the Zone Information Table, or ZIT (discussed in section 7.5.1). RTMP is used by the routers to exchange this routing information, thereby keeping their respective tables current and minimizing internetwork processing delays.

RTMP has three different packets: Data, Request, and Response (see Figures 7-12a and 7-12b). The Data packet (DDP type 1) is used to maintain the routing tables and contains routing tuples (network number and distance) which are the table entries to be exchanged. RTMP Request (DDP type 5) and RTMP Response (DDP type 1) packets are used by non-router nodes to obtain information about the routers connected to their network. Phase 2 has added a fourth packet, a Route Data Request (RDR) packet that is used to obtain information on demand from any router.

Figure 7-12a
AppleTalk RTMP Packets (Phase 1)

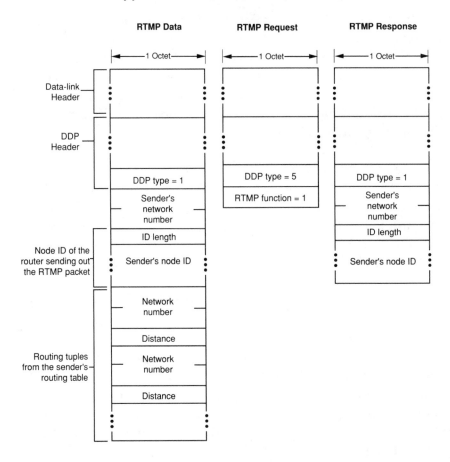

Figure 7-12b
AppleTalk RTMP Packets (Phase 2)

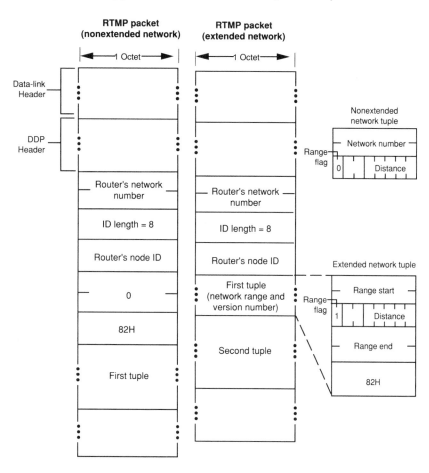

An example of four RTMP Request packets is shown in Figure 7-13 (also extracted from Figure 7-4). Frame 99 is a Phase 1 broadcast from a routing entity (kahuna), network 29225, node 147. Frame 100 is a broadcast from another routing entity (VAX1), network 29225, node 254. Frame 101 is a Phase 2 multicast from macrouter to all AppleTalk nodes (delineated by the destination address 090007FFFFFFH) on network 2000. Frame 102 is a Phase 1 broadcast from macrouter, network 29225, node 141. Note that macrouter is handling both Phase 1 and Phase 2 protocols, and is running the Apple

Phase 2 Upgrade Utility. This utility is provided with AppleTalk routers to permit interoperability of Phase 1 and 2 routers.

AppleTalk Phase 2 networks change the RTMP header information to accommodate the extended addressing discussed in section 7.2. The tuple within the RTMP data packet can contain a network number or network range information. See reference [7-4] Section 5 and [7-5] Section 4 for specific details.

Figure 7-13
AppleTalk Routing Table Maintenance Protocol Example

```
Sniffer Network Analyzer data from 22-Feb-90 at 08:57:38,
file A:VLOGLOCK.ENC, Page 1

- - - - - - - - - - - - - - - Frame 99 - - - - - - - - - - - - - - - -

RTMP:----- RTMP Data  -----
RTMP:
RTMP:  Net         = 29225
RTMP:  Node ID length = 8 bits
RTMP:  Node ID     = 147
RTMP:  Tuple 1 : Version 2
RTMP:  Tuple 2 : Net = 104, Distance = 1
RTMP:  Tuple 3 : Net = 106, Distance = 1
RTMP:  Tuple 4 : Net = 110, Distance = 1
RTMP:  Tuple 5 : Net = 111, Distance = 1
RTMP:  Tuple 6 : Net = 103, Distance = 1
RTMP:  Tuple 7 : Net = 107, Distance = 1
RTMP:  Tuple 8 : Net = 108, Distance = 1
RTMP:  Tuple 9 : Net = 29225, Distance = 0
RTMP:  Tuple 10 : Net = 102, Distance = 1
RTMP:  Tuple 11 : Net = 200, Distance = 0
RTMP:  Tuple 12 : Net = 105, Distance = 1
RTMP:  Tuple 13 : Net = 115, Distance = 0
RTMP:  Tuple 14 : Net = 1000, Distance = 0
RTMP:
RTMP:[Normal end of "RTMP Data ".]
RTMP:
```

Figure 7-13 (continued)

```
- - - - - - - - - - - - - - - Frame 100 - - - - - - - - - - - - - - - - -

RTMP:----- RTMP Data  -----
RTMP:
RTMP:  Net           = 29225
RTMP:  Node ID length = 8 bits
RTMP:  Node ID       = 254
RTMP:  Tuple 1 : Net = 12345, Distance = 0
RTMP:  Tuple 2 : Net = 29225, Distance = 0
RTMP:  Tuple 3 : Net = 3000, Distance = 1
RTMP:  Tuple 4 : Net = 500, Distance = 1
RTMP:  Tuple 5 : Net = 2000, Distance = 1
RTMP:  Tuple 6 : Net = 104, Distance = 2
RTMP:  Tuple 7 : Net = 107, Distance = 2
RTMP:  Tuple 8 : Net = 108, Distance = 2
RTMP:  Tuple 9 : Net = 110, Distance = 2
RTMP:  Tuple 10 : Net = 102, Distance = 2
RTMP:  Tuple 11 : Net = 103, Distance = 2
RTMP:  Tuple 12 : Net = 200, Distance = 1
RTMP:  Tuple 13 : Net = 105, Distance = 2
RTMP:  Tuple 14 : Net = 115, Distance = 1
RTMP:  Tuple 15 : Net = 111, Distance = 2
RTMP:  Tuple 16 : Net = 106, Distance = 2
RTMP:  Tuple 17 : Net = 1000, Distance = 1
RTMP:  Tuple 18 : Net = 37413, Distance = 1
RTMP:
RTMP:[Normal end of "RTMP Data ".]
RTMP:

- - - - - - - - - - - - - - - Frame 101 - - - - - - - - - - - - - - - - -

RTMP:----- RTMP Data  -----
RTMP:
RTMP:  Net           = 2000
RTMP:  Node ID length = 8 bits
RTMP:  Node ID       = 10
RTMP:  Tuple 1 : Cable range = 2000 to 2000 (Version 2)
RTMP:  Tuple 2 : Net = 37413, Distance = 2
RTMP:  Tuple 3 : Net = 12345, Distance = 1
RTMP:  Tuple 4 : Cable range = 3000 to 3000 (Version 2)
RTMP:  Tuple 5 : Net = 500, Distance = 0
RTMP:  Tuple 6 : Net = 1000, Distance = 1
RTMP:  Tuple 7 : Net = 115, Distance = 1
RTMP:  Tuple 8 : Net = 105, Distance = 2
RTMP:  Tuple 9 : Net = 200, Distance = 1
RTMP:  Tuple 10 : Net = 102, Distance = 2
RTMP:  Tuple 11 : Net = 108, Distance = 2
RTMP:  Tuple 12 : Net = 107, Distance = 2
```

Figure 7-13 (continued)

```
RTMP:   Tuple 13 : Net = 103, Distance = 2
RTMP:   Tuple 14 : Net = 111, Distance = 2
RTMP:   Tuple 15 : Net = 110, Distance = 2
RTMP:   Tuple 16 : Net = 106, Distance = 2
RTMP:   Tuple 17 : Net = 104, Distance = 2
RTMP:   Tuple 18 : Net = 29225, Distance = 0
RTMP:[Normal end of "RTMP Data ".]
RTMP:
- - - - - - - - - - - - - - - - Frame 102 - - - - - - - - - - - - - - - - -

RTMP:----- RTMP Data   -----
RTMP:
RTMP:   Net            = 29225
RTMP:   Node ID length = 8 bits
RTMP:   Node ID        = 141
RTMP:   Tuple 1 : Version 2
RTMP:   Tuple 2 : Net = 3000, Distance = 0
RTMP:   Tuple 3 : Net = 500, Distance = 0
RTMP:   Tuple 4 : Net = 29225, Distance = 0
RTMP:   Tuple 5 : Net = 2000, Distance = 0
RTMP:
RTMP:[Normal end of "RTMP Data ".]
RTMP:
```

7.5 | AppleTalk Higher Layer Protocols

Four Session Layer protocols are used by AppleTalk. Zone Information Protocol supports the routing process. Printer Access Protocol establishes connections between workstations and servers (usually print servers). AppleTalk Session Protocol establishes and tears down sessions to transfer data between two entities. AppleTalk Data Stream Protocol establishes and maintains full-duplex streams of data between two entities.

At the Presentation and Application Layers, the AppleTalk Filing Protocol is used to handle remote file access, and PostScript is the page description protocol used with the LaserWriter printers.

We'll look at each protocol individually.

7.5.1 Zone Information Protocol

An AppleTalk zone is a logical grouping of networks that is designated in order to think about the internet in smaller segments. In AppleTalk Phase 1, a particular network can belong to only one zone, although a zone may contain several networks. In AppleTalk Phase 2, there is no strict relationship between zone names and network numbers, so two nodes could have the same network number but still fall in different zones.

ZIP is used for two major purposes: to allow NBP to determine which networks belong within which zones (see section 7.4.2); and to help routers maintain their tables (see section 7.4.4). ZIP and RTMP are considered peers — both are implemented by the routers and exchange data regarding the internet. The ZIP data is structured in a Zone Information Table (ZIT), and new zone information is transmitted to the routers via an assigned socket known as the Zone Information Socket (ZIS).

There are several different types of ZIP packets. Query and Response packets (DDP type=6) are used to transmit information to and from the ZIS of a router. The Function code within the ZIP header (see Figure 7-14a) indicates a Query or Response. The Query packets are the same for Phase 1 and 2. The Response packets are also the same for both phases unless the zone list will not fit inside the packet. In that case, an Extended ZIP Reply packet (ZIP function=8) is used. New Phase 2 packets, ZIP GetNetInfo and NetInfoReply (see Figure 7-14b) are used when the node boots up. GetNetInfo is a broadcast to the ZIS; NetInfoReply is returned to the requesting node and socket. Reference [7-5] provides further details on the various ZIP packets.

Figure 7-14a
AppleTalk ZIP Query and Reply Packets

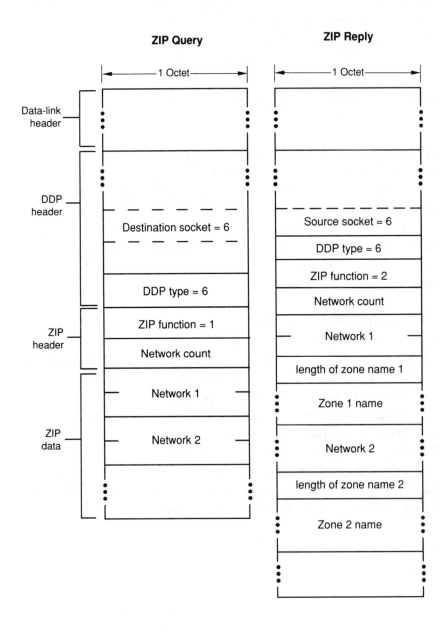

Figure 7-14b
AppleTalk ZIP GetNetInfo and ZIP NetInfo Reply Packets

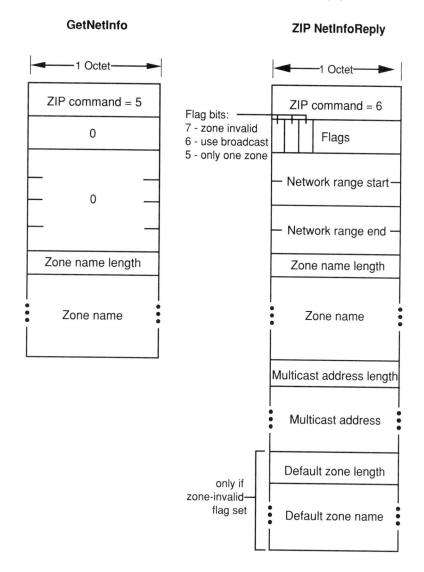

7.5.2 | Printer Access Protocol

PAP was originally used to handle communications between Macintosh computers and LaserWriter printers, but it is now used as a general purpose format for printer-dependent communications. PAP is a client of both NBP and ATP and defines its dialogue as PostScript when the LaserWriter is used.

When a workstation wishes to access the printer, a PAPOpen command is issued. The PAP then obtains the address of the server's Session Listening Socket (SLS) from NBP. Once the session has been opened, the client can receive data from the far end using PAPRead calls, or write data to the far end using PAPWrite calls. The session is terminated when the PAPClose call is issued. A number of other PAP packets, all of which are delineated by the PAP function field (see Figure 7-15), are used to transfer data and obtain status information.

The PAP header begins with the four-octet User Data field of the ATP header and may continue into the ATP Data field, if necessary. The ATP User Data field is for the use of the ATP client (which is the next higher layer protocol), and is not examined by ATP. The first octet contains the Connection ID, which is a PAP-generated identification of this particular connection. (SendStatus requests and Status replies put a 0 in this field.) The next field is the PAP Function, which defines that particular packet. SendData packets place a sequence number in the next two octets — Data packets place an EOF; all other PAP packets fill octets three and four with 0. Phase 1 and 2 PAP packets are the same.

An example PAP packet, OpenConn, is shown in Figure 7-15. We'll see these protocols in use later when we analyze a print job.

Figure 7-15
AppleTalk PAP packets

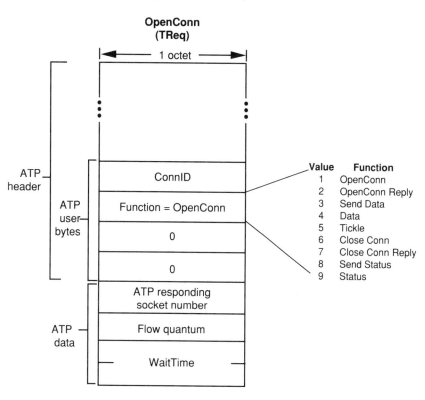

7.5.3 | AppleTalk Session Protocol

There must be a mechanism to establish communication between a workstation and a server, i.e. the session. In AppleTalk, the AppleTalk Session Protocol (ASP) is used for this purpose. Similar to PAP, ASP is a client of ATP and provides four basic services. The first two, Opening and Closing are self explanatory. The third, Session Request Handling, conveys commands and replies between the workstation and the server. The fourth, Session Management, determines the current status of the remote end (known as tickling), and assures the reliability of the session packets.

The ASP header is completely contained within the ATP User Data field (four octets) and begins with an SPFunction field that defines one of the nine ASP packet types (see Figure 7-16). For the OpenSessReply packet, this field contains the Server Session Socket (SSS), which is the end point socket in the connection. The second octet contains either the Workstation Session Socket (WSS) or Session ID. The third and fourth octets are used for the ASP version number, error codes, or they are set to 0, depending upon the packet being transmitted. Packets requiring data, such as the Command or Write packets, use the ATP data field, as necessary.

The AppleTalk Filing Protocol (AFP), which is a Presentation Layer protocol, is a client of the ASP services and is used to manipulate files that reside on a remote workstation or server. Another function of AFP is to translate file formats between end-users. Translators for Macintosh, Apple II, and MS-DOS files are available. A complete discussion of AFP is beyond the scope of this book, but you can refer to Section V of Reference [7-5] for further details.

Figure 7-16
AppleTalk ASP Packets

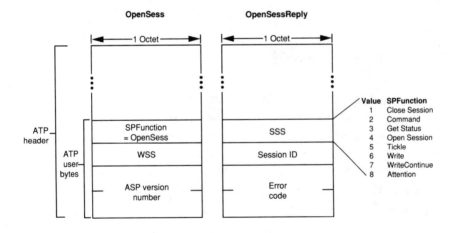

7.5.4   AppleTalk Data Stream Protocol

The last AppleTalk higher layer protocol we will examine is the AppleTalk Data Stream Protocol (ADSP). Where PAP and ASP have distinct clients using their services (PostScript and AFP, respectively), ADSP is designed to be a general purpose Session Layer protocol. It establishes and maintains full-duplex data streams of information between two AppleTalk sockets. It also includes flow control via sequence numbers to assure that a fast sender does not overwhelm a slow receiver with too much data.

The ADSP header (see Figure 7-17) is DDP Type=7 and begins with a two-octet SourceConnID which, with the socket number at each end, identifies this connection. The sequence counters follow next, including the PktFirstByteSeq (four octets), which identifies the sequence number of the first data byte in the sequence; the PktNextRcvSeq (four octets), which is a piggyback acknowledgement of the last packet received at this node; and finally RecvWdw (two octets), which is the receive window used for flow control.

The last field in the ADSP header is the Descriptor, which identifies the type of ADSP packet being transmitted. If the control bit is set, this is a Control packet (see table on Figure 7-17). If the control bit is not set, the packet is a data packet. The Ack Request forces the receiving end to send an immediate acknowledgement; the EOM bit indicates the logical end of message in a data stream; and the Attention bit indicates an attention packet.

Figure 7-17
AppleTalk ADSP Packet

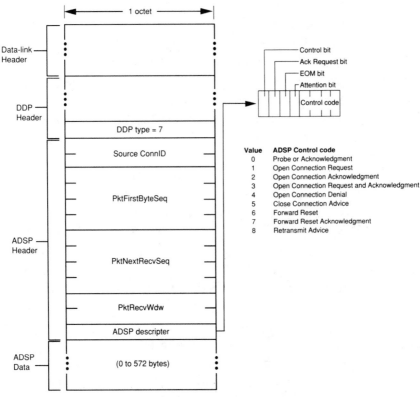

<table>
<tr><th>Value</th><th>ADSP Control code</th></tr>
<tr><td>0</td><td>Probe or Acknowledgment</td></tr>
<tr><td>1</td><td>Open Connection Request</td></tr>
<tr><td>2</td><td>Open Connection Acknowledgment</td></tr>
<tr><td>3</td><td>Open Connection Request and Acknowledgment</td></tr>
<tr><td>4</td><td>Open Connection Denial</td></tr>
<tr><td>5</td><td>Close Connection Advice</td></tr>
<tr><td>6</td><td>Forward Reset</td></tr>
<tr><td>7</td><td>Forward Reset Acknowledgment</td></tr>
<tr><td>8</td><td>Retransmit Advice</td></tr>
</table>

7.6 | Protocol Analysis with AppleTalk

To complete our study of the AppleTalk protocols, let's examine the details of two common operations: printing to a LaserWriter located on another AppleTalk network, and accessing a file on the same network.

In the first example, to access the printer, the client (maciicx, which is a Phase 2 node) must communicate with the router (macrouter, which is running both Phase 1 and 2 in the AppleTalk Upgrade Utility) that provides the connection to the other network. The printing process begins in frame 2 of Figure 7-18, and includes two ZIP packets (frames 31 and 32) that provide zone information to the client. The internet router tables are updated with the RTMP packets broadcast from the Phase 1 servers, such as kahuna (frame 1) and VAX1 (frame 14). The NBP request to find the name LaserWriter in frame 46 initiates the logical connection. The PAP connection is started in frame 59, and confirmed in frame 68. Actual transfer of the data begins in frame 72.

Figure 7-18
AppleTalk Printing Analysis Summary

Sniffer Network Analyzer data from 22-Feb-90 at 08:16:14, A:PRINTDIR.ENC, Page 1

SUMMARY		Delta T	Destination	Source	Summary
M	1		Broadcast	kahuna	RTMP R Node=29225.147 Routing ent=14
	2	2.9267	macrouter	maciicx	ATP C ID=22641 LEN=6
	3	0.0009	VAX1	macrouter	ATP C ID=22641 LEN=6
	4	0.0251	macrouter	VAX1	ATP R ID=22641 LEN=10 NS=0 (Last)
	5	0.0009	maciicx	macrouter	ATP R ID=22641 LEN=10 NS=0 (Last)
	6	0.0009	macrouter	maciicx	ATP D ID=22641
	7	0.0009	VAX1	macrouter	ATP D ID=22641
	8	1.3676	macrouter	maciicx	ATP C ID=22642 LEN=6
	9	0.0009	VAX1	macrouter	ATP C ID=22642 LEN=6
	10	0.0263	macrouter	VAX1	ATP R ID=22642 LEN=10 NS=0 (Last)
	11	0.0008	maciicx	macrouter	ATP R ID=22642 LEN=10 NS=0 (Last)
	12	0.0009	macrouter	maciicx	ATP D ID=22642
	13	0.0009	VAX1	macrouter	ATP D ID=22642
	14	1.5151	Broadcast	VAX1	RTMP R Node=29225.254 Routing ent=18
	15	1.1516	090007FFFFFF	macrouter'	RTMP R Node=2000.10 Routing ent=18
	16	0.0053	Broadcast	macrouter	RTMP R Node=29225.141 Routing ent=5
	17	0.7878	macrouter	maciicx	ATP C ID=22250 LEN=0
	18	0.0009	VAX1	macrouter	ATP C ID=22250 LEN=0
	19	0.8687	ISO End Stns	VAX1	ISO_IP Routing Exchange ESH PDU,S=0
	20	0.9652	DEC Routers	VAX1	DRP ROUTER Hello S=6.14 BLKSZ=148
	21	0.3644	Broadcast	kahuna	RTMP R Node=29225.147 Routing ent=14
	22	0.3303	macrouter	maciicx	ATP C ID=22643 LEN=6
	23	0.0009	VAX1	macrouter	ATP C ID=22643 LEN=6
	24	0.0402	macrouter	VAX1	ATP R ID=22643 LEN=10 NS=0 (Last)
	25	0.0008	maciicx	macrouter	ATP R ID=22643 LEN=10 NS=0 (Last)
	26	0.0009	macrouter	maciicx	ATP D ID=22643
	27	0.0009	VAX1	macrouter	ATP D ID=22643
	28	0.2614	DEC Endnode	VAX1	DRP ROUTER Hello S=6.14 BLSZ=1498
	29	2.1530	macrouter	maciicx	ATP C ID=22225 LEN=0

Figure 7-18 (continued)

```
30    0.0009   VAX1              macrouter     ATP C ID=22225 LEN=0
31    1.6075   macrouter         maciicx       ZIP C GetZoneList INDEX=1
32    0.0027   maciicx           macrouter     ZIP R GetZoneList ZONES=EBC
33    0.8932   macrouter         VAX1          ATP C ID=45289 LEN=0
34    0.0008   maciicx           macrouter     ATP C ID=45289 LEN=0
35    0.5625   Broadcast         VAX1          RTMP R Node=29225.254 Routing ent=18
36    0.3739   macrouter         maciicx       NBP C Request ID=68
37    0.0119   maciicx           macrouter     NBP R Lookup ID=68 N=1
38    0.7761   090007FFFFFF      macrouter     RTMP R Node=2000.10 Routing ent=18
39    0.0051   Broadcast         macrouter     RTMP R Node=29225.141 Routing ent=5
40    0.4220   macrouter         maciicx       ATP C ID=22645 LEN=6
41    0.0009   VAX1              macrouter     ATP C ID=22645 LEN=6
42    0.0196   macrouter         VAX1          ATP R ID=22645 LEN=10 NS=0 (Last)
43    0.0009   maciicx           macrouter     ATP R ID=22645 LEN=10 NS=0 (Last)
44    0.0010   macrouter         maciicx       ATP D ID=22645
45    0.0009   VAX1              macrouter     ATP D ID=22645
46    0.2243   macrouter         maciicx       NBP C Request ID=68 (=:LaserWriter@
47    0.0117   maciicx           macrouter     NBP R Lookup ID=68 N=1
48    0.8289   macrouter         maciicx       ATP C ID=22646 LEN=6
49    0.0009   VAX1              macrouter     ATP C ID=22646 LEN=6
50    0.0205   macrouter         VAX1          ATP R ID=22646 LEN=10 NS=0 (Last)
51    0.0008   maciicx           macrouter     ATP R ID=22646 LEN=10 NS=0 (Last)
52    0.0010   macrouter         maciicx       ATP D ID=22646
53    0.0009   VAX1              macrouter     ATP D ID=22646
54    1.4464   Broadcast         kahuna        RTMP R Node=29225.147 Routing ent=14
55    4.1898   macrouter         maciicx       NBP C Request ID=69 (Demo
56    0.0124   maciicx           macrouter     NBP R Lookup ID=69 N=1
57    0.0025   macrouter         maciicx       PAP C OpenConn ID=111 RW=248 Q=8 T=0
58    1.4270   DEC Routers       VAX1          DRP ROUTER  Hello  S=6.14   BLSZ=1498
59    0.1208   macrouter         maciicx       PAP C OpenConn ID=111 RW=248 Q=8 T=0
60    0.0996   Broadcast         VAX1          RTMP R Node=29225.254 Routing ent=18
61    0.3505   macrouter         maciicx       ATP C ID=22648 LEN=6
62    0.0009   VAX1              macrouter     ATP C ID=22648 LEN=6
63    0.0412   macrouter         VAX1          ATP R ID=22648 LEN=10 NS=0 (Last)
64    0.0008   maciicx           macrouter     ATP R ID=22648 LEN=10 NS=0 (Last)
65    0.0010   macrouter         maciicx       ATP D ID=22648
66    0.0009   VAX1              macrouter     ATP D ID=22648
67    0.3839   DEC Endnode       VAX1          DRP ROUTER Hello S=6.14   BLKSZ=1498
68    0.2694   maciicx           macrouter     PAP R OpenConnRepl ID=111 RS=247 Q=8
69    0.0009   macrouter         maciicx       ATP D ID=22647
70    0.0012   macrouter         maciicx       PAP C Tickle ID=111
71    0.0044   maciicx           macrouter     PAP C Tickle ID=111
72    0.0086   macrouter         maciicx       PAP C SendData ID=111 SEQ=1
73    0.0374   macrouter         VAX1          ATP C ID=256 LEN=0
74    0.0009   maciicx           macrouter     ATP C ID=256 LEN=0
75    0.0492   090007FFFFFF      macrouter     RTMP R Node=2000.10 Routing ent=18
76    0.0051   Broadcast         macrouter     RTMP R Node=29225.141 Routing ent=5
77    0.4288   maciicx           macrouter     PAP C SendData ID=111 SEQ=1
```

Figure 7-18 (continued)

```
78   0.0015   macrouter    maciicx      PAP R Data ID=111 LEN=228 More data
79   0.0151   maciicx      macrouter    ATP D ID=61457
80   0.0044   maciicx      macrouter    PAP C SendData ID=111 SEQ=2
81   0.0207   maciicx      macrouter    PAP R Data ID=111 LEN=2 More data
82   0.0009   macrouter    maciicx      ATP D ID=22650
83   0.0022   macrouter    maciicx      PAP C SendData ID=111 SEQ=2
84   0.0027   macrouter    maciicx      PAP R Data ID=111 LEN=6 End of data
85   0.0082   maciicx      macrouter    ATP D ID=61458
86   0.0143   maciicx      macrouter    PAP R Data ID=111 LEN=0 End of data
```

Figure 7-19 shows the details of three frames at the end of the printing sequence. Frame 84 is a PAP packet sent from the maciicx to the macrouter and containing six octets of data, which is indicated to be the last of the transaction (see the PAP header). Frame 85 is transmitted from the macrouter and releases the connection. Frame 86 shows the PAP header indicating the end of file. In summary, macrouter is routing between Phase 1 and Phase 2 networks. While these networks are on the same cable, they are logically different.

Figure 7-19
AppleTalk Printing Analysis Details

```
Sniffer Network Analyzer data from 22-Feb-90 at 08:16:14, file A:PRINTDIR.ENC

- - - - - - - - - - - - - - - - Frame 84 - - - - - - - - - - - - - - - - -

DLC:   ----- DLC Header -----
DLC:
DLC:   Frame 84 arrived at  08:16:42.3016 ; frame size is 60 (003C hex) bytes.
DLC:   Destination: Station 3Com  580975, macrouter
DLC:   Source     : Station DECnet006418, maciicx
DLC:   802.2 LLC length = 35
DLC:
LLC:   ----- LLC Header -----
LLC:
LLC:   DSAP = AA, SSAP = AA, Command, Unnumbered frame: UI
LLC:
SNAP:  ----- SNAP frame -----
SNAP:
SNAP:  Vendor ID = 080007 (Apple)
SNAP:  Type = 809B (AppleTalk)
SNAP:
```

Figure 7-19 (continued)

```
DDP:----- DDP header -----
DDP:
DDP:  Hop count          = 0
DDP:  Length             = 27
DDP:  Checksum           = 0000
DDP:  Destination Network Number = 500
DDP:  Destination Node          = 246
DDP:  Destination Socket        = 181
DDP:  Source Network Number     = 2000
DDP:  Source Node               = 7
DDP:  Source Socket             = 248
DDP:  DDP protocol type = 3 (ATP)
DDP:
ATP:----- ATP header -----
ATP:
ATP:  Client          = (PAP)
ATP:  Function        = 2 (Response)
ATP:  Control field   = 10
ATP:          ...1 .... = Last reply for this transaction
ATP:  Response sequence = 0
ATP:  Transaction id    = 61458
ATP:  User data         = 6F040100
ATP:
PAP:----- PAP header -----
PAP:
PAP:  Connection ID    = 111
PAP:  PAP type         = 4 (Data)
PAP:  EOF              = 1 (End of data)
PAP:
PAP:  [6 byte(s) of data]
PAP:
PAP:[Normal end of "PAP header".]
PAP:
DLC:  Frame padding: 11 bytes


- - - - - - - - - - - - - - - - Frame 85 - - - - - - - - - - - - - - - -


DLC:  ----- DLC Header -----
DLC:
DLC:  Frame 85 arrived at  08:16:42.3098 ; frame size is 60 (003C hex) bytes.
DLC:  Destination: Station DECnet006418, maciicx
DLC:  Source     : Station 3Com   580975, macrouter
DLC:  802.2 LLC length = 29
DLC:
LLC:  ----- LLC Header -----
LLC:
LLC:  DSAP = AA, SSAP = AA, Command, Unnumbered frame: UI
LLC:
```

Figure 7-19 (continued)

```
SNAP: ----- SNAP frame -----
SNAP:
SNAP: Vendor ID = 080007 (Apple)
SNAP: Type = 809B (AppleTalk)
SNAP:
DDP:----- DDP header -----
DDP:
DDP:  Hop count          = 1
DDP:  Length             = 21
DDP:  Checksum           = 0000
DDP:  Destination Network Number = 2000
DDP:  Destination Node           = 7
DDP:  Destination Socket         = 248
DDP:  Source Network Number      = 500
DDP:  Source Node                = 246
DDP:  Source Socket              = 181
DDP:  DDP protocol type = 3 (ATP)
DDP:
ATP:----- ATP header -----
ATP:
ATP:  Function           = 3 (Release)
ATP:  Transaction id     = 61458
ATP:  User data          = 6F040000
ATP:
ATP:[Normal end of "ATP header".]
ATP:
DLC:  Frame padding: 17 bytes


- - - - - - - - - - - - - - - - - Frame 86 - - - - - - - - - - - - - - - - - -


DLC:  ----- DLC Header -----
DLC:
DLC:  Frame 86 arrived at  08:16:42.3241 ; frame size is 60 (003C hex) bytes.
DLC:  Destination: Station DECnet006418, maciicx
DLC:  Source      : Station 3Com  580975, macrouter
DLC:  802.2 LLC length = 29
DLC:
LLC:  ----- LLC Header -----
LLC:
LLC:  DSAP = AA, SSAP = AA, Command, Unnumbered frame: UI
LLC:
SNAP: ----- SNAP frame -----
SNAP:
SNAP: Vendor ID = 080007 (Apple)
SNAP: Type = 809B (AppleTalk)
SNAP:
```

Figure 7-19 (continued)

```
DDP:----- DDP header -----
DDP:
DDP:   Hop count          = 1
DDP:   Length             = 21
DP:    Checksum           = 0000
DDP:   Destination Network Number = 2000
DDP:   Destination Node           = 7
DDP:   Destination Socket         = 246
DDP:   Source Network Number      = 500
DDP:   Source Node                = 246
DDP:   Source Socket              = 247
DDP:   DDP protocol type = 3 (ATP)
DDP:
ATP:----- ATP header -----
ATP:
ATP:   Client            = (PAP)
ATP:   Function          = 2 (Response)
ATP:   Control field     = 10
ATP:            ...1 .... = Last reply for this transaction
ATP:   Response sequence = 0
ATP:   Transaction id    = 22651
ATP:   User data         = 6F040100
ATP:
PAP:----- PAP header -----
PAP:
PAP:   Connection ID     = 111
PAP:   PAP type          = 4 (Data)
PAP:   EOF               = 1 (End of data)
PAP:
PAP:
PAP:[Normal end of "PAP header".]
PAP:
DLC:   Frame padding: 17 bytes
```

The second example (Figure 7-20) demonstrates how to access a file that exists on a Phase 1 server (VAX1). The macrouter begins sending VAX1 NBP packets beginning in frame 14 to locate the appropriate name. Frame 17 begins the VAX1 response, which continues through frame 114. Also note the RTMP packets sent from the servers in frames 3 and 4, and the ECHO packets in frames 105 and 106. An AFP login to VAX1 occurs in frames 124 and 125, the remote volume (Alisa) is opened in frame 130, and file parameters are obtained beginning in frame 133. The file access then proceeds.

Figure 7-20
AppleTalk File Access Analysis Summary

Sniffer Network Analyzer data from 22-Feb-90 at 09:21:14,
file A:VAXFILE.ENC, Page 1

SUMMARY	Delta T	Destination	Source	Summary
M 1		DEC Routers	VAX1	DRP L1 Route S=6.14
2	0.0087	DEC Routers	VAX1	DRP L1 Route S=6.14
3	0.6053	Broadcast	kahuna	RTMP R Node=29225.147 Routing
4	3.0256	Broadcast	VAX1	RTMP R Node=29225.254 Routing
5	0.9437	090007FFFFFF	macrouter	RTMP R Node=2000.10 Routing
6	0.0053	Broadcast	macrouter	RTMP R Node=29225.141 Routing
7	2.4150	ISO End Stns	VAX1	ISO_IP Routing Exchange ESH
8	3.6218	Broadcast	kahuna	RTMP R Node=29225.147 Routing
9	0.7939	DEC Routers	VAX1	DRP ROUTER Hello S=6.14
10	1.0000	DEC Endnode	VAX1	DRP ROUTER Hello S=6.14
11	1.2206	Broadcast	VAX1	RTMP R Node=29225.254 Routing
12	0.9544	090007FFFFFF	macrouter	RTMP R Node=2000.10 Routing
13	0.0052	Broadcast	macrouter	RTMP R Node=29225.141 Routing
14	3.4537	VAX1	macrouter	NBP C Lookup ID=3
15	0.0021	VAX1	macrouter	NBP C Lookup ID=3
16	0.0014	Broadcast	macrouter	NBP C Lookup ID=3
17	0.0029	macrouter	VAX1	NBP R Lookup ID=3 N=1
18	0.0054	macrouter	VAX1	NBP R Lookup ID=3 N=1
19	0.0598	macrouter	VAX1	NBP R Lookup ID=3 N=1
20	0.8590	VAX1	macrouter	NBP C Lookup ID=3
21	0.0022	VAX1	macrouter	NBP C Lookup ID=3
22	0.0014	Broadcast	macrouter	NBP C Lookup ID=3
23	0.0029	macrouter	VAX1	NBP R Lookup ID=3 N=1
24	0.0052	macrouter	VAX1	NBP R Lookup ID=3 N=1
25	0.0684	macrouter	VAX1	NBP R Lookup ID=3 N=1
26	0.8506	VAX1	macrouter	NBP C Lookup ID=3
27	0.0022	VAX1	macrouter	NBP C Lookup ID=3
28	0.0014	Broadcast	macrouter	NBP C Lookup ID=3
29	0.0029	macrouter	VAX1	NBP R Lookup ID=3 N=1
30	0.0045	macrouter	VAX1	NBP R Lookup ID=3 N=1
31	0.0591	macrouter	VAX1	NBP R Lookup ID=3 N=1
32	0.6454	Broadcast	kahuna	RTMP R Node=29225.147 Routing
33	0.2154	VAX1	macrouter	NBP C Lookup ID=3 (
34	0.0022	VAX1	macrouter	NBP C Lookup ID=3 (
35	0.0014	Broadcast	macrouter	NBP C Lookup ID=3 (
36	0.0033	macrouter	VAX1	NBP R Lookup ID=3 N=1 1
37	0.0045	macrouter	VAX1	NBP R Lookup ID=3 N=1 1
38	0.0613	macrouter	VAX1	NBP R Lookup ID=3 N=1 1
39	0.8581	VAX1	macrouter	NBP C Lookup ID=3
40	0.0022	VAX1	macrouter	NBP C Lookup ID=3
41	0.0014	Broadcast	macrouter	NBP C Lookup ID=3

Figure 7-20 (continued)

```
42   0.0042   macrouter           VAX1            NBP R Lookup ID=3 N=1
43   0.0040   macrouter           VAX1            NBP R Lookup ID=3 N=1
44   0.1282   macrouter           VAX1            NBP R Lookup ID=3 N=1
45   1.7226   Broadcast           VAX1             RTMP R Node=29225.254 Routing
46   0.2484   VAX1                macrouter       NBP C Lookup ID=4
47   0.0021   VAX1                macrouter       NBP C Lookup ID=4
48   0.0014   Broadcast           macrouter       NBP C Lookup ID=4 (
49   0.0040   macrouter           VAX1            NBP R Lookup ID=4 N=1 1
50   0.0040   macrouter           VAX1            NBP R Lookup ID=4 N=1 1
51   0.0688   macrouter           VAX1            NBP R Lookup ID=4 N=1 1
52   0.6150   090007FFFFFF macrouter             RTMP R Node=2000.10 Routing e
53   0.0052   Broadcast           macrouter        RTMP R Node=29225.141 Routing
54   0.2301   VAX1                macrouter       NBP C Lookup ID=4 (
55   0.0022   VAX1                macrouter       NBP C Lookup ID=4 (
56   0.0014   Broadcast           macrouter       NBP C Lookup ID=4 (
57   0.0029   macrouter           VAX1            NBP R Lookup ID=4 N=1 1
58   0.0045   macrouter           VAX1            NBP R Lookup ID=4 N=1
59   0.0571   macrouter           VAX1            NBP R Lookup ID=4 N=1
60   0.8627   VAX1                macrouter       NBP C Lookup ID=4
61   0.0022   VAX1                macrouter       NBP C Lookup ID=4
62   0.0014   Broadcast           macrouter       NBP C Lookup ID=4
63   0.0029   macrouter           VAX1            NBP R Lookup ID=4 N=1
64   0.0045   macrouter           VAX1            NBP R Lookup ID=4 N=1
65   0.0603   macrouter           VAX1            NBP R Lookup ID=4 N=1
66   0.8595   VAX1                macrouter       NBP C Lookup ID=4
67   0.0022   VAX1                macrouter       NBP C Lookup ID=4
68   0.0014   Broadcast           macrouter       NBP C Lookup ID=4
69   0.0029   macrouter           VAX1            NBP R Lookup ID=4 N=1
70   0.0045   macrouter           VAX1            NBP R Lookup ID=4 N=1
71   0.0645   macrouter           VAX1            NBP R Lookup ID=4 N=1
72   0.6621   DEC Routers         VAX1            DRP ROUTER  Hello  S=6.14
73   0.1930   VAX1                macrouter       NBP C Lookup ID=4
74   0.0021   VAX1                macrouter       NBP C Lookup ID=4
75   0.0015   Broadcast           macrouter       NBP C Lookup ID=4
76   0.0029   macrouter           VAX1            NBP R Lookup ID=4 N=1
77   0.0057   macrouter           VAX1            NBP R Lookup ID=4 N=1
78   0.0609   macrouter           VAX1            NBP R Lookup ID=4 N=1
79   0.7337   DEC Endnode         VAX1            DRP ROUTER  Hello  S=6.14
80   1.2879   VAX1                macrouter       NBP C Lookup ID=5
81   0.0022   VAX1                macrouter       NBP C Lookup ID=5
82   0.0014   Broadcast           macrouter       NBP C Lookup ID=5
83   0.0042   macrouter           VAX1            NBP R Lookup ID=5 N=1
84   0.0040   macrouter           VAX1            NBP R Lookup ID=5 N=1
85   0.0643   macrouter           VAX1            NBP R Lookup ID=5 N=1
86   0.8546   VAX1                macrouter       NBP C Lookup ID=5
87   0.0022   VAX1                macrouter       NBP C Lookup ID=5
88   0.0013   Broadcast           kahuna           RTMP R Node=29225.147 Routing
89   0.0002   Broadcast           macrouter       NBP C Lookup ID=5
```

Figure 7-20 (continued)

```
90   0.0053   macrouter       VAX1        NBP R Lookup ID=5 N=1
91   0.0078   macrouter       VAX1        NBP R Lookup ID=5 N=1
92   0.0634   macrouter       VAX1        NBP R Lookup ID=5 N=1
93   0.8506   VAX1            macrouter   NBP C Lookup ID=5
94   0.0022   VAX1            macrouter   NBP C Lookup ID=5
95   0.0014   Broadcast       macrouter   NBP C Lookup ID=5
96   0.0030   macrouter       VAX1        NBP R Lookup ID=5 N=1
97   0.0045   macrouter       VAX1        NBP R Lookup ID=5 N=1
98   0.0614   macrouter       VAX1        NBP R Lookup ID=5 N=1
99   0.8582   VAX1            macrouter   NBP C Lookup ID=5
100  0.0022   VAX1            macrouter   NBP C Lookup ID=5
101  0.0014   Broadcast       macrouter   NBP C Lookup ID=5
102  0.0029   macrouter       VAX1        NBP R Lookup ID=5 N=1
103  0.0046   macrouter       VAX1        NBP R Lookup ID=5 N=1
104  0.0643   macrouter       VAX1        NBP R Lookup ID=5 N=1
105  0.1972   VAX1            macrouter   ECHO C LEN=585
106  0.0325   macrouter       VAX1        ECHO R LEN=585
107  0.0212   VAX1            macrouter   ASP C GetStat
108  0.0283   macrouter       VAX1        ASP R GetStat LEN=374
109  0.5760   VAX1            macrouter   NBP C Lookup ID=5
110  0.0022   VAX1            macrouter   NBP C Lookup ID=5
111  0.0014   Broadcast       macrouter   NBP C Lookup ID=5
112  0.0029   macrouter       VAX1        NBP R Lookup ID=5 N=1
113  0.0050   macrouter       VAX1        NBP R Lookup ID=5 N=1
114  0.0577   macrouter       VAX1        NBP R Lookup ID=5 N=1
115  0.1392   Broadcast       VAX1         RTMP R Node=29225.254 Routing
116  0.9547   090007FFFFFF    macrouter    RTMP R Node=2000.10 Routing
117  0.0052   Broadcast       macrouter    RTMP R Node=29225.141 Routing
118  6.0474   Broadcast       kahuna       RTMP R Node=29225.147 Routing
119  1.5739   VAX1            macrouter   ASP C OpenSess WSS=250
120  0.0241   macrouter       VAX1        ASP R OpenSess SSS=131 ID=5
121  0.0119   macrouter       VAX1        ASP C Tickle ID=5
122  0.0045   VAX1            macrouter   ATP D ID=1123
123  0.0008   VAX1            macrouter   ASP C Tickle ID=5
124  0.0009   VAX1            macrouter   AFP C Login AFPVersion 2.0
125  0.2813   macrouter       VAX1        AFP R OK
126  0.0151   VAX1            macrouter   ATP D ID=1125
127  0.0034   VAX1            macrouter   AFP C GetSrvrParms
128  0.0462   macrouter       VAX1        AFP R OK 3 volumes
129  0.0158   VAX1            macrouter   ATP D ID=1126
130  0.3032   VAX1            macrouter    AFP C OpenVol Volume="Alisa
131  0.2905   macrouter       VAX1        AFP R OK
132  0.0152   VAX1            macrouter   ATP D ID=1127
133  0.0008   VAX1            macrouter    AFP C GetFileDirParms VolID=3
134  0.1446   macrouter       VAX1        AFP R OK
135  0.0164   VAX1            macrouter   ATP D ID=1128
136  0.0008   VAX1            macrouter   AFP C CloseVol VolID=3
137  0.0224   DEC Routers     VAX1         DRP ROUTER  Hello  S=6.14
```

Figure 7-20 (continued)

```
138    0.1086   macrouter    VAX1         AFP R OK
139    0.0155   VAX1         macrouter    ATP D ID=1129
140    0.0143   VAX1         macrouter    AFP C OpenVol Volume="Alisa
141    0.0819   Broadcast    VAX1         RTMP R Node=29225.254 Routing
142    0.2347   macrouter    VAX1         AFP R OK
143    0.0151   VAX1         macrouter    ATP D ID=1130
144    0.0008   VAX1         macrouter    AFP C GetFileDirParms VolID=1
145    0.1388   macrouter    VAX1         AFP R OK
146    0.0149   VAX1         macrouter    ATP D ID=1131
147    0.0008   VAX1         macrouter    AFP C CloseVol VolID=1
```

The details of the AFP open volume packet (see Figure 7-21) demonstrates how the AppleTalk protocols are logically connected (review Figure 7-1). The LAP header points to the long DDP header (layer 3), the DDP header indicates the ATP header (layer 4), the ATP header's client is ASP (layer 5), and finally the ASP header and data includes the AFP command, bit map, and volume name (Alisa Demo Volume) at layers 6 and 7. Frame 131 from VAX1 to macrouter confirms the opening of the volume. See reference [7-8] for further information on protocol analysis with the Network General Sniffer.

Figure 7-21
AppleTalk File Access Analysis Details

```
Sniffer Network Analyzer data from 22-Feb-90 at 09:21:14,
file A:VAXFILE.ENC, Page 1


- - - - - - - - - - - - - - - - - - - Frame 130 - - - - - - - - - - - - - - - - - -

DLC:   ----- DLC Header -----
DLC:
DLC:   Frame 130 arrived at  09:21:59.8455 ; frame size is 60 (003C hex) bytes.
DLC:   Destination: Station DECnet000E18, VAX1
DLC:   Source      : Station 3Com  580975, macrouter
DLC:   Ethertype = 809B (AppleTalk)
DLC:
LAP:----- LAP header -----
LAP:
LAP:   Destination node  = 254
LAP:   Source node       = 141
LAP:   LAP protocol type = 2 (Long DDP)
LAP:
```

Figure 7-21 (continued)

```
DDP:----- DDP header -----
DDP:
DDP:    Hop count          = 1
DDP:    Length             = 43
DDP:    Checksum           = 0000
DDP:    Destination Network Number = 37413
DDP:    Destination Node          = 5
DDP:    Destination Socket        = 131
DDP:    Source Network Number     = 3000
DDP:    Source Node               = 117
DDP:    Source Socket             = 250
DDP:    DDP protocol type = 3 (ATP)
DDP:
ATP:----- ATP header -----
ATP:
ATP:    Client             = (ASP)
ATP:    Function           = 1 (Request)
ATP:    Control field      = 2X
ATP:            ..1. .... = Exactly-once transaction
ATP:    Request bitmap     = 01
ATP:            .... ...1 = Request bitmap
ATP:    Transaction id     = 1127
ATP:    User data          = 02050002
ATP:
ASP:----- ASP header -----
ASP:
ASP:    SPCmdType                 = 2 (Command)
ASP:    Session ID                = 5
ASP:    Sequence                  = 2
ASP:
AFP:----- AFP -----
AFP:
AFP:    FP command         = 24 (OpenVol)
AFP:    Vol bitmap         = 0020
AFP:    .... ...0  .... .... = No volume name
AFP:    .... ....  0... .... = No bytes total
AFP:    .... ....  .0.. .... = No bytes free
AFP:    .... ....  ..1. .... = Volume ID
AFP:    .... ....  ...0 .... = No backup date
AFP:    .... ....  .... 0... = No modify date
AFP:    .... ....  .... .0.. = No creation date
AFP:    .... ....  .... ..0. = No signature
AFP:    .... ....  .... ...0 = No attributes
AFP:
AFP:    Volume name        = "Alisa Demo Volume"
AFP:
AFP:
AFP:[Normal end of "AFP".]
```

Figure 7-21 (continued)

```
- - - - - - - - - - - - - - - - Frame 131 - - - - - - - - - - - - - - - - - - -

DLC:   ----- DLC Header -----
DLC:
DLC:   Frame 131 arrived at  09:22:00.1361 ; frame size is 60 (003C hex) bytes.
DLC:   Destination: Station 3Com   580975, macrouter
DLC:   Source      : Station DECnet000E18, VAX1
DLC:   Ethertype = 809B (AppleTalk)
DLC:
LAP:----- LAP header -----
LAP:
LAP:   Destination node  = 141
LAP:   Source node       = 254
LAP:   LAP protocol type = 2 (Long DDP)
LAP:
DDP:----- DDP header -----
DDP:
DDP:   Hop count           = 2
DDP:   Length              = 25
DDP:   Checksum            = 0000
DDP:   Destination Network Number = 3000
DDP:   Destination Node        = 117
DDP:   Destination Socket      = 250
DDP:   Source Network Number   = 37413
DDP:   Source Node             = 5
DDP:   Source Socket           = 131
DDP:   DDP protocol type = 3 (ATP)
DDP:
ATP:----- ATP header -----
ATP:
ATP:   Client          = (ASP)
ATP:   Function        = 2 (Response)
ATP:   Control field   = 10
ATP:           ...1 .... = Last reply for this transaction
ATP:   Response sequence = 0
ATP:   Transaction id    = 1127
 ATP:  User data         = 00000000
ATP:
ASP:----- ASP header -----
ASP:
ASP:   SPCmdType (reply)           = (Command)
ASP:   Command result             = 0
ASP:
AFP:----- AFP -----
AFP:
AFP:   FP reply        = (OpenVol)
AFP:   Error           = 0 (NoErr)
AFP:   Vol bitmap      = 0020
```

Figure 7-21 (continued)

```
AFP:  .... ...0   .... ....  = No volume name
AFP:  .... ....   0... ....  = No bytes total
AFP:  .... ....   .0.. ....  = No bytes free
AFP:  .... ....   ..1. ....  = Volume ID
AFP:  .... ....   ...0 ....  = No backup date
AFP:  .... ....   .... 0...  = No modify date
AFP:  .... ....   .... .0..  = No creation date
AFP:  .... ....   .... ..0.  = No signature
AFP:  .... ....   .... ...0  = No attributes
AFP:
AFP:  Volume ID        = 3
AFP:
AFP:
AFP:[Normal end of "AFP".]
AFP:
```

It's easy to see why Apple Computer decided to distinguish between "LocalTalk" and "AppleTalk." AppleTalk is an excellent example of a well-designed network architecture. Each building block has a specific purpose, and relies upon the layers above and below for completeness. All network operating systems should fit together so well!

7.7 | References

[7-1] Apple Computer Inc., *Inside Macintosh*, Volumes I-V, Addison-Wesley Publishing Co., Inc., 1985

[7-2] Apple Computer Inc., *AppleTalk Network System Overview*, Addison-Wesley Publishing Co., Inc., 1989.

[7-3] Mike Rogers and Virginia Bare, *Hands-On AppleTalk*, Brady, Division of Simon and Schuster, Inc., 1989.

[7-4] Apple Computer Inc., *Inside AppleTalk*, Addison-Wesley Publishing Co., Inc., 1989.

[7-5]   Apple Computer Inc., "AppleTalk Phase 2 Protocol Specification, and Addendum to Inside AppleTalk", document ADPA #C0144LL/A, 1989.

[7-6]   Apple Computer Inc., AppleTalk Phase 2 Introduction and Upgrade Guide, document 030-2175-A, 1989.

[7-7]   Apple Computer, Inc., AppleTalk Internet Router Administrator's Guide, document 030-2175-A, 1989.

[7-8]   Ethernet Network Portable Protocol Analyzer Operation and Reference Manual, Network General Corp., 1986–1988.

CHAPTER EIGHT

Evaluating Network Operating Systems

Every author reserves the right to be surprised at the reasons people buy his books. This project was undertaken primarily to educate LAN administrators, and secondly to provide information to software developers. In general, this book is for anyone who requires a bit-level understanding of the software that controls his or her network's functions.

I suspect, however, that there is another, perhaps larger audience who could be most accurately described as "shoppers"; those individuals who are evaluating LAN and/or WAN network operating systems (NOSs) with an eye toward a future purchase. Dissecting the various layers of a networking software architecture as we have done in Chapters 3 - 7 certainly provides some insight into the NOS's operations.

However, there are other factors that should be considered during the evaluation process. These include:

1. Define the end-user applications for your network. Two factors to consider are the application programs themselves and NOS utilities. For application programs, the issue is "will it run under my NOS?" For example, Novell provides a software compatibility database known as NetWire on the CompuServe Information Service. Call CompuServe at (800) 484-8990 or (614) 457-8650) for further information. Banyan has an excellent application directory (reference [6-10]). Built-in or available utilities, such as electronic mail, can be extremely useful. 3Com's 3+Mail or Banyan's Chat are good examples of

these services. Check with various vendors and be sure you understand what you need before you buy.

2. Consider any needs to support multiple operating systems, such as DOS, OS/2, UNIX, or Macintosh. The OS/2-based NOSs, such as 3+Open and IBM LAN Server, support both DOS and OS/2 environments. AppleTalk is obviously strong for the Macintosh. Portable NetWare is designed to support UNIX, VMS, and other operating systems. Make sure that you consider future expansion and all the possible users of your LAN before you make a NOS commitment.

3. Is there a reason to select one hardware platform over another? Make sure that the entire network, including hardware, cabling, and software, is considered as part of the overall design. Consider the CPU (80x86 or 680x0), and any bus requirements or advantages or disadvantages between choosing the PC, AT, MicroChannel, and EISA. NetWare and VINES have 80386 versions available, and the IBM OS/2 LAN Server is part of the Communication Manager and IBM's Systems Application Architecture. Look for EISA-compatible NOSs to appear in the near future.

4. Consider workstation and server RAM requirements, as well as other hardware constraints that may affect the server. These include whether to use a dedicated or non-dedicated server, hard disk requirements, the number of parallel and serial ports, video display, etc.

5. Although it is not really a protocol issue, fault tolerance is important. Three schemes are most common. The first is disk mirroring or disk duplexing. This configuration provides duplicate disks and/or controllers, thus assuring that two copies of the network data exist in the event of a hardware failure. A second fault tolerant scheme is transaction tracking, which is used for lengthy operations such as accounting and database operations. This scheme assures that either all of an operation's transactions are completed, or that none of them are completed. NetWare, 3+, and 3+Open have strengths here.

6. An issue related to fault tolerance is a network's susceptibility to power failures. Both Novell and Banyan servers accept direct inputs from an activated uninterruptible power supply (UPS), thus shutting down the server in an orderly fashion so that file corruption does not occur.

7. Determine what internetworking might be required, either now or in the future? Those operating systems based upon XNS do especially well with internetworking, as do systems with built-in TCP/IP, since those protocols were designed to support the U.S. Department of Defense's internetworking requirements. Administrators with networks requiring WAN connections should consider Banyan VINES, because its StreetTalk global naming service easily supports large networks. Multiple protocol stacks, such as XNS or TCP/IP, are easily handled with 3Com's Demand Protocol Architecture. Novell's internal routing allows multiple hardware architectures, such as Ethernet and ARCNET, to be internetworked inside the server, thus eliminating the need for an additional hardware component.

8. Is connectivity to a mainframe or other host required? If so, consider SNA compatibility. Not surprisingly, IBM's PC LAN and OS/2 LAN Server are excellent choices for mainframe support.

9. Ease of administration, including comprehensive reference material, on-line help, and factory support, are crucial. Also consider the user interface and its friendliness, as well as the rigors involved in installing the NOS. Check vendor references from users that support similar applications, network size, etc., and consider their experiences. Also look for users' groups that can provide technical, practical, and moral support.

10. Security is a growing concern for many network users. The manner in which passwords are transmitted across the transmission medium (encrypted or not), and the manner in which user logins and remote access attempts are monitored can be significant. Since the definition of "multi-level security" varies with each vendor, understand how each

NOS implements security. Also consider file, directory, and volume restrictions, as well as read and write permissions. Other security features may be available with a specific NOS as well. For example, Banyan's VanGuard security has a provision to discourage hackers; if an unauthorized individual attempts to login and fails five times, that workstation is locked and must be rebooted.

11. Understand the limitations as well as the strengths of each NOS you consider. By understanding these limitations, the optimization of the various network parameters, such as those for the IBM PC LAN Program discussed in Chapter 5, can proceed in an orderly fashion instead of by trial and error. Secondly, develop network benchmarks, such as average and peak network utilization, so that growth patterns can be predicted. The effects of adding more workstations or servers need to be considered. Many subtle problems, such as the NetWare caching example offered in Chapter 3, do not surface until the network is stressed. Finally, consider hardware, software, and cabling limits as part of the initial network design, and develop a plan to reach beyond those capacities as growth demands over then next three to five years.

12. And finally, don't forget to consider the network analysis tools themselves (see section 2.6). Unless you plan to write your own protocol interpreter, make sure that the tool you select is capable of interpreting all of the important protocols on your LAN.

Good luck, and may your net work.

About the Author

Mark A. Miller, P.E., is president of DigiNet Corporation, a Denver-based data communication engineering firm specializing in the design of local area and wide area communication networks. He develops and teaches courses in local area network troubleshooting, PC and Macintosh networking, T-1 networks, and packet switching and the X.25 protocol. Mark is also a registered professional engineer and is author of *LAN Troubleshooting Handbook* (M&T Books, 1989).

Index

A Library of Networking References from M&T Books!

More Networking Books ...

LAN Troubleshooting Handbook

by Mark A. Miller, P.E.

This book is specifically for users and administrators who need to identify problems and maintain a LAN that is already installed. Topics include LAN standards, the OSI model, network documentation, LAN test equipment, cable system testing, and more. Addressed are specific issues associated with troubleshooting the four most popular LAN architectures: ARCNET, Token Ring®, Ethernet®, and StarLAN™. Each are closely examined to pinpoint the problems unique to its design and the hardware. Handy checklists to assist in solving each architecture's unique network difficulties are also included.

Book & Disk (MS-DOS)   *Item #056-7*   *$39.95*
Book only   *Item #054-0*   *$29.95*

Building Local Area Networks with Novell's NetWare

by Patrick H. Corrigan and Aisling Guy

From the basic components to complete network installation, here is the practical guide that PC system integrators will need to build and implement PC LANs in this rapidly growing market. The specifics of building and maintaining PC LANs, including hardware configurations, software development, cabling, selection criteria, installation, and on-going management are described in a clear "how-to" manner with numerous illustrations and sample LAN management forms. *Building Local Area Networks* gives particular emphasis to Novell's NetWare, Version 2.1. Additional topics covered include the OS/2 LAN manager, Tops, Banyan VINES™, internetworking, host computer gateways, and multisystem networks that link PCs, Apples, and mainframes.

Book & Disk (MS-DOS)   *Item #025-7*   *$39.95*
Book only   *Item #010-9*   *$29.95*

More Networking Books ...

NetWare® Supervisor's Guide

By John T. McCann, Adam T. Ruef, and Steven L. Guengerich

Written for network administrators, consultants, installers, and power users of all versions of NetWare, including NetWare 386. Where other books provide information on using NetWare at a workstation level, this definitive reference focuses on how to administer NetWare. Contained are numerous examples which include understanding and using NetWare's undocumented commands and utilities, implementing system fault tolerant LANs, refining installation parameters to improve network performance, and more.

Book only   *Item #111-3*   *$24.95*

NetWare® 386 User's Guide

by Christine Milligan

NetWare 386 User's Guide is a complete guide to using and understanding Novell's NetWare 386. It is an excellent reference for all NetWare users working with, or considering upgrading to NetWare 386. Detailed tutorials cover tasks such as logging in, working with directories and files, and printing over a network. Complete explanations of the basic concepts underlying NetWare 386, along with a summary of the differences between NetWare 286 and 386, are included. Advanced users will benefit from the information on managing workstation environments and the troubleshooting index that fully examines NetWare 386 error messages.

Book only   *Item #101-6*   *$29.95*

More Networking Books ...

NetWare® Administrator's Guide

by Tom Kieffer

This comprehensive guide is for all NetWare administrators responsible for the daily management of a Netware network. Through in-depth discussions and detailed explanations, administrators will learn how to increase their network's performance and simplify file server management. All utilities available from the console are thoroughly examined. Readers will learn how to link a Netware network to other networks, set up and manage remote access services, keep track of cabling layouts, monitor network operations, manage shared resources, and much more.

Book only   *Item #125-3*   *$34.95*

LAN Basics
An Introduction to Local Area Networks

by Greg Nunemacher

A complete introduction to local area networks (LANs), this book is a must for anyone who needs to know basic LAN principles. It includes a complete overview of LANs, clearly defining what a LAN is, the functions of a LAN, and how LANs fit into the field of telecommunications. The author discusses the specifics of building a LAN, including the required hardware and software, an overview of the types of products availlable, deciding what products to, purchase, and assembling the pieces into a working LAN system. LAN Basics also includes case studies that illustrate how LAN principles work. Particular focus is given to Ethernet and Token-Ring.

Book only   *Item #127-X*   *$29.95*

More Networking Books ...

The NetWare® Manual Makers
Complete Kits for Creating Customized
NetWare Manuals

These unique packages are a must for all Netware administrators and supervisors responsible for training network users. The NetWare Manual Makers enable the user to create network training manuals specific to their individual sites. The book is a printed version of the manual that is generated using the accompanying disk. It includes general "how-to" information on using a network, as well as fill-in-the-blank sections that help administrators explain and document procedures unique to a particular site. The disk files are provided in WordPerfect and ASCII formats. The WordPerfect file creates a manual that looks exactly like the one in the book. The ASCII file can be imported into any desktop publishing or word processing software.

The NetWare® 286 Manual Maker
The Complete Kit for Creating Customized
NetWare 286 Manuals

by Christine Milligan

Book/Disk   *Item #119-9*   *$49.95*

The NetWare® 386 Manual Maker
The Complete Kit for Creating Customized
NetWare 386 Manuals

by Christine Milligan

Book/Disk   *Item #120-2*   *$49.95*

The NetWare for Macintosh™ Manual Maker
The Complete Kit for Creating Customized Net-
Ware for Macintosh™ Manuals

by Kelley J. P. Lindberg

Book/Disk   *Item #130-X*   *$49.95*

More Networking Books ...

LAN Protocol Handbook

by Mark A. Miller, P.E.

This is a must for all network administrators and software developers requiring in-depth knowledge of the internal protocols of the most popular network software. It illustrates the techniques of protocol analysis— the step-by-step process of unraveling LAN software failures. Detailed are how Ethernet, IEEE 802.3, IEEE 802.5, and ARCNET networks transmit frames of information between workstations. From that foundation, it presents LAN performnce measurements, protocol analysis methods, and protocol analyzer products. Individual chapters thoroughly discuss Novell's Netware, 3Com's 3+™ and 3+Open™, IBM Token-Ring™ related protocols, and more!

Book only   *Item 099-0*   *$34.95*

More Networking Books ...

NetWare® for Macintosh User's Guide

by Kelley J. P. Lindberg

NetWare for Macintosh User's Guide is the definitive reference to using Novell's NetWare on Macintosh computers. Whether a novice or advanced user, this comprehensive text provides the information readers need to get the most from their NetWare network. It includes an overview of network operations and detailed explanations of all NetWare for Macintosh menu and command line utilities. Detailed tutorials cover such tasks as logging in, working with directories and files, and printing over a network. Advanced users will benefit from the information on managing workstation environments as well as the troubleshooting index that fully examines Netware for Macintosh error messages.

Book only   *Item #126-1*   *$29.95*

To Order: Return this form with your payment to **M&T Books**, 501 Galveston Drive, Redwood City, CA 94063 or **CALL TOLL-FREE 1-800-533-4372** (in California, call 1-800-356-2002). Ask for operator 7085.

❏ **YES!** Please send me the following: ❏ Check enclosed, payable to **M&T Books**.

Item#	Description	Qty	Price

Charge my ❏ Visa ❏ MC ❏ AmEx

Card No. _____ Exp. Date _____

Signature _____

Subtotal _____

CA residents add sales tax —%_____

Add $3.50 per item for shipping and handling _____

TOTAL _____

Name _____

Address _____

City _____

State _____ Zip_____

Note: Prices subject to change without notice. Disks may be returned for exchange only if damaged in transit.

Order the
LAN Protocol Handbook
Demonstration Disks

Here is your opportunity to survey six different protocol analyzers and see the principles of the book in action! The set of seven demonstration disks are for those who wish to pursue the techniques of protocol analysis or consider the purchase of an analysis tool.

The analyzers will give you a clear view of your network so that you can better control and manage your LAN, as well as pinpoint trouble spots. The *LAN Protocol Handbook* demo disks are packed with detailed demonstration programs for LANalyzer®, LAN Watch®, The Sniffer® for Token-Ring and Ethernet, SpiderAnalyzer® 320-R for Token-Ring, and LANVista®. Because each of these analyzers have their own unique merits, by surveying the demo programs you will receive enough information to choose an analyzer that best suits your specific needs.

Requirements: IBM PC/XT/AT compatible with at least 640K after booting. Requires DOS version 2.0 or later. Either a color or mono display may be used.

To Order: Return this coupon with your payment to:
M&T Books
501 Galveston Drive
Redwood City, CA 94063
Or **CALL TOLL-FREE 1-800-533-4372 (in CA 1-800-356-2002)**

☐ **YES!** Please send me the *LAN Protocol Handbook* demo disks!
Demonstration disks (set of 7) ___$39.95___
CA residents add 7.25% sales tax _____
Total _____

☐ Check enclosed, payable to M&T Books.
Charge my   ☐ VISA   ☐ MC   ☐ AmEx
Card no. _____Exp. Date _____
Signature_____
Name _____
Address _____
City _____ State _____ Zip _____

Note: Disks may be returned for a replacement if damaged. No refunds or credits given. The demonstration disks are not an attempt to provide comprehensive reviews nor offer endorsements of any particular products.

7092